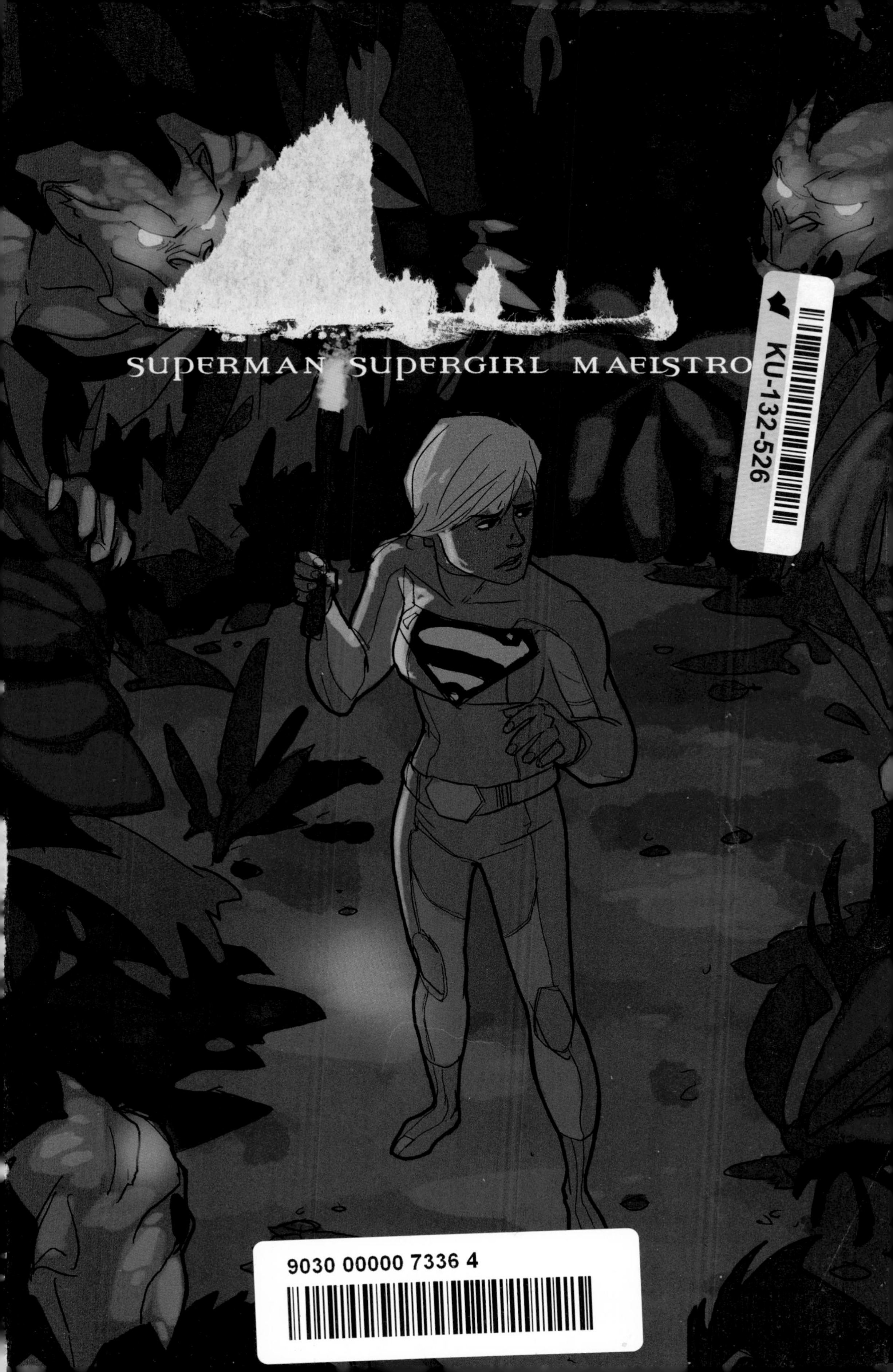
SUPERMAN SUPERGIRL MAELSTRO

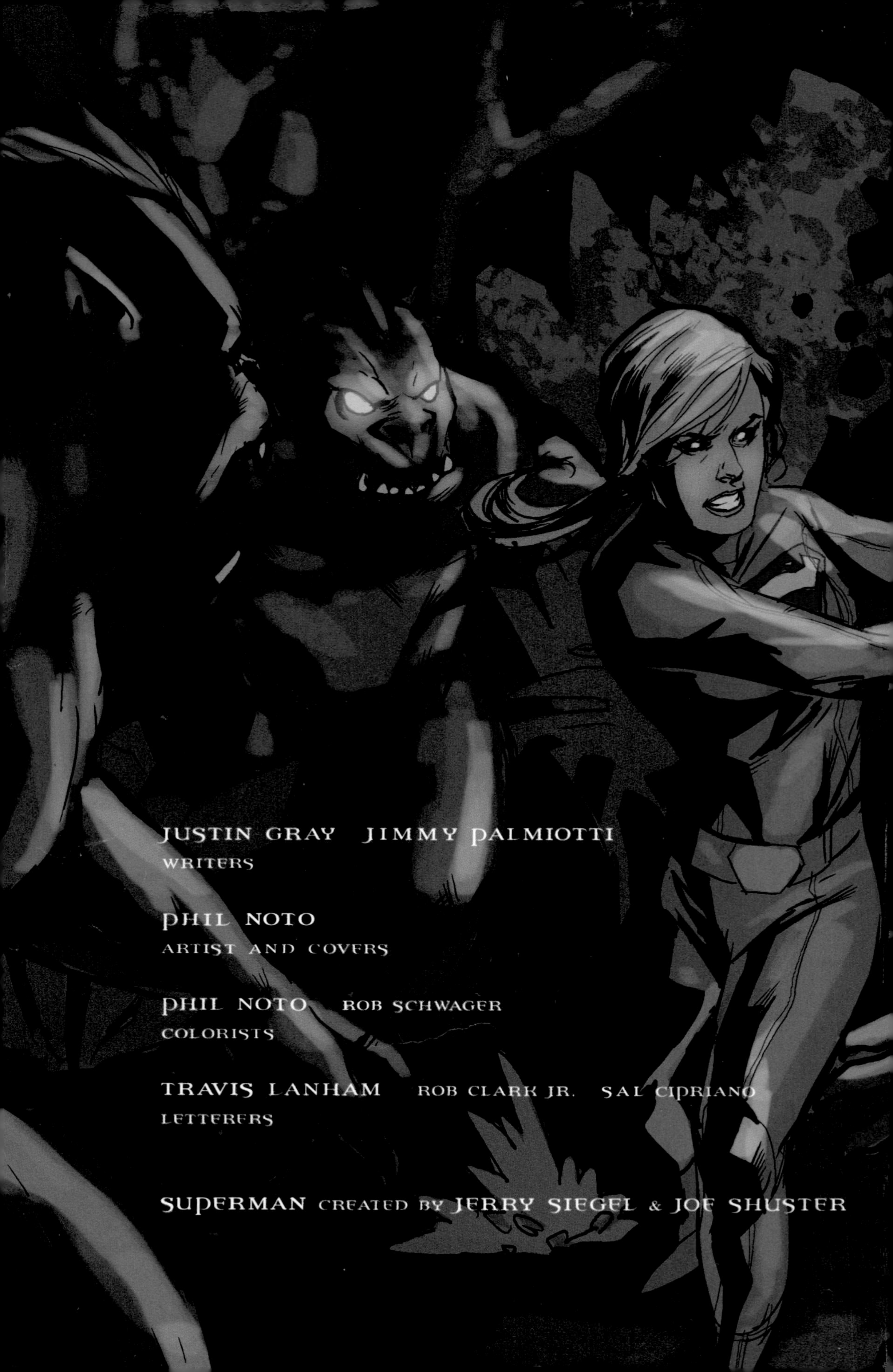

JUSTIN GRAY JIMMY PALMIOTTI
WRITERS

PHIL NOTO
ARTIST AND COVERS

PHIL NOTO ROB SCHWAGER
COLORISTS

TRAVIS LANHAM ROB CLARK JR. SAL CIPRIANO
LETTERERS

SUPERMAN CREATED BY JERRY SIEGEL & JOE SHUSTER

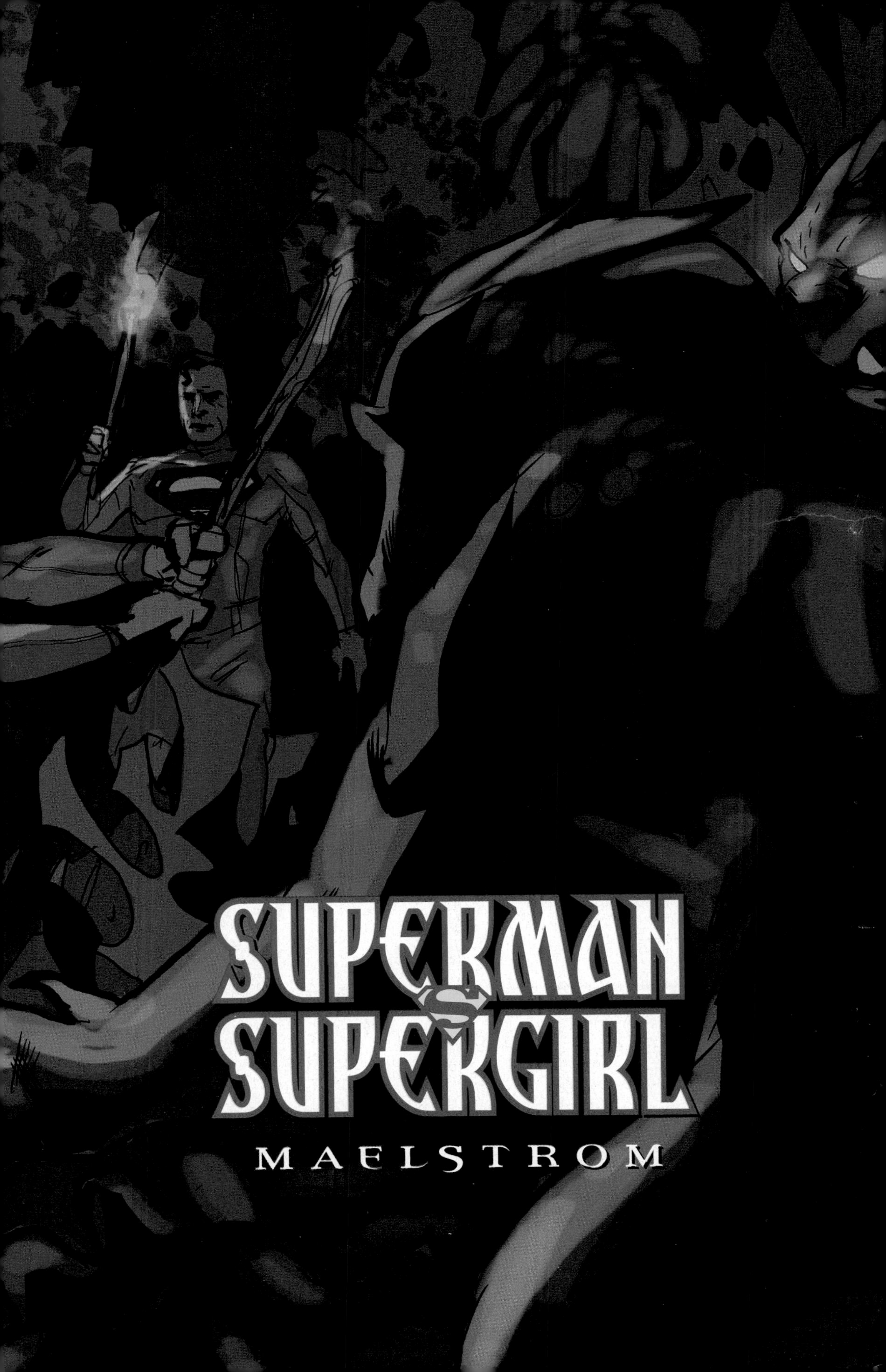

SUPERMAN SUPERGIRL

MAELSTROM

Dan DiDio SVP-Executive Editor
Michael Siglain Editor-original series
Harvey Richards Assist. Editor-original series
Georg Brewer VP-Design & DC Direct Creative
Bob Harras Group Editor-Collected Editions
Peter Hamboussi Editor
Robbin Brosterman Design Director-Books

DC COMICS

Paul Levitz President & Publisher
Richard Bruning SVP-Creative Director
Patrick Caldon EVP-Finance & Operations
Amy Genkins SVP-Business & Legal Affairs
Jim Lee Editorial Director-WildStorm
Gregory Noveck SVP-Creative Affairs
Steve Rotterdam SVP-Sales & Marketing
Cheryl Rubin SVP-Brand Management

Cover by Phil Noto

SUPERMAN/SUPERGIRL: MAELSTROM
Published by DC Comics.

DC Comics, 1700 Broadway, New York, NY 10019
A Warner Bros. Entertainment Company
Printed by World Color Press, Inc,
St-Romuald, QC, Canada 11/04/09
First Printing. ISBN: 978-1-4012-2508-7

SUSTAINABLE FORESTRY INITIATIVE Certified Fiber Sourcing
www.sfiprogram.org
Fiber used in this product line meets the sourcing requirements of the SFI program. www.sfiprogram.org PWC-SFICOC-260

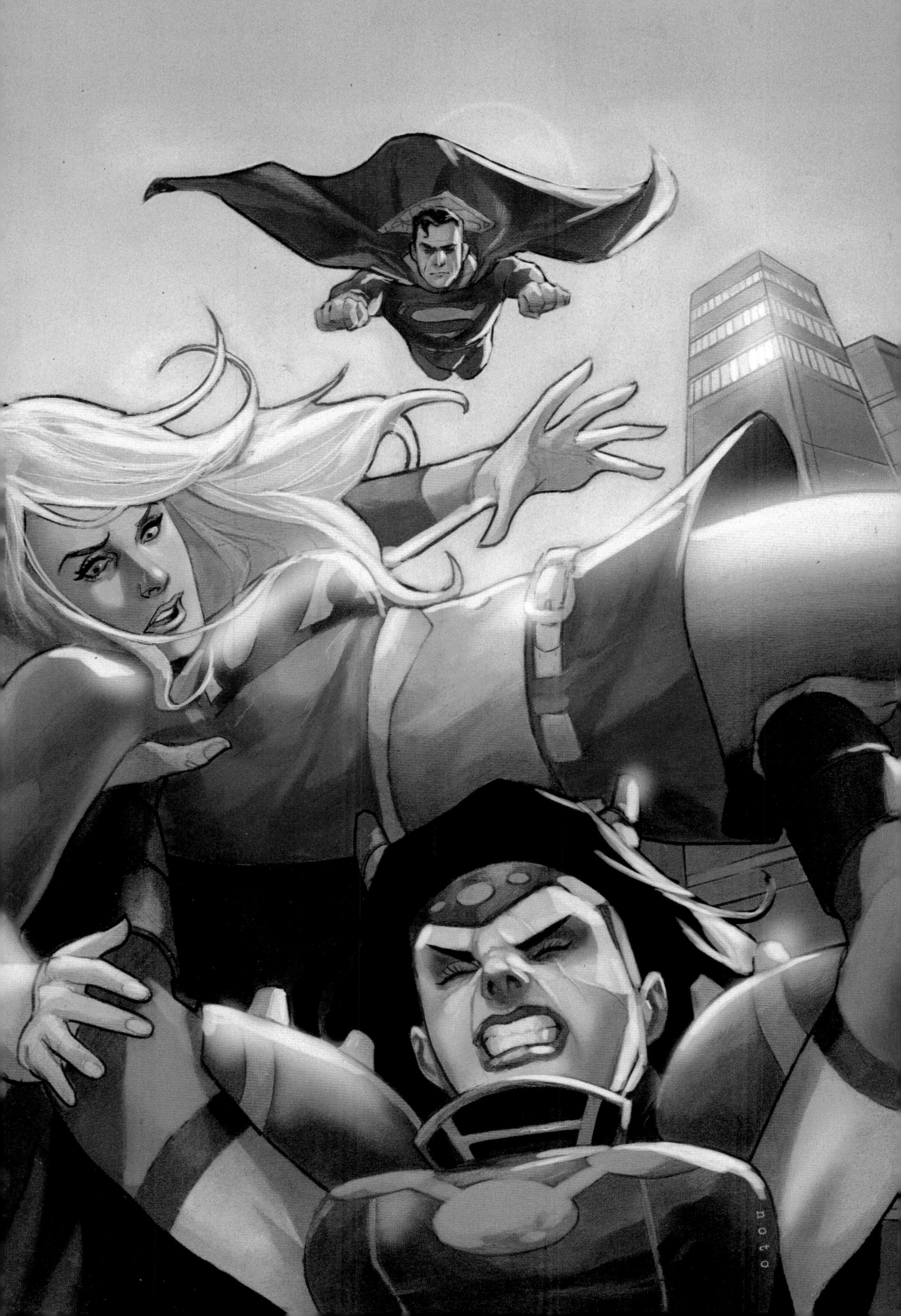
noto

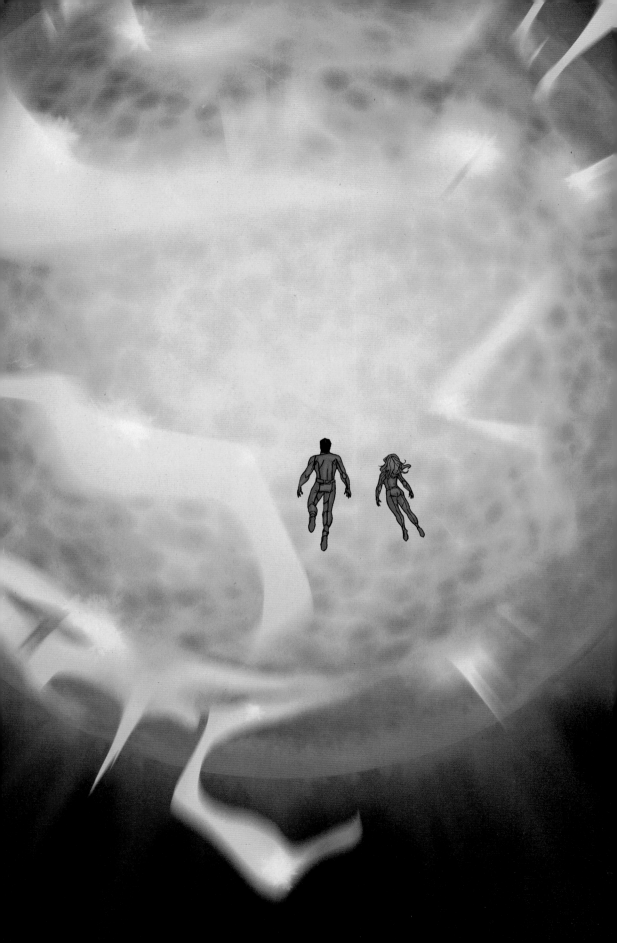

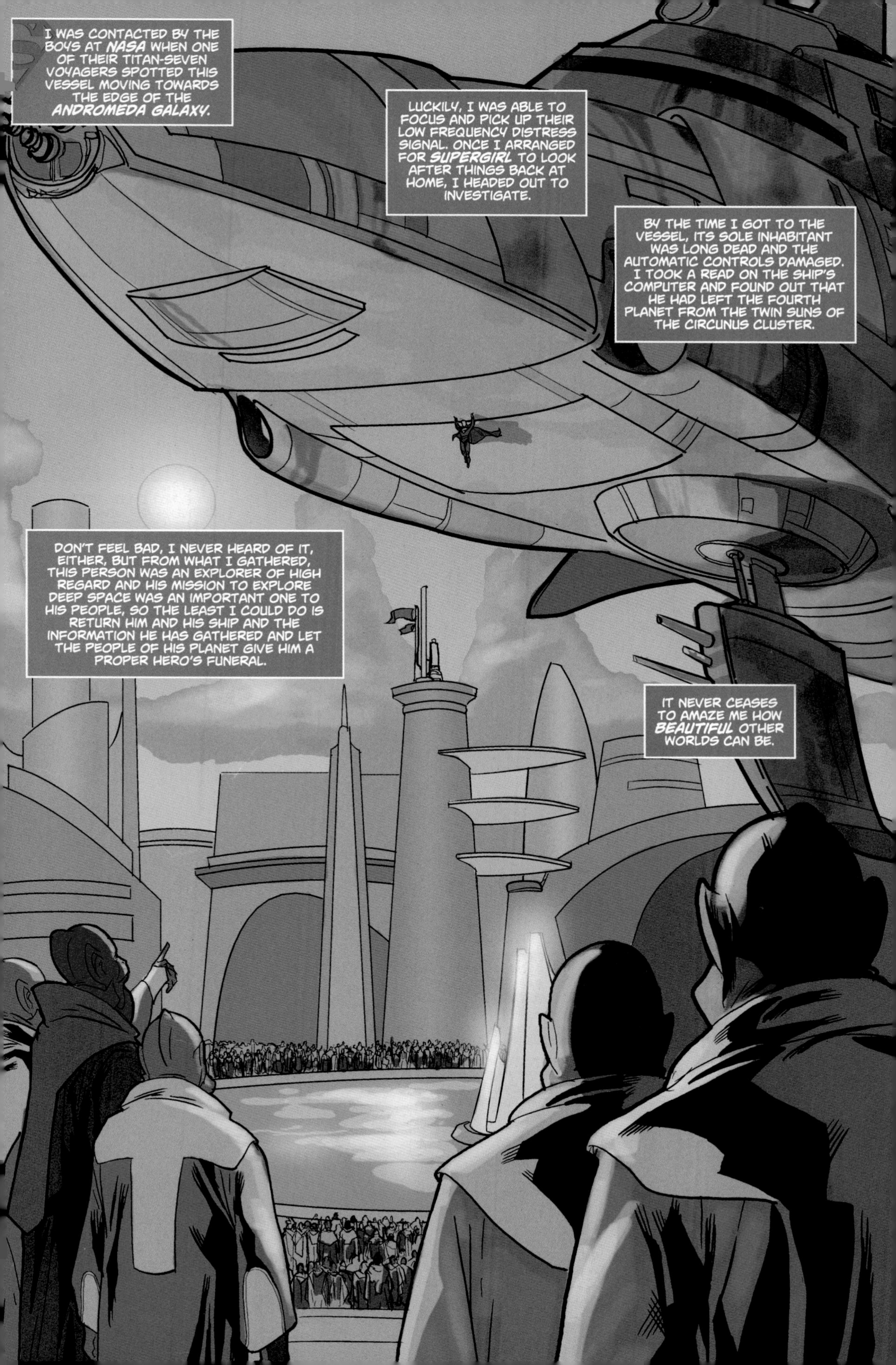
I WAS CONTACTED BY THE BOYS AT NASA WHEN ONE OF THEIR TITAN-SEVEN VOYAGERS SPOTTED THIS VESSEL MOVING TOWARDS THE EDGE OF THE ANDROMEDA GALAXY.
LUCKILY, I WAS ABLE TO FOCUS AND PICK UP THEIR LOW FREQUENCY DISTRESS SIGNAL. ONCE I ARRANGED FOR SUPERGIRL TO LOOK AFTER THINGS BACK AT HOME, I HEADED OUT TO INVESTIGATE.
BY THE TIME I GOT TO THE VESSEL, ITS SOLE INHABITANT WAS LONG DEAD AND THE AUTOMATIC CONTROLS DAMAGED. I TOOK A READ ON THE SHIP'S COMPUTER AND FOUND OUT THAT HE HAD LEFT THE FOURTH PLANET FROM THE TWIN SUNS OF THE CIRCUNUS CLUSTER.
DON'T FEEL BAD, I NEVER HEARD OF IT, EITHER, BUT FROM WHAT I GATHERED, THIS PERSON WAS AN EXPLORER OF HIGH REGARD AND HIS MISSION TO EXPLORE DEEP SPACE WAS AN IMPORTANT ONE TO HIS PEOPLE, SO THE LEAST I COULD DO IS RETURN HIM AND HIS SHIP AND THE INFORMATION HE HAS GATHERED AND LET THE PEOPLE OF HIS PLANET GIVE HIM A PROPER HERO'S FUNERAL.
IT NEVER CEASES TO AMAZE ME HOW BEAUTIFUL OTHER WORLDS CAN BE.

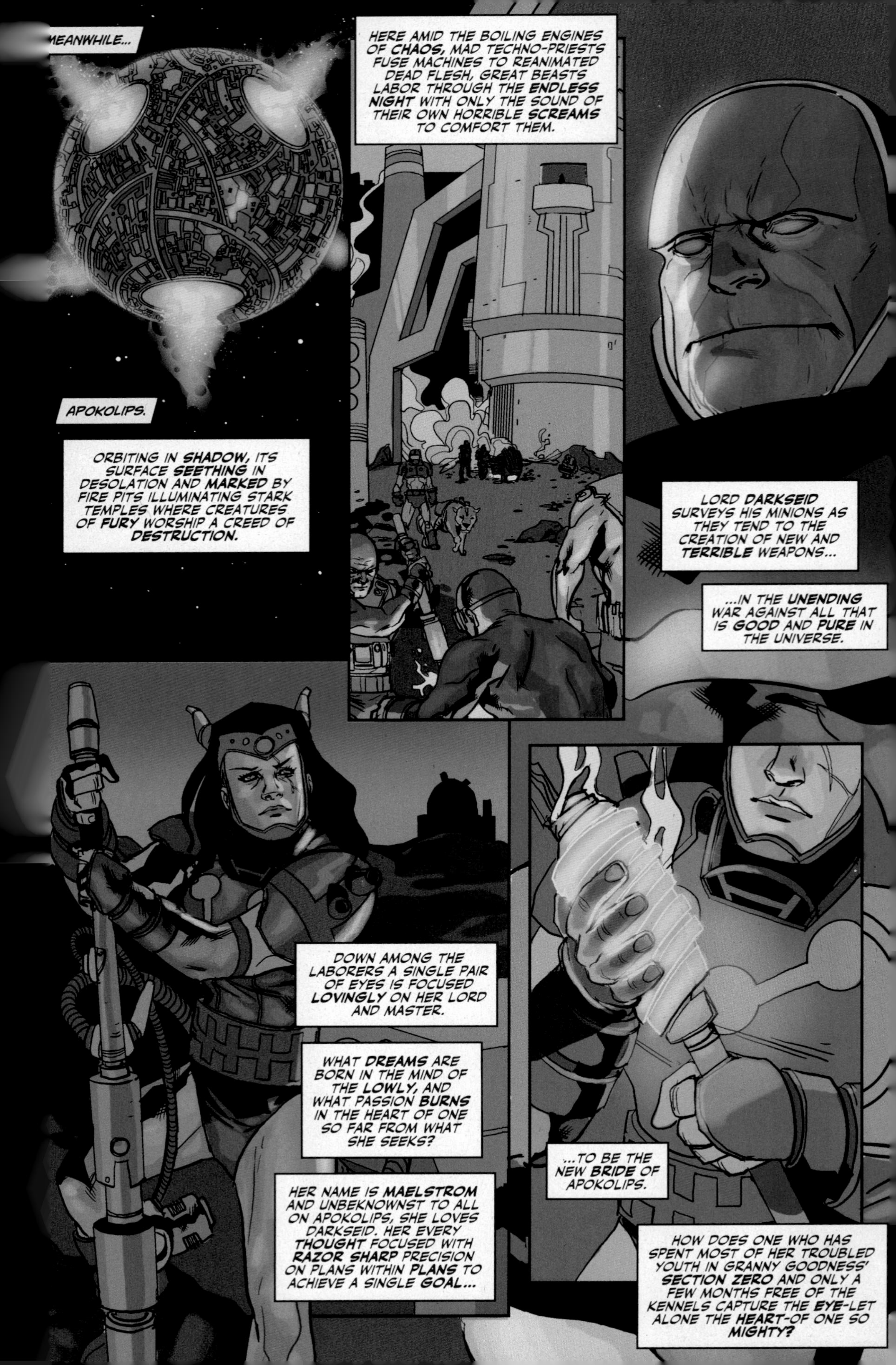
MEANWHILE...
APOKOLIPS.
ORBITING IN SHADOW, ITS SURFACE SEETHING IN DESOLATION AND MARKED BY FIRE PITS ILLUMINATING STARK TEMPLES WHERE CREATURES OF FURY WORSHIP A CREED OF DESTRUCTION.
HERE AMID THE BOILING ENGINES OF CHAOS, MAD TECHNO-PRIESTS FUSE MACHINES TO REANIMATED DEAD FLESH, GREAT BEASTS LABOR THROUGH THE ENDLESS NIGHT WITH ONLY THE SOUND OF THEIR OWN HORRIBLE SCREAMS TO COMFORT THEM.
LORD DARKSEID SURVEYS HIS MINIONS AS THEY TEND TO THE CREATION OF NEW AND TERRIBLE WEAPONS...
...IN THE UNENDING WAR AGAINST ALL THAT IS GOOD AND PURE IN THE UNIVERSE.
DOWN AMONG THE LABORERS A SINGLE PAIR OF EYES IS FOCUSED LOVINGLY ON HER LORD AND MASTER.
WHAT DREAMS ARE BORN IN THE MIND OF THE LOWLY, AND WHAT PASSION BURNS IN THE HEART OF ONE SO FAR FROM WHAT SHE SEEKS?
HER NAME IS MAELSTROM AND UNBEKNOWNST TO ALL ON APOKOLIPS, SHE LOVES DARKSEID. HER EVERY THOUGHT FOCUSED WITH RAZOR SHARP PRECISION ON PLANS WITHIN PLANS TO ACHIEVE A SINGLE GOAL...
...TO BE THE NEW BRIDE OF APOKOLIPS.
HOW DOES ONE WHO HAS SPENT MOST OF HER TROUBLED YOUTH IN GRANNY GOODNESS' SECTION ZERO AND ONLY A FEW MONTHS FREE OF THE KENNELS CAPTURE THE EYE-LET ALONE THE HEART-OF ONE SO MIGHTY?

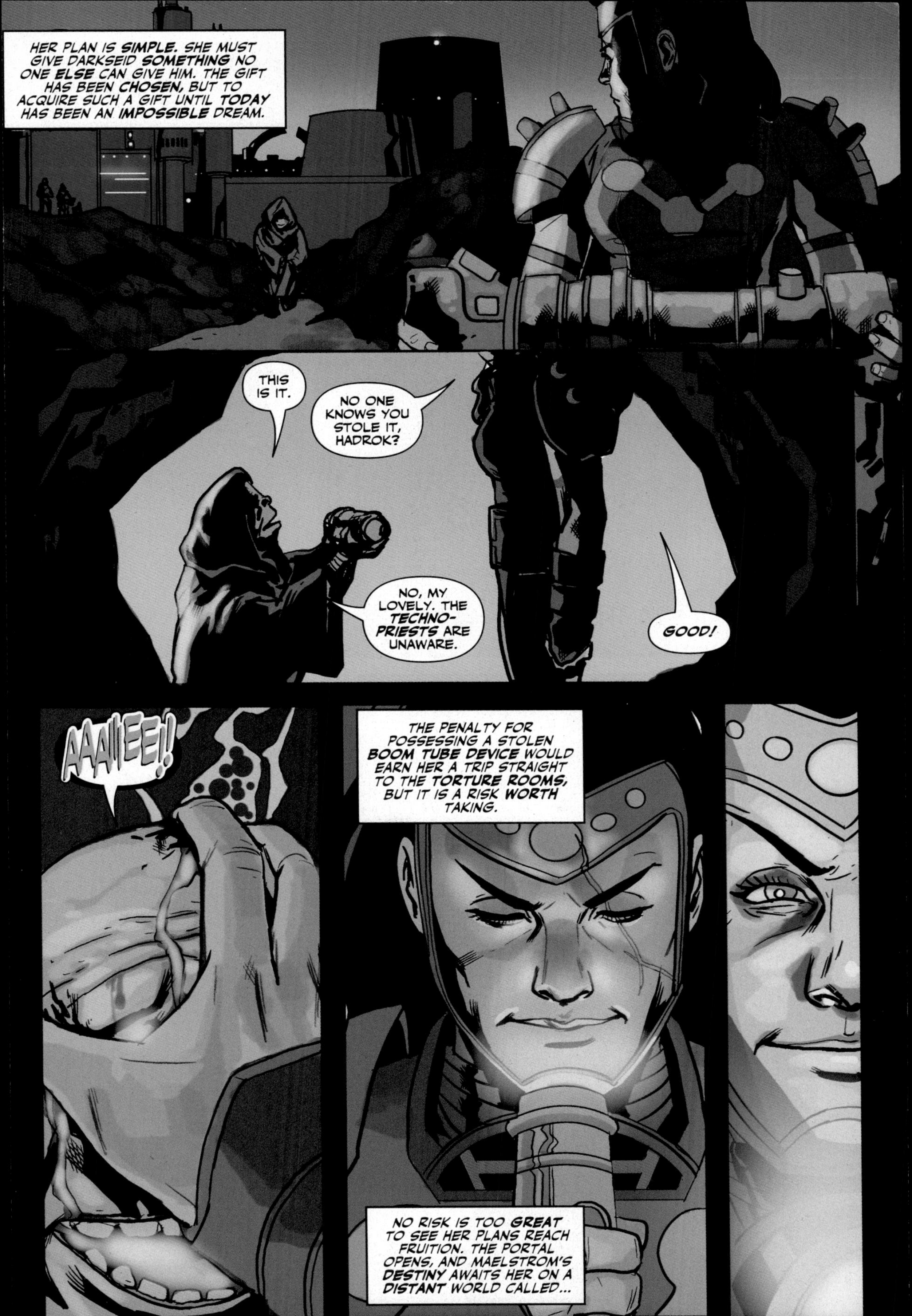
HER PLAN IS SIMPLE. SHE MUST GIVE DARKSEID SOMETHING NO ONE ELSE CAN GIVE HIM. THE GIFT HAS BEEN CHOSEN, BUT TO ACQUIRE SUCH A GIFT UNTIL TODAY HAS BEEN AN IMPOSSIBLE DREAM.
THIS IS IT.
NO ONE KNOWS YOU STOLE IT, HADROK?
NO, MY LOVELY. THE TECHNO-PRIESTS ARE UNAWARE.
GOOD!
AAAIIEE!!
THE PENALTY FOR POSSESSING A STOLEN BOOM TUBE DEVICE WOULD EARN HER A TRIP STRAIGHT TO THE TORTURE ROOMS, BUT IT IS A RISK WORTH TAKING.
NO RISK IS TOO GREAT TO SEE HER PLANS REACH FRUITION. THE PORTAL OPENS, AND MAELSTROM'S DESTINY AWAITS HER ON A DISTANT WORLD CALLED...

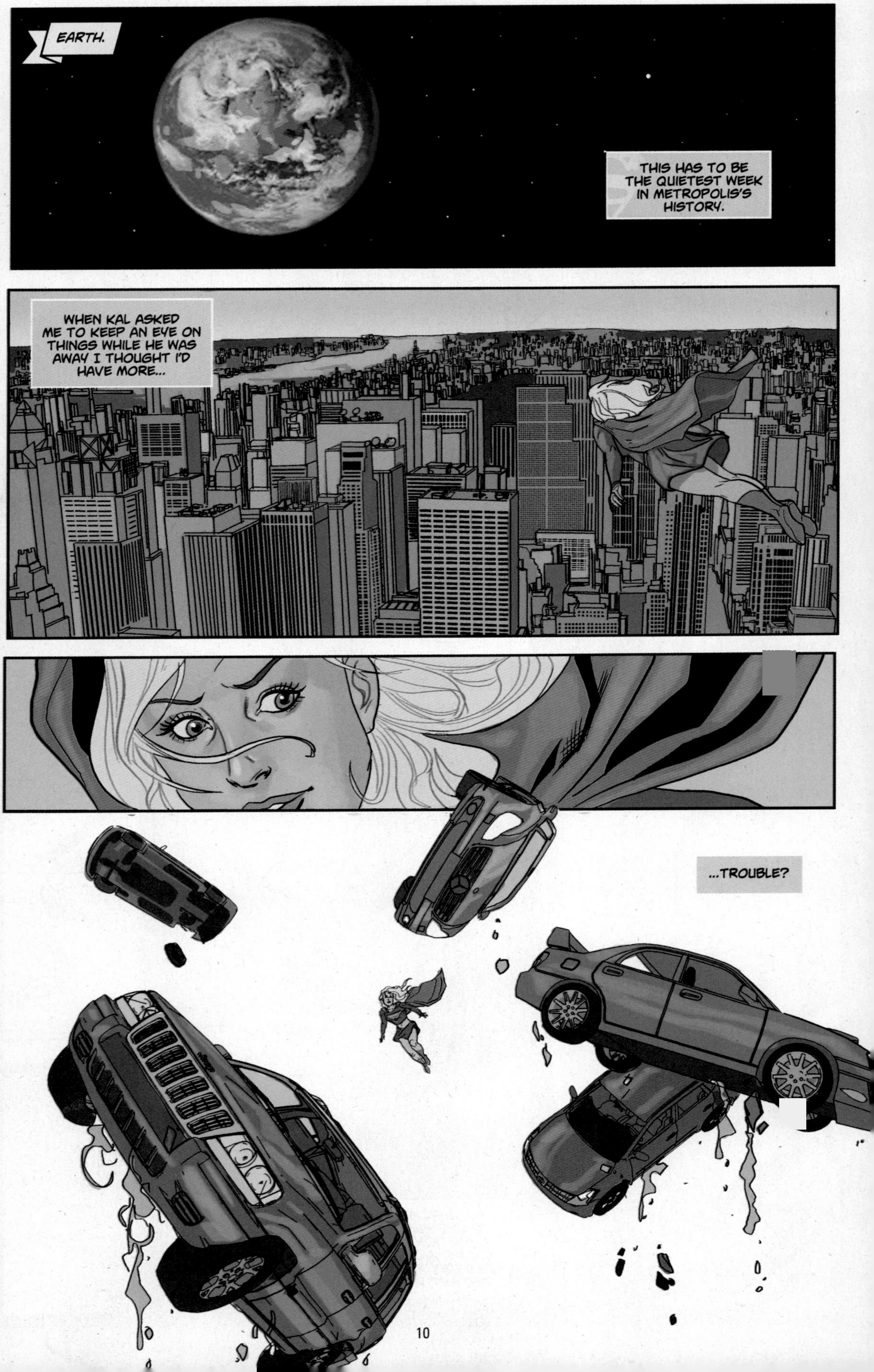
EARTH.
THIS HAS TO BE THE QUIETEST WEEK IN METROPOLIS'S HISTORY.
WHEN KAL ASKED ME TO KEEP AN EYE ON THINGS WHILE HE WAS AWAY I THOUGHT I'D HAVE MORE...
...TROUBLE?

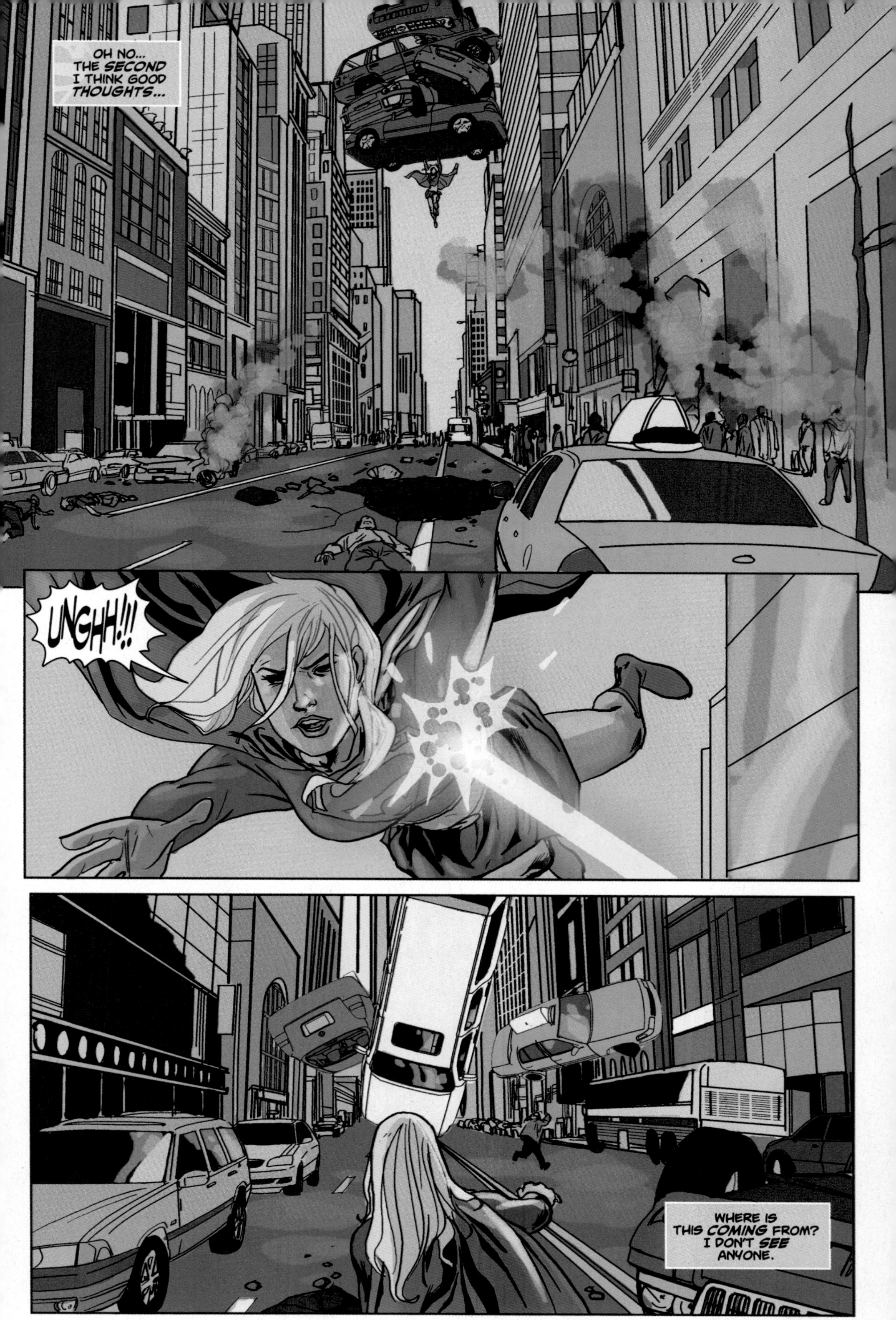
OH NO... THE SECOND I THINK GOOD THOUGHTS...
UNGHH!!!
WHERE IS THIS COMING FROM? I DON'T SEE ANYONE.

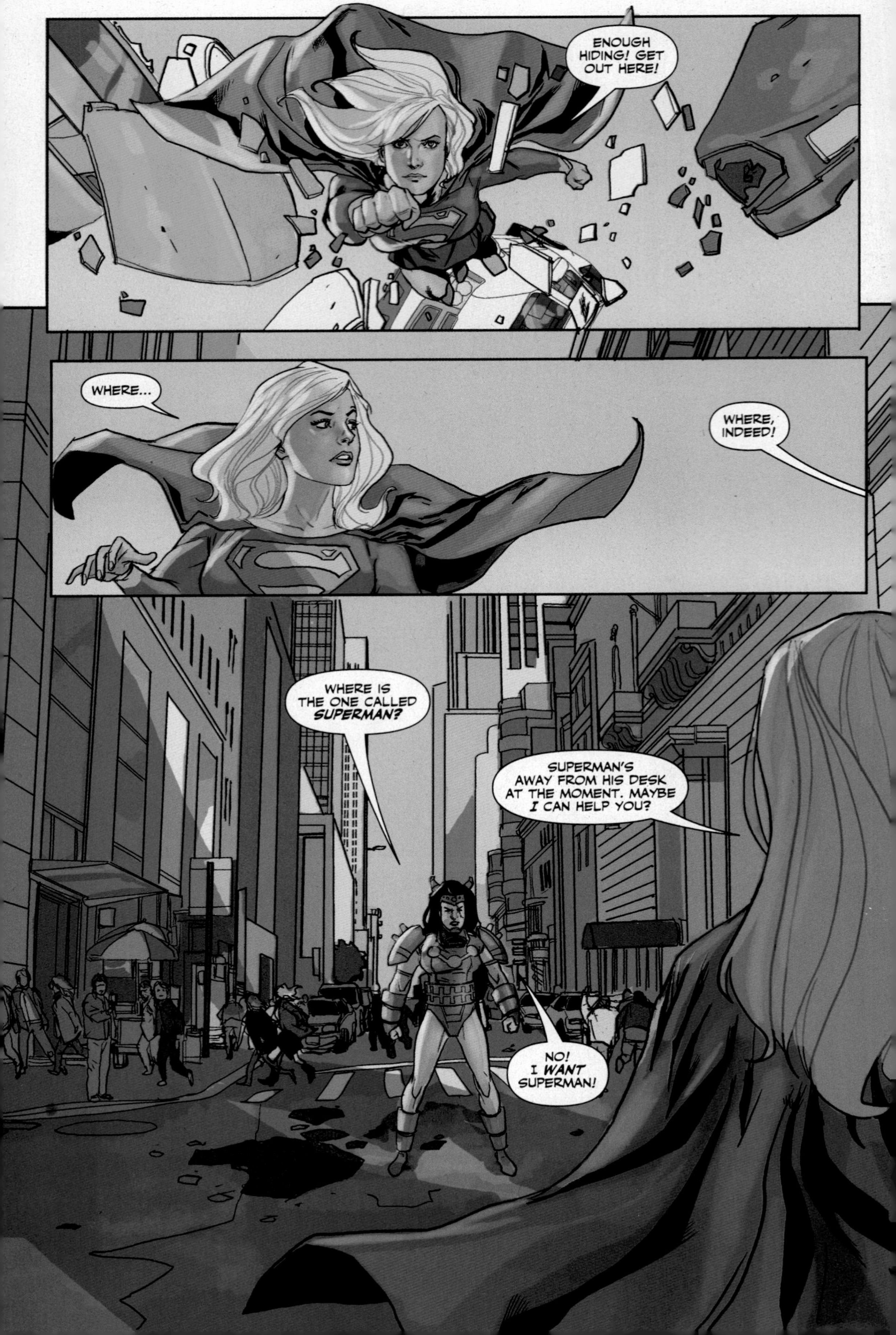
ENOUGH HIDING! GET OUT HERE!
WHERE...
WHERE, INDEED!
WHERE IS THE ONE CALLED *SUPERMAN?*
SUPERMAN'S AWAY FROM HIS DESK AT THE MOMENT. MAYBE *I* CAN HELP YOU?
NO! I *WANT* SUPERMAN!

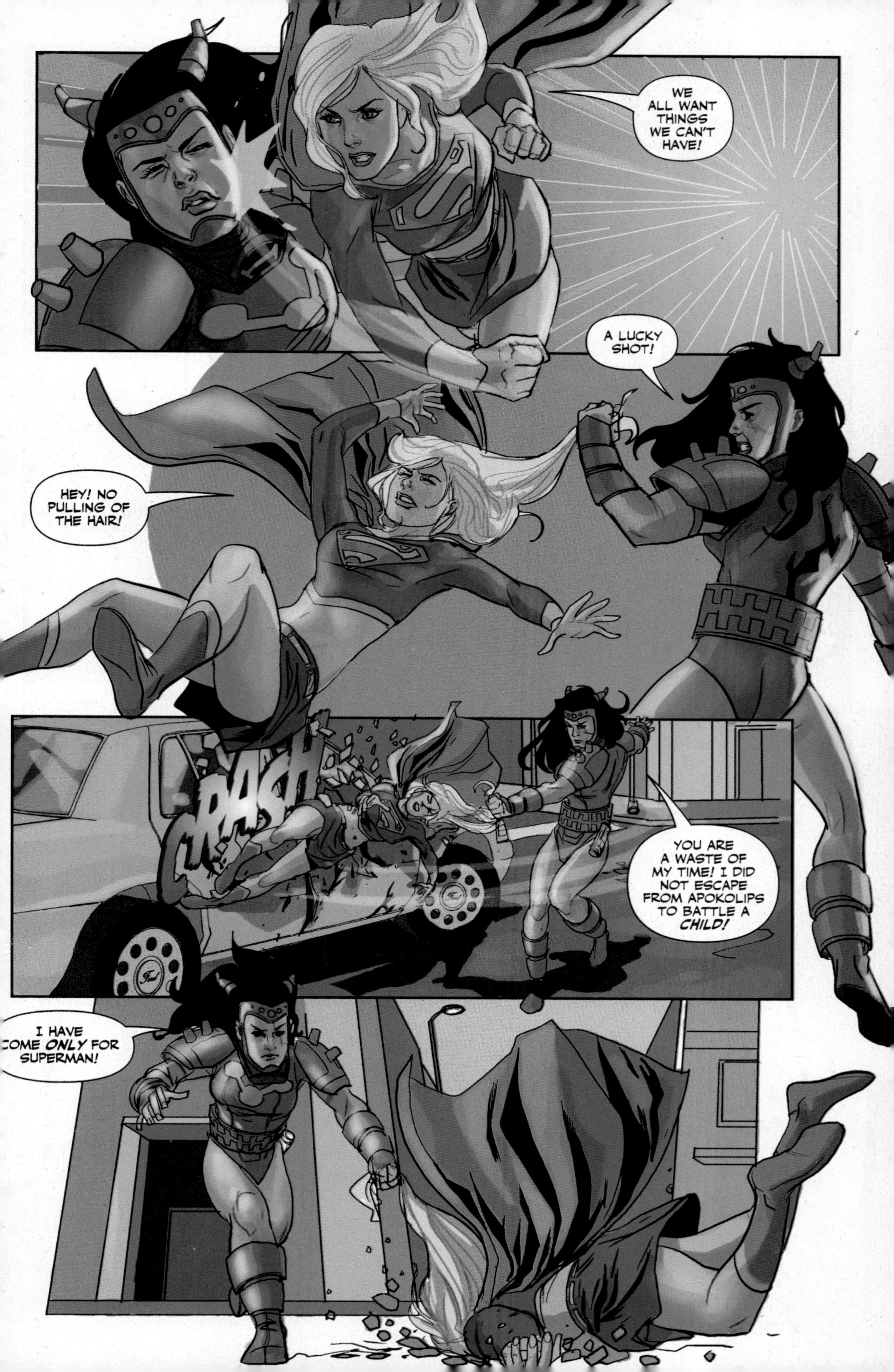
WE ALL WANT THINGS WE CAN'T HAVE!
A LUCKY SHOT!
HEY! NO PULLING OF THE HAIR!
CRASH
YOU ARE A WASTE OF MY TIME! I DID NOT ESCAPE FROM APOKOLIPS TO BATTLE A CHILD!
I HAVE COME ONLY FOR SUPERMAN!

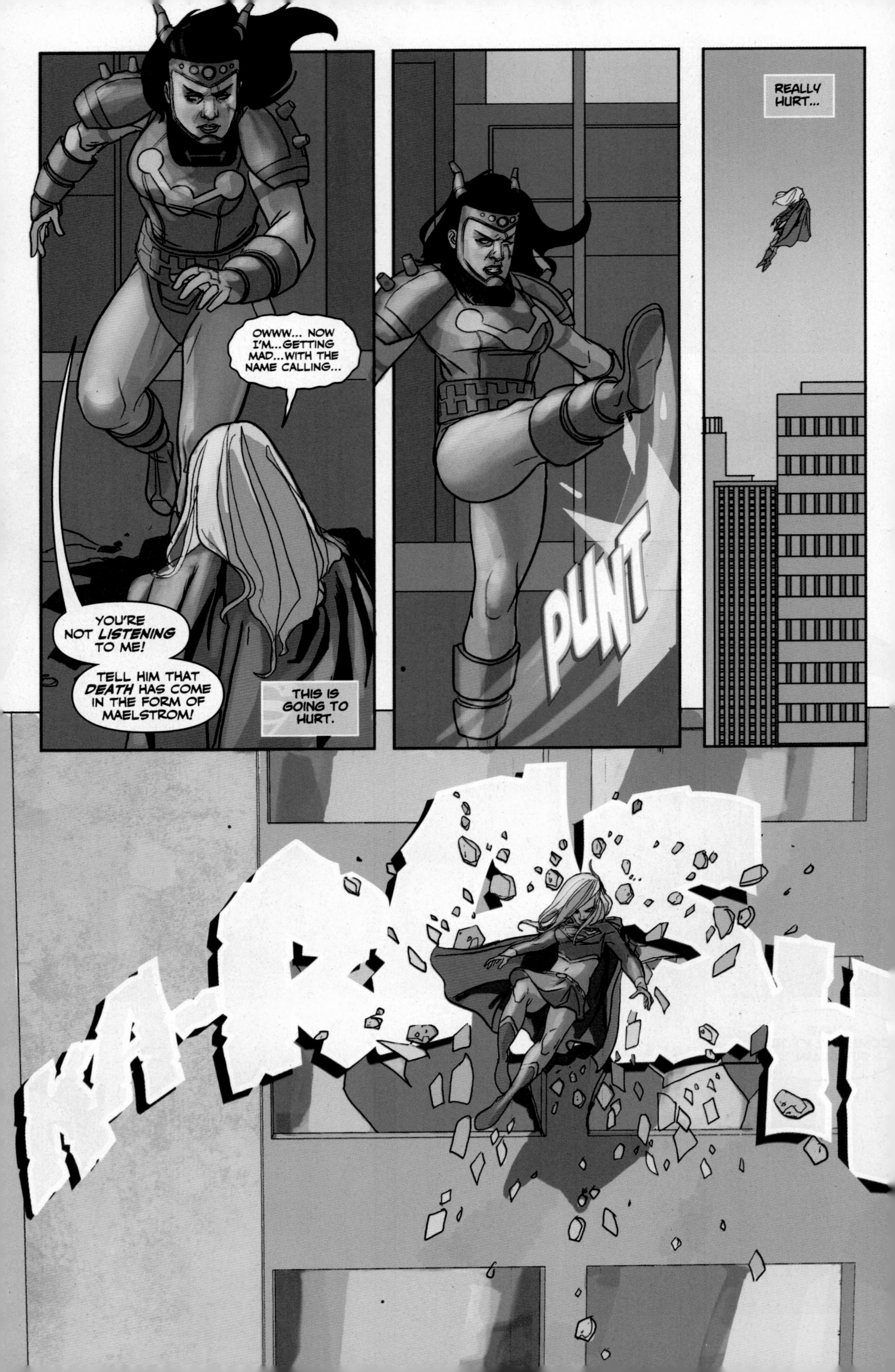

OWWW... NOW I'M...GETTING MAD...WITH THE NAME CALLING...
YOU'RE NOT *LISTENING* TO ME!
TELL HIM THAT *DEATH* HAS COME IN THE FORM OF MAELSTROM!
THIS IS GOING TO HURT.
PUNT
REALLY HURT...
KA-BLASH

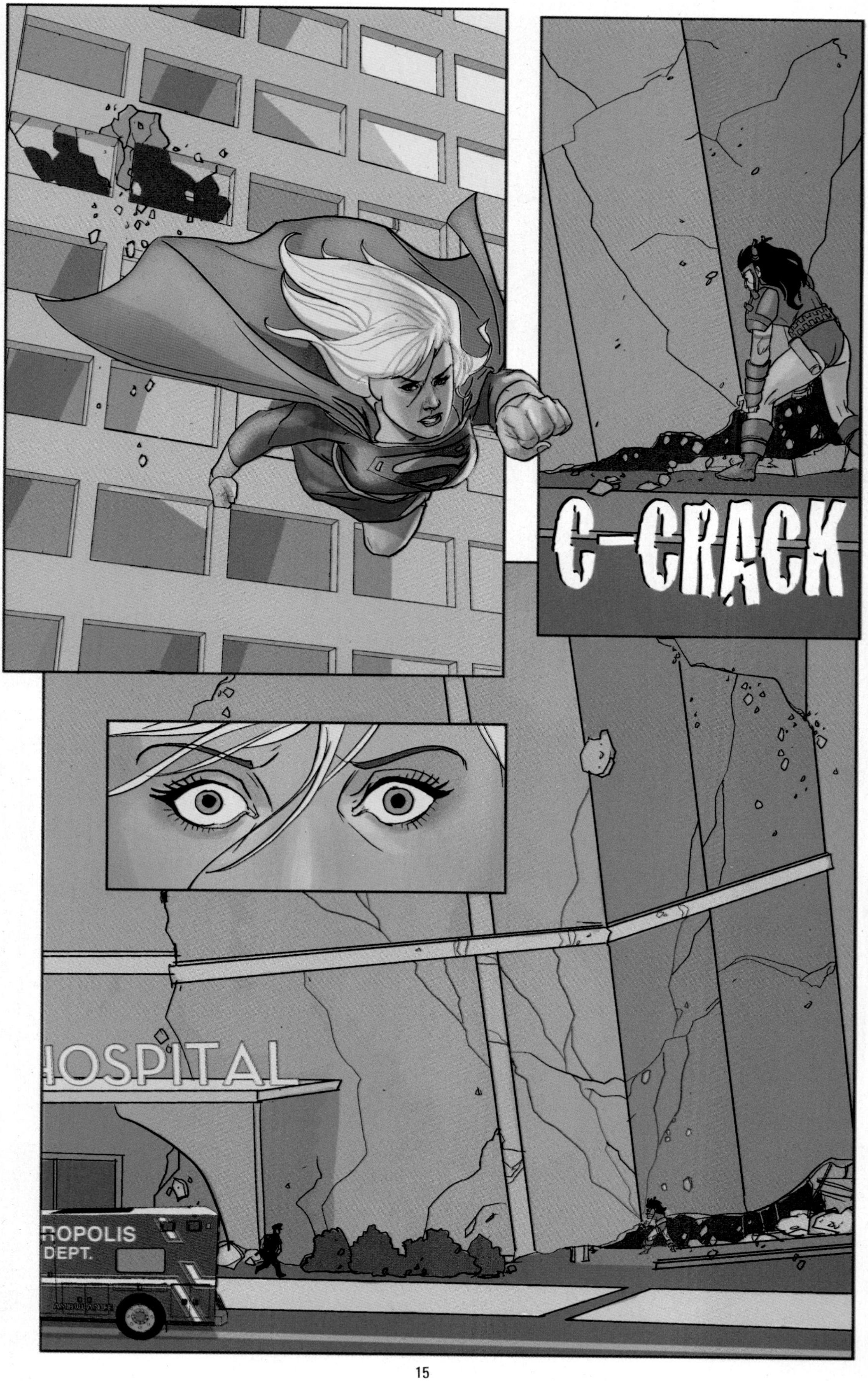
C-CRACK
HOSPITAL
ROPOLIS
DEPT.

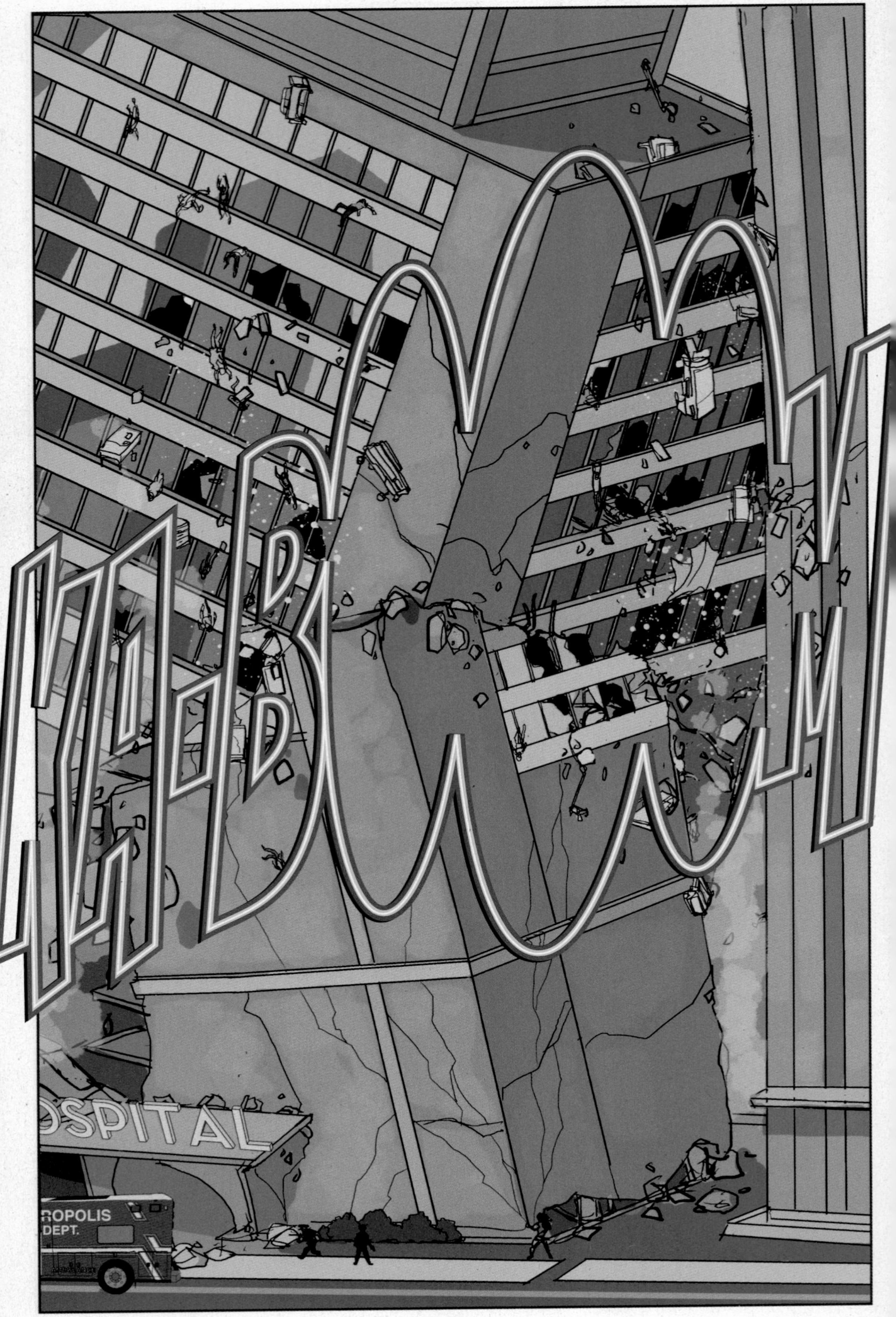
KABOOM
OSPITAL
ROPOLIS
DEPT.

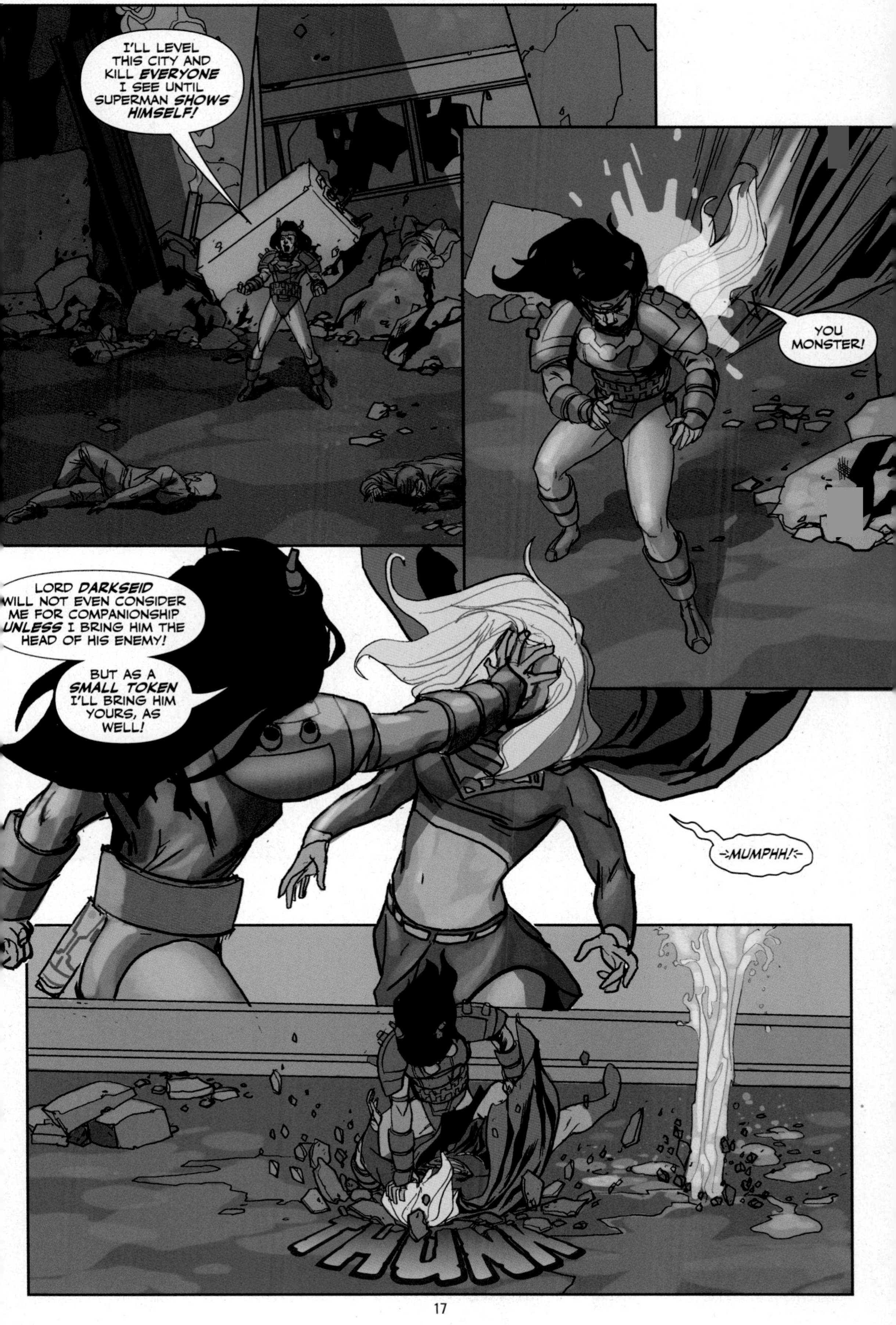
I'LL LEVEL THIS CITY AND KILL EVERYONE I SEE UNTIL SUPERMAN SHOWS HIMSELF!
YOU MONSTER!
LORD DARKSEID WILL NOT EVEN CONSIDER ME FOR COMPANIONSHIP UNLESS I BRING HIM THE HEAD OF HIS ENEMY!
BUT AS A SMALL TOKEN I'LL BRING HIM YOURS, AS WELL!
MUMPHH!
THUNK

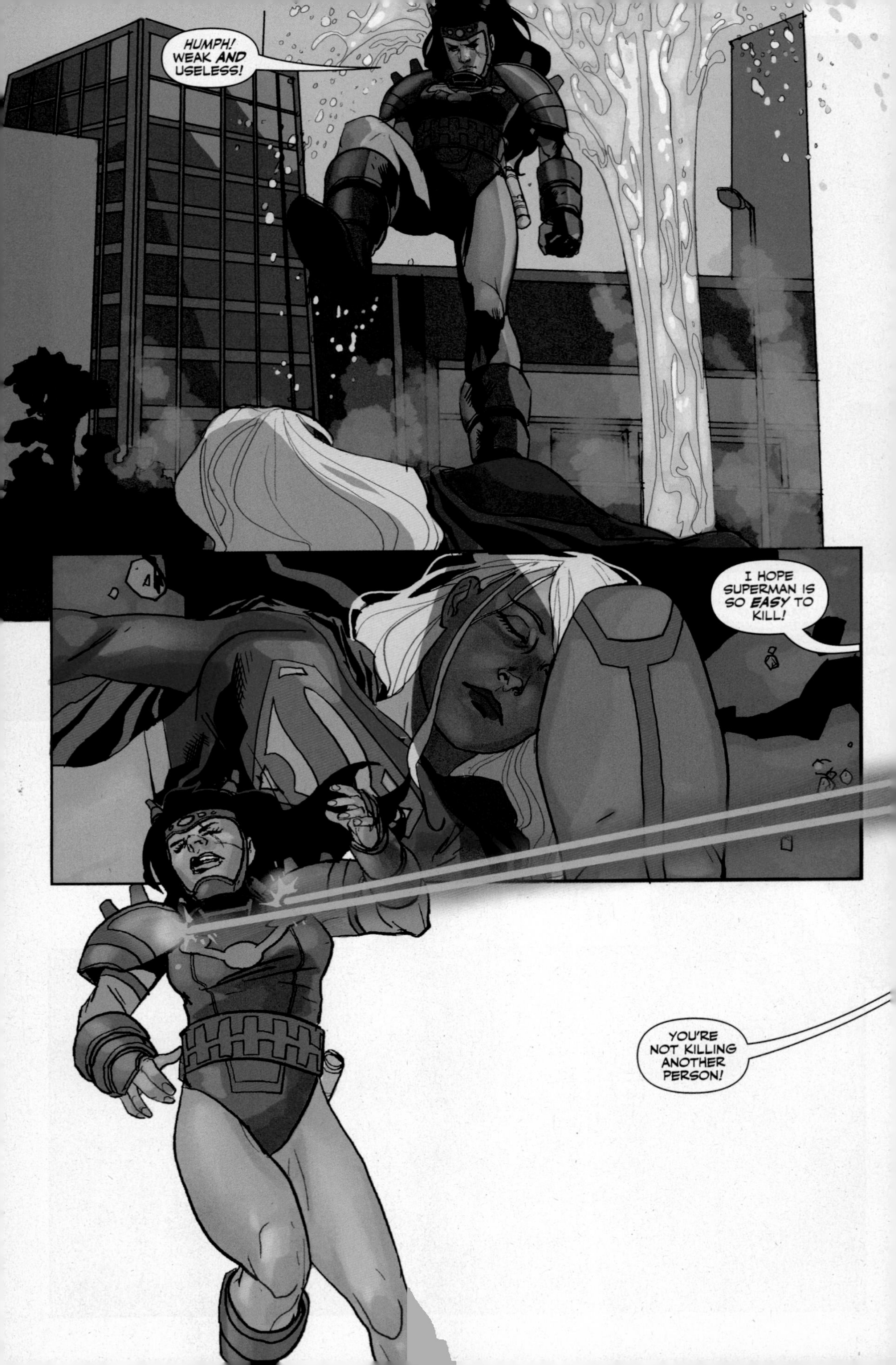
HUMPH! WEAK AND USELESS!
I HOPE SUPERMAN IS SO EASY TO KILL!
YOU'RE NOT KILLING ANOTHER PERSON!

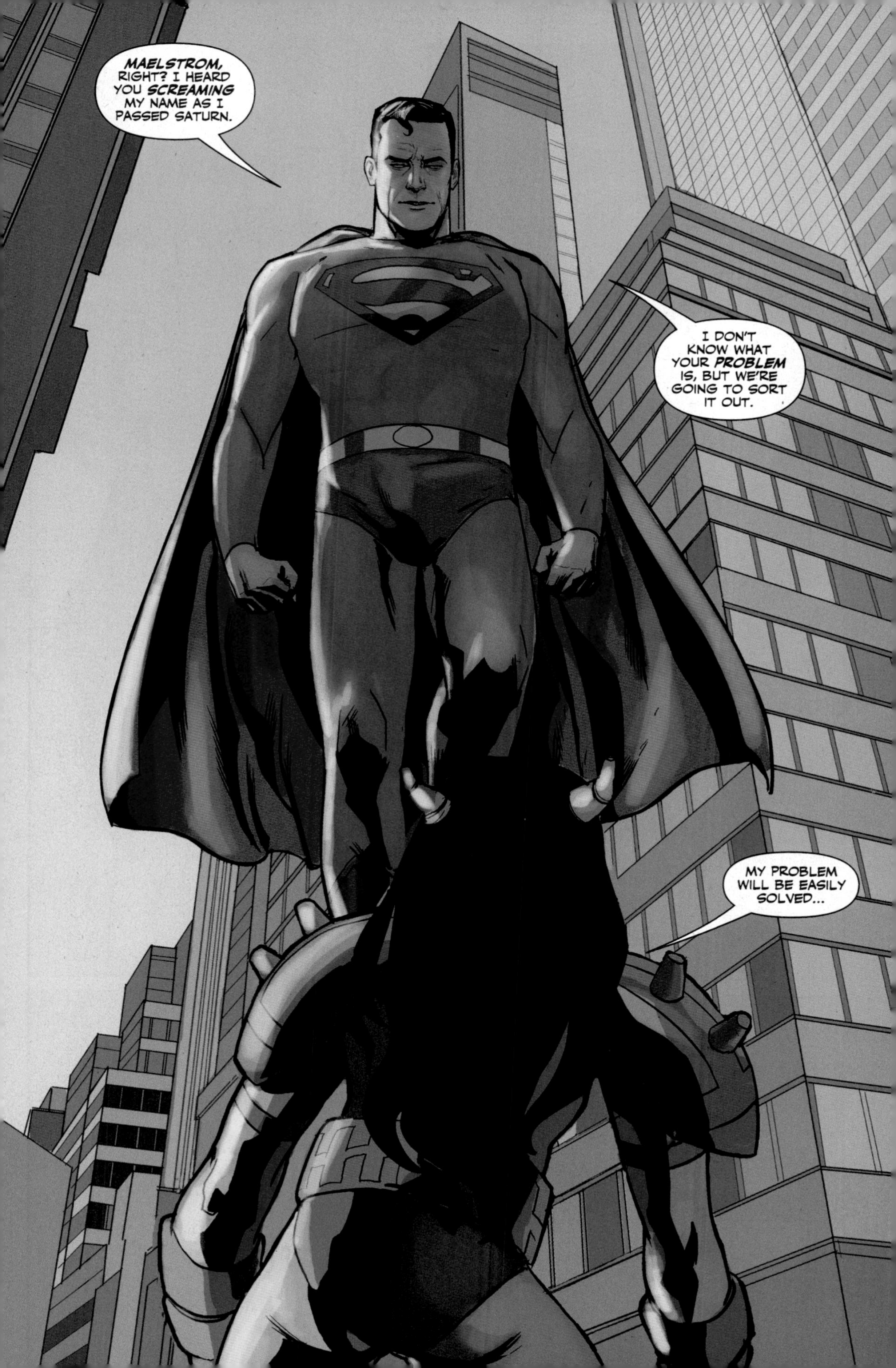
MAELSTROM, RIGHT? I HEARD YOU SCREAMING MY NAME AS I PASSED SATURN.
I DON'T KNOW WHAT YOUR PROBLEM IS, BUT WE'RE GOING TO SORT IT OUT.
MY PROBLEM WILL BE EASILY SOLVED...

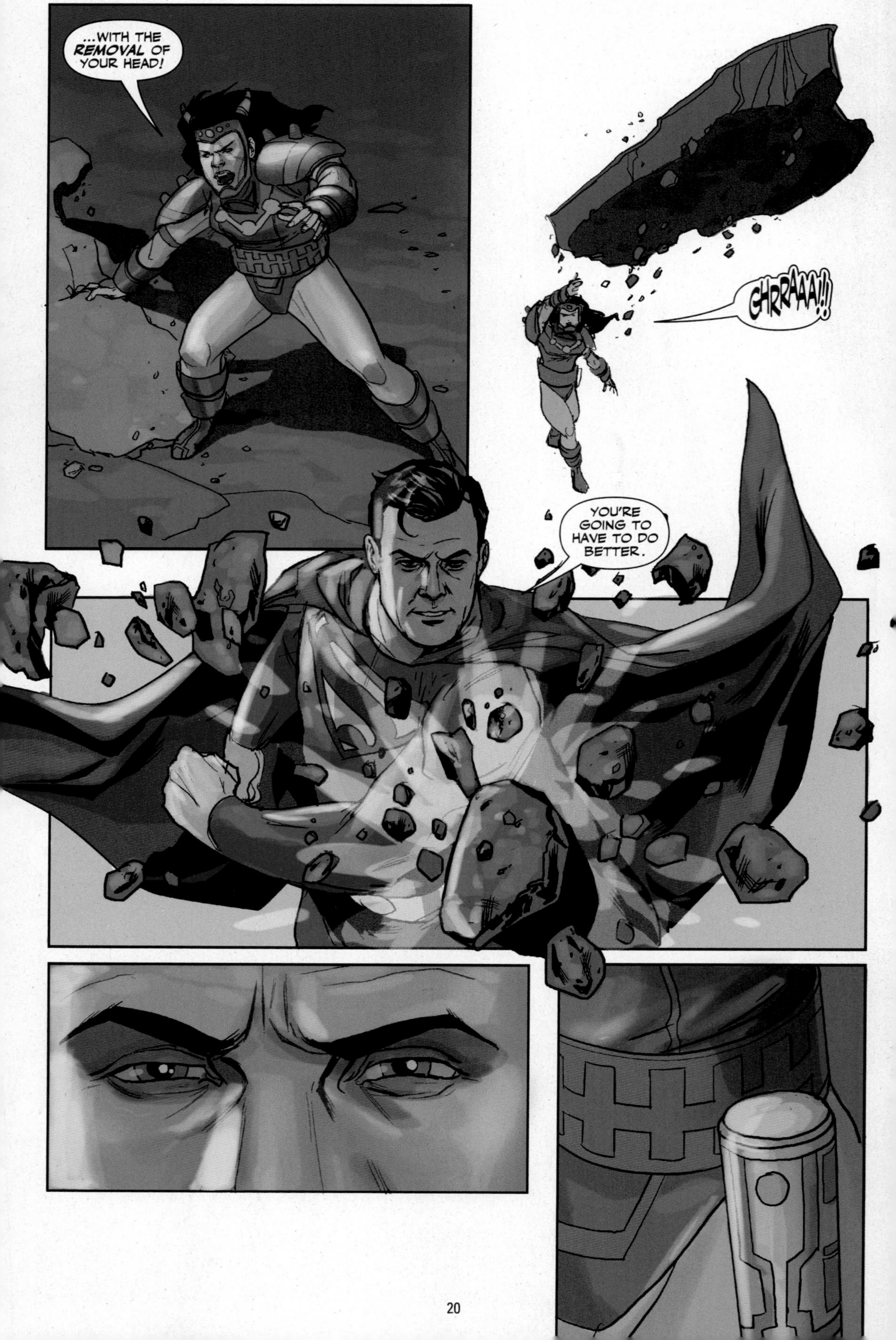
...WITH THE *REMOVAL* OF YOUR HEAD!
GHRRAAA!!!
YOU'RE GOING TO HAVE TO DO BETTER.

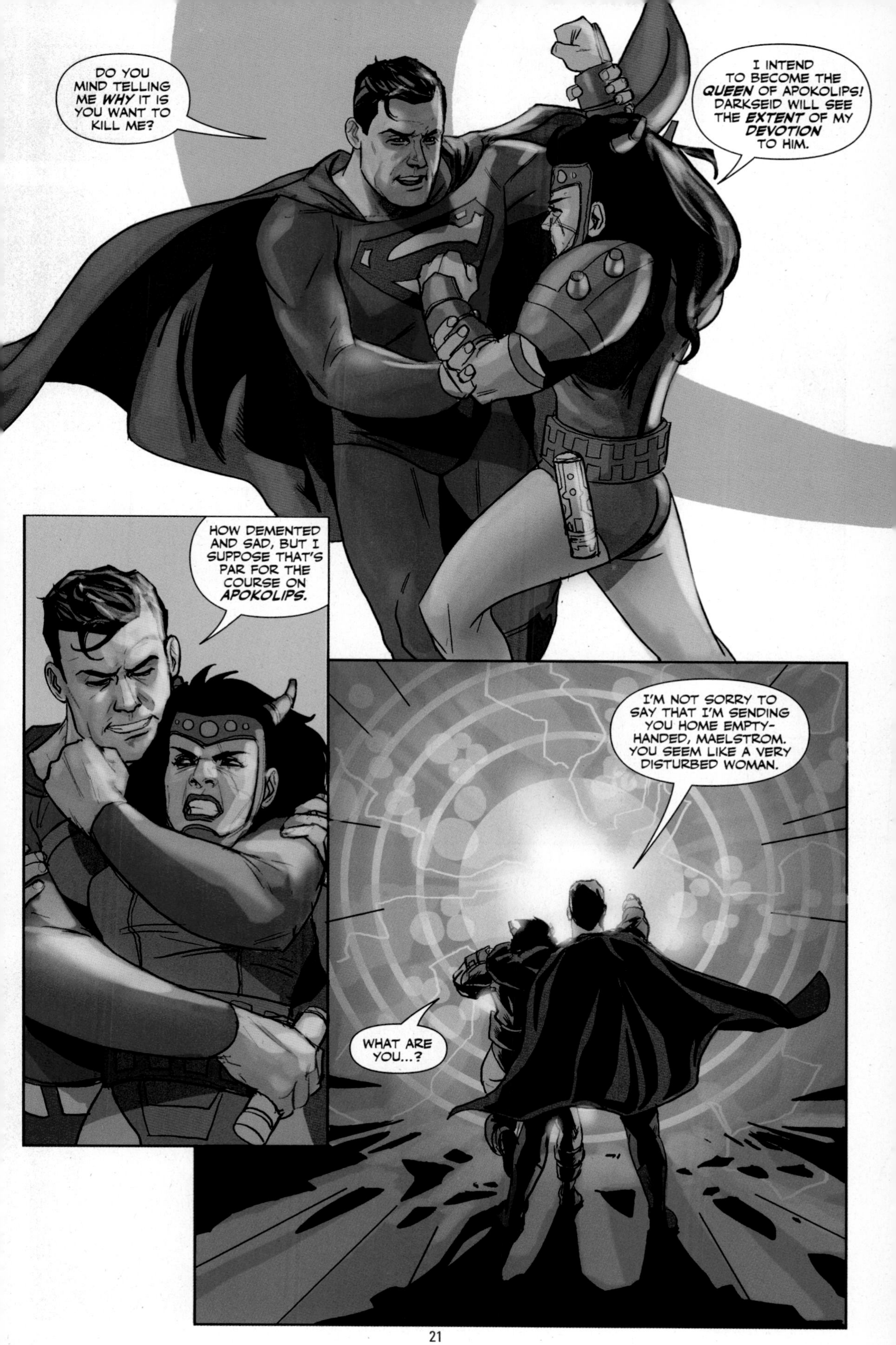
DO YOU MIND TELLING ME *WHY* IT IS YOU WANT TO KILL ME?
I INTEND TO BECOME THE *QUEEN* OF APOKOLIPS! DARKSEID WILL SEE THE *EXTENT* OF MY *DEVOTION* TO HIM.
HOW DEMENTED AND SAD, BUT I SUPPOSE THAT'S PAR FOR THE COURSE ON *APOKOLIPS.*
I'M NOT SORRY TO SAY THAT I'M SENDING YOU HOME EMPTY-HANDED, MAELSTROM. YOU SEEM LIKE A VERY DISTURBED WOMAN.
WHAT ARE YOU...?

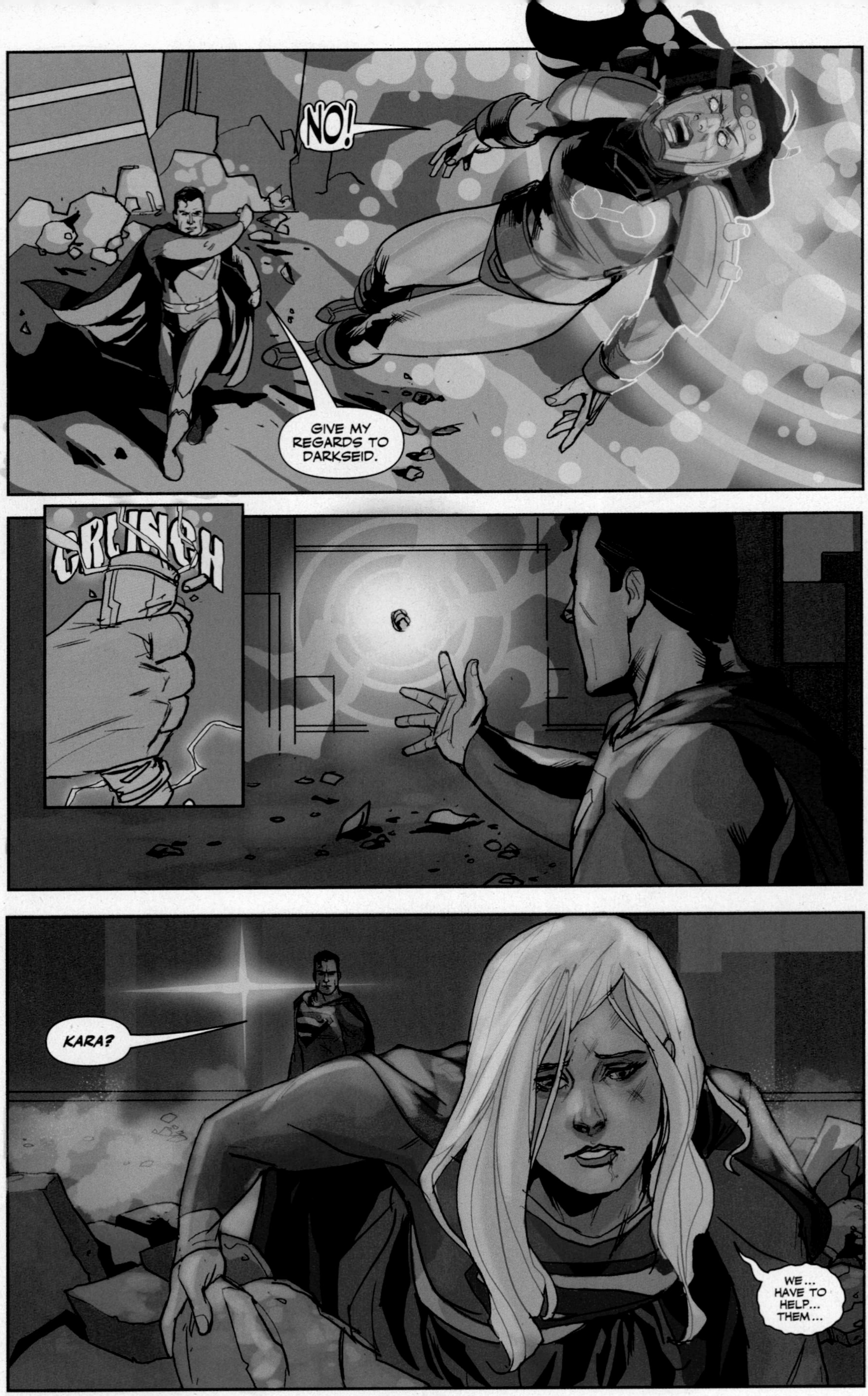
NO!
GIVE MY REGARDS TO DARKSEID.
CRUNCH
KARA?
WE... HAVE TO HELP... THEM...

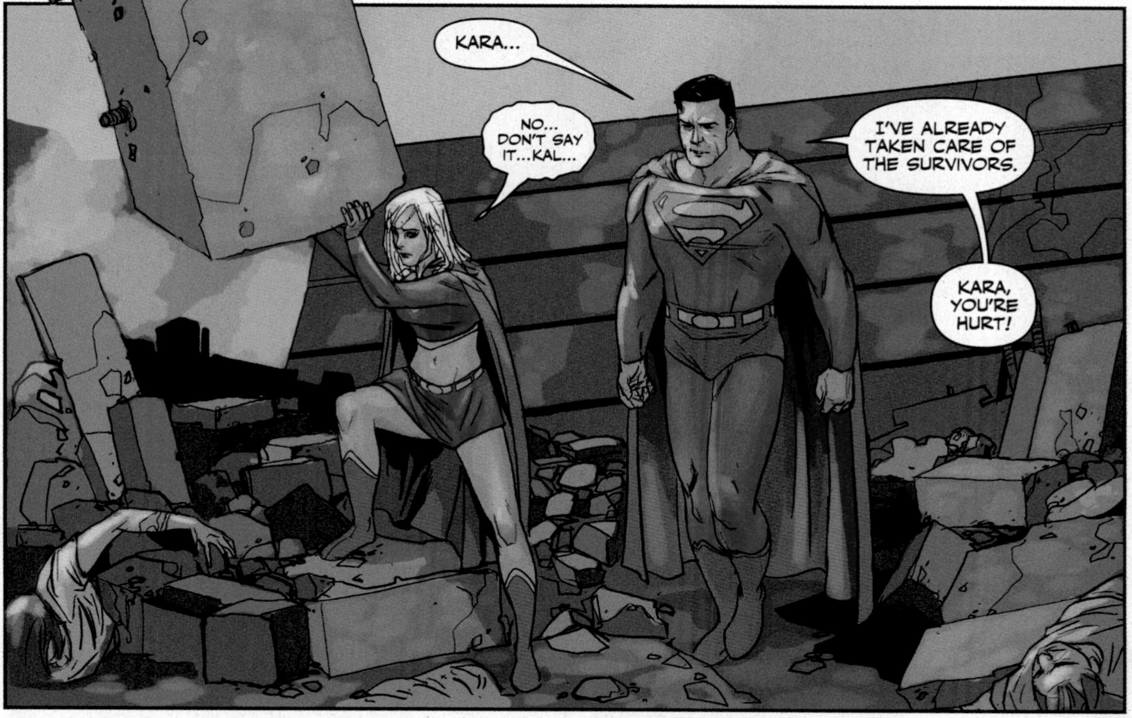
KARA...
NO... DON'T SAY IT...KAL...
I'VE ALREADY TAKEN CARE OF THE SURVIVORS.
KARA, YOU'RE HURT!

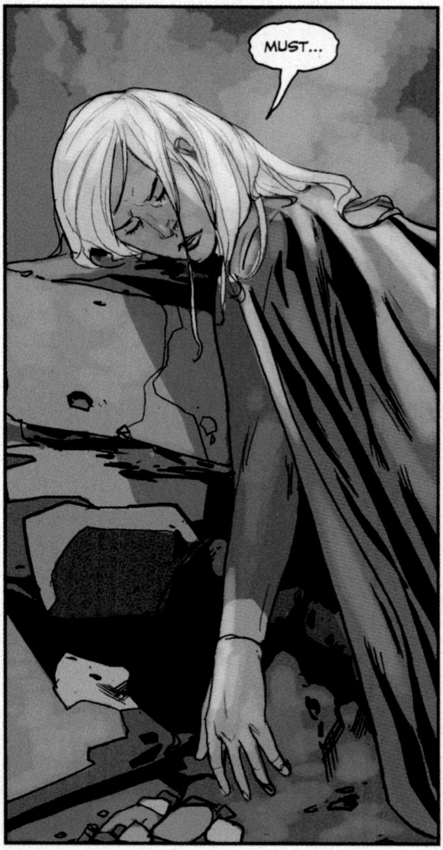
MUST...

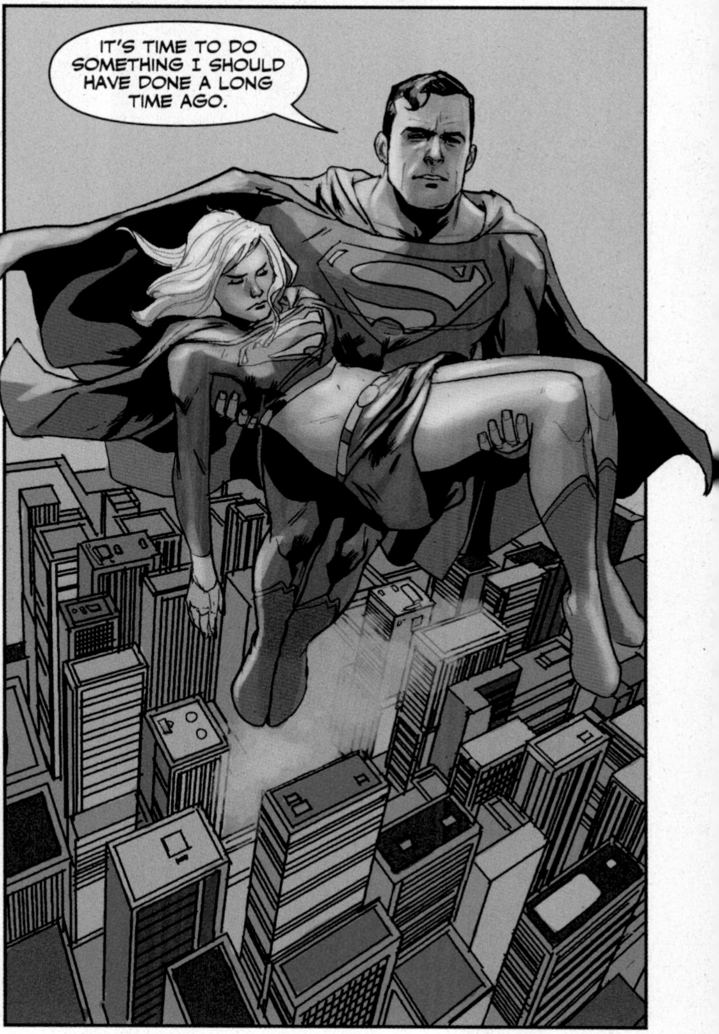
IT'S TIME TO DO SOMETHING I SHOULD HAVE DONE A LONG TIME AGO.

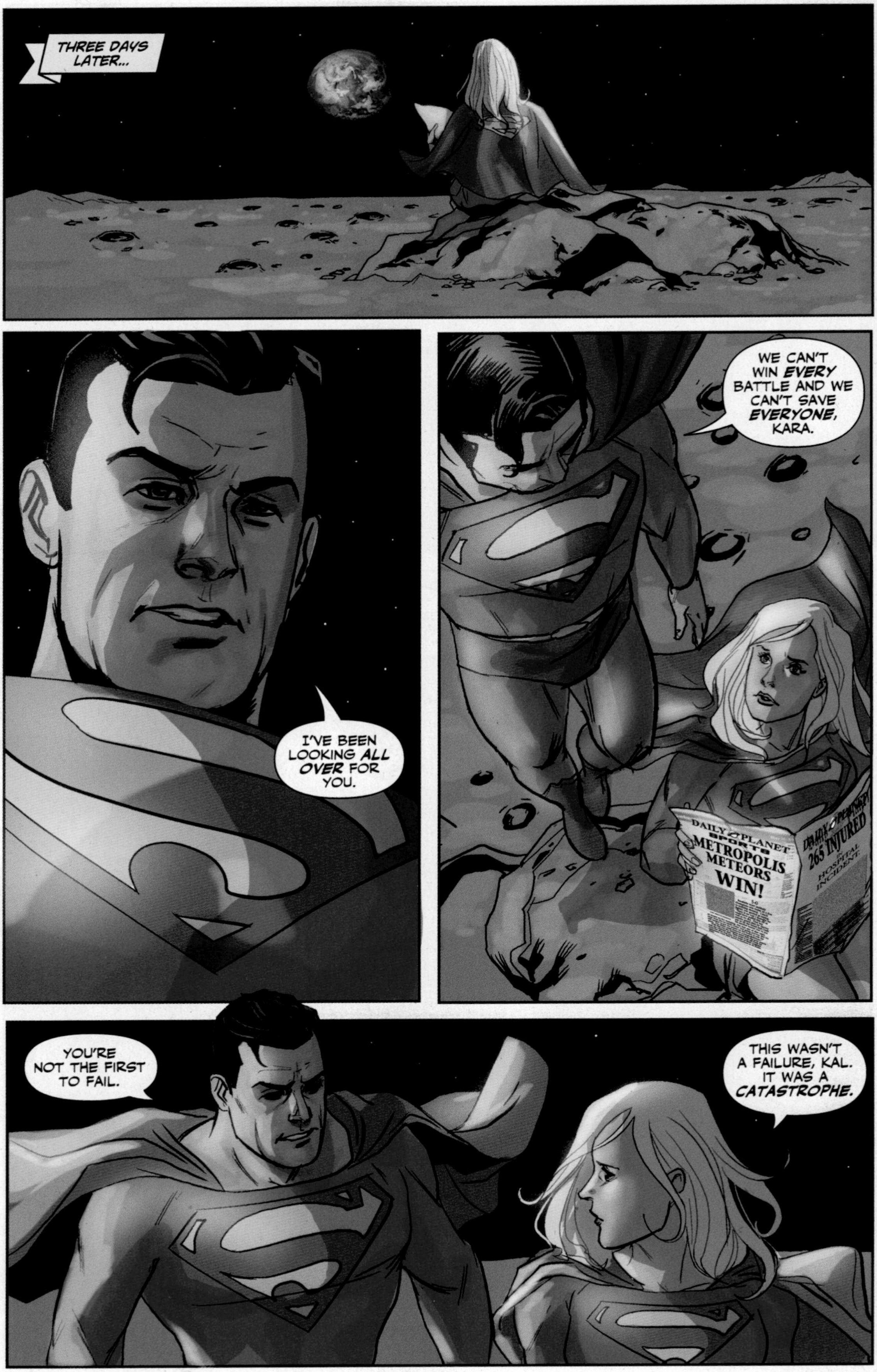
THREE DAYS LATER...
I'VE BEEN LOOKING ALL OVER FOR YOU.
WE CAN'T WIN EVERY BATTLE AND WE CAN'T SAVE EVERYONE, KARA.
DAILY PLANET SPORTS
METROPOLIS METEORS WIN!
265 INJURED
HOSPITAL INCIDENT
YOU'RE NOT THE FIRST TO FAIL.
THIS WASN'T A FAILURE, KAL. IT WAS A CATASTROPHE.

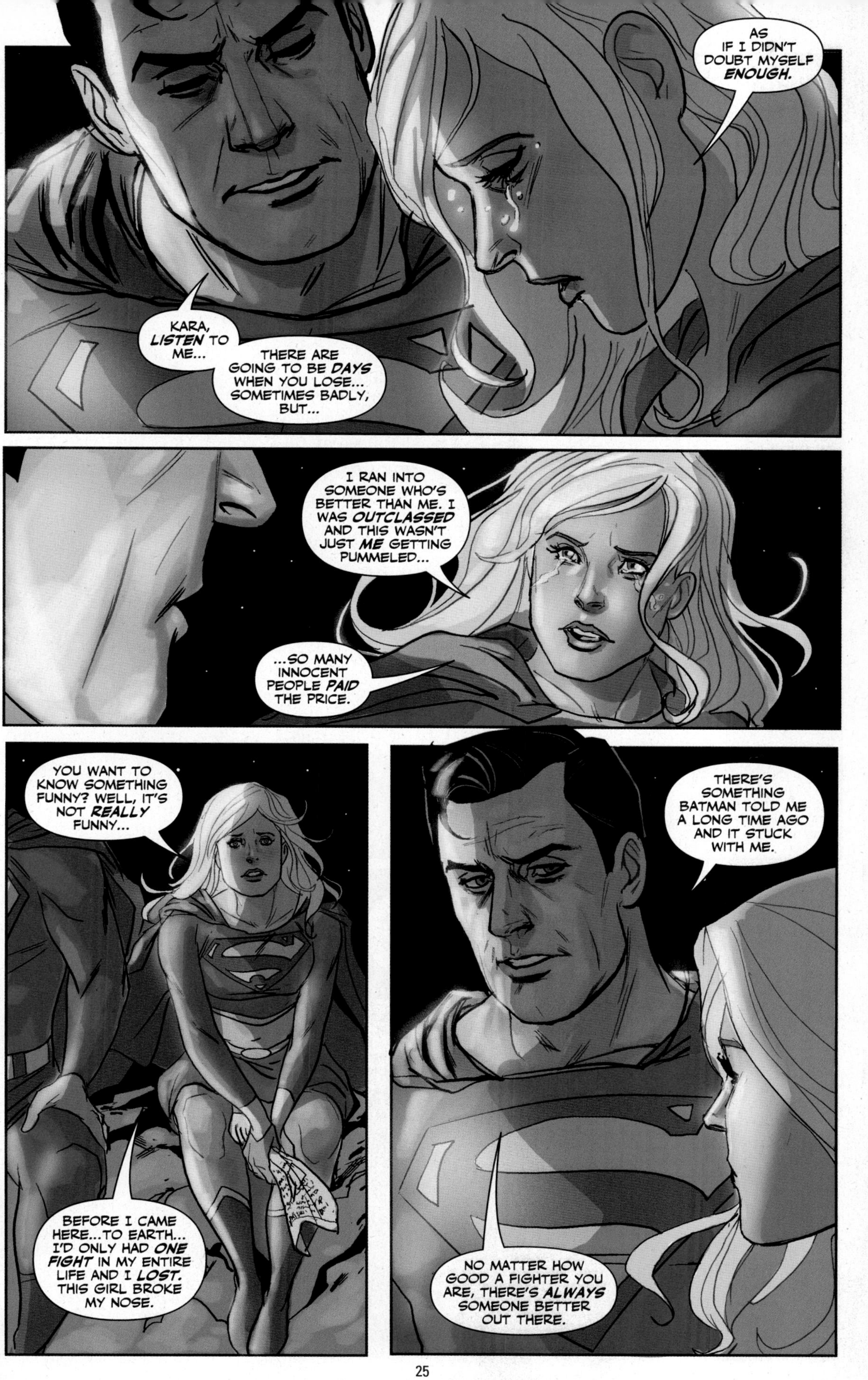
AS IF I DIDN'T DOUBT MYSELF ENOUGH.
KARA, LISTEN TO ME...
THERE ARE GOING TO BE DAYS WHEN YOU LOSE... SOMETIMES BADLY, BUT...
I RAN INTO SOMEONE WHO'S BETTER THAN ME. I WAS OUTCLASSED AND THIS WASN'T JUST ME GETTING PUMMELED...
...SO MANY INNOCENT PEOPLE PAID THE PRICE.
YOU WANT TO KNOW SOMETHING FUNNY? WELL, IT'S NOT REALLY FUNNY...
BEFORE I CAME HERE...TO EARTH... I'D ONLY HAD ONE FIGHT IN MY ENTIRE LIFE AND I LOST. THIS GIRL BROKE MY NOSE.
THERE'S SOMETHING BATMAN TOLD ME A LONG TIME AGO AND IT STUCK WITH ME.
NO MATTER HOW GOOD A FIGHTER YOU ARE, THERE'S ALWAYS SOMEONE BETTER OUT THERE.

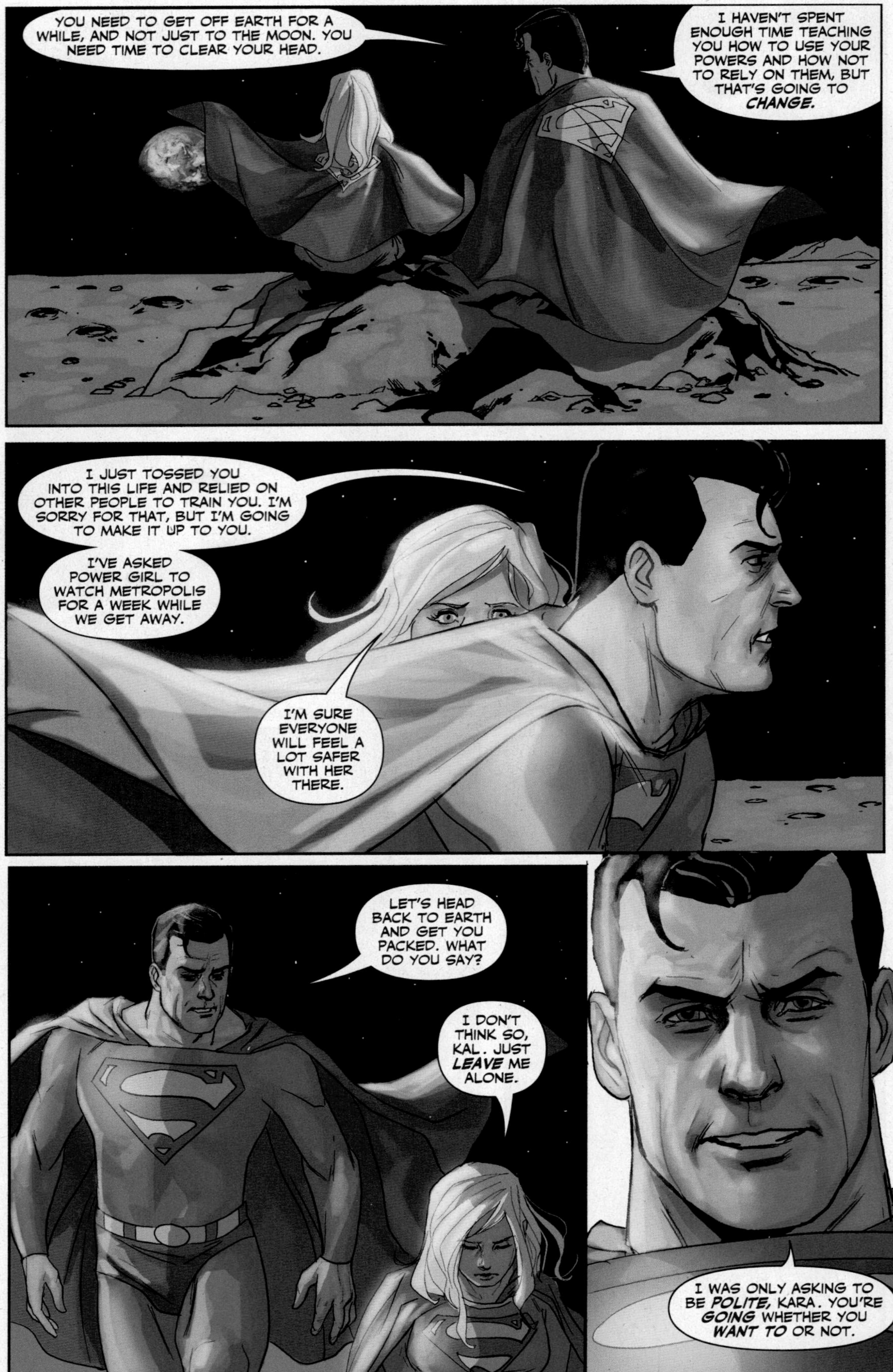
YOU NEED TO GET OFF EARTH FOR A WHILE, AND NOT JUST TO THE MOON. YOU NEED TIME TO CLEAR YOUR HEAD.
I HAVEN'T SPENT ENOUGH TIME TEACHING YOU HOW TO USE YOUR POWERS AND HOW NOT TO RELY ON THEM, BUT THAT'S GOING TO *CHANGE.*
I JUST TOSSED YOU INTO THIS LIFE AND RELIED ON OTHER PEOPLE TO TRAIN YOU. I'M SORRY FOR THAT, BUT I'M GOING TO MAKE IT UP TO YOU.
I'VE ASKED POWER GIRL TO WATCH METROPOLIS FOR A WEEK WHILE WE GET AWAY.
I'M SURE EVERYONE WILL FEEL A LOT SAFER WITH HER THERE.
LET'S HEAD BACK TO EARTH AND GET YOU PACKED. WHAT DO YOU SAY?
I DON'T THINK SO, KAL. JUST *LEAVE* ME ALONE.
I WAS ONLY ASKING TO BE *POLITE,* KARA. YOU'RE *GOING* WHETHER YOU *WANT TO* OR NOT.

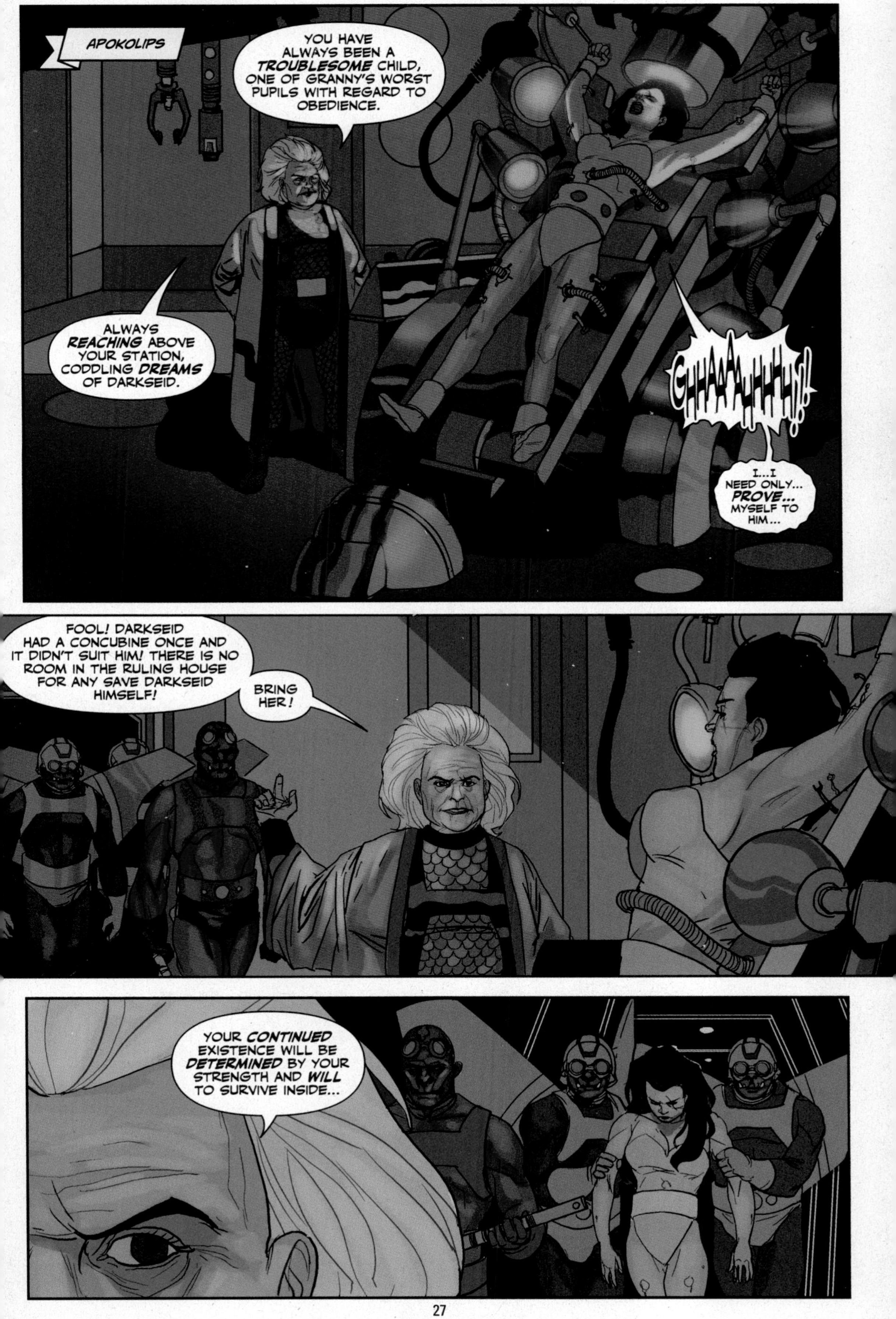
APOKOLIPS
YOU HAVE ALWAYS BEEN A TROUBLESOME CHILD, ONE OF GRANNY'S WORST PUPILS WITH REGARD TO OBEDIENCE.
ALWAYS REACHING ABOVE YOUR STATION, CODDLING DREAMS OF DARKSEID.
GHHAAAAAHHHH!!
I...I NEED ONLY... PROVE... MYSELF TO HIM...
FOOL! DARKSEID HAD A CONCUBINE ONCE AND IT DIDN'T SUIT HIM! THERE IS NO ROOM IN THE RULING HOUSE FOR ANY SAVE DARKSEID HIMSELF!
BRING HER!
YOUR CONTINUED EXISTENCE WILL BE DETERMINED BY YOUR STRENGTH AND WILL TO SURVIVE INSIDE...

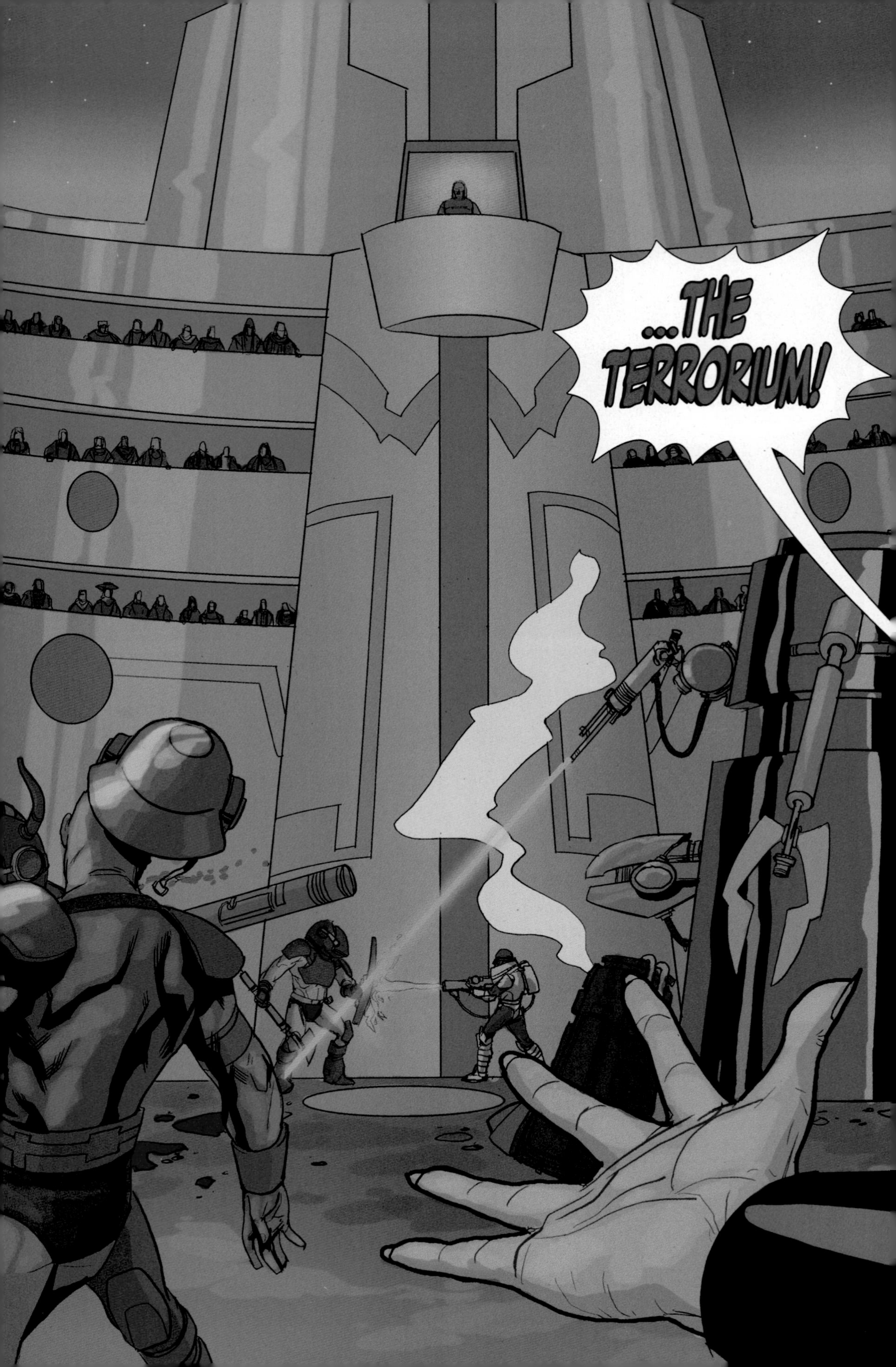
...THE TERRORIUM!

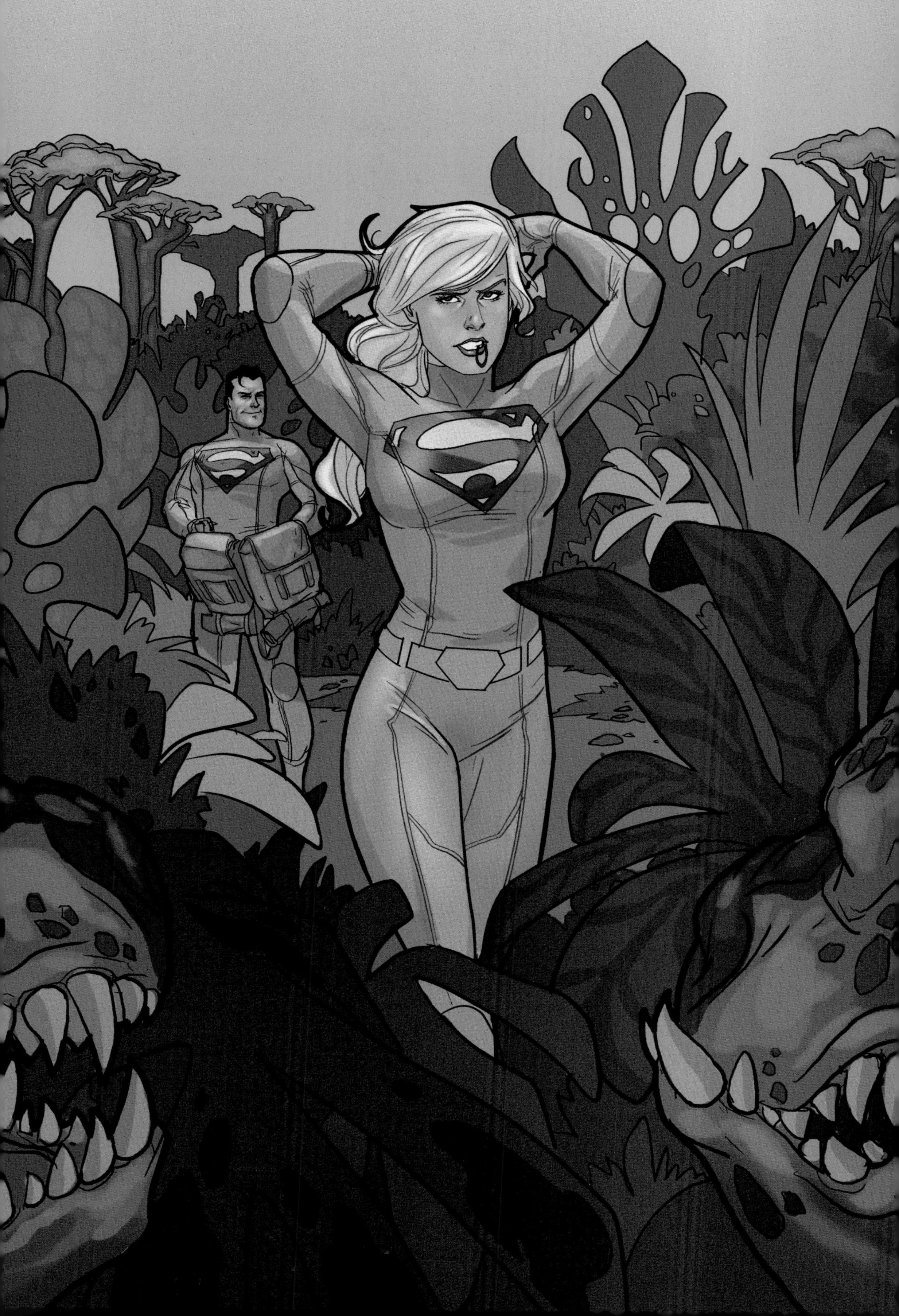

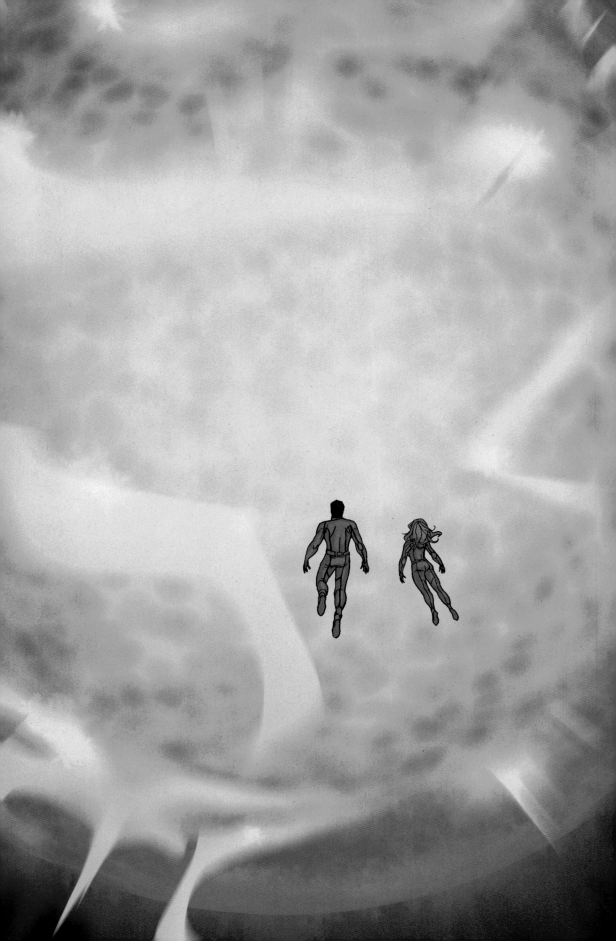

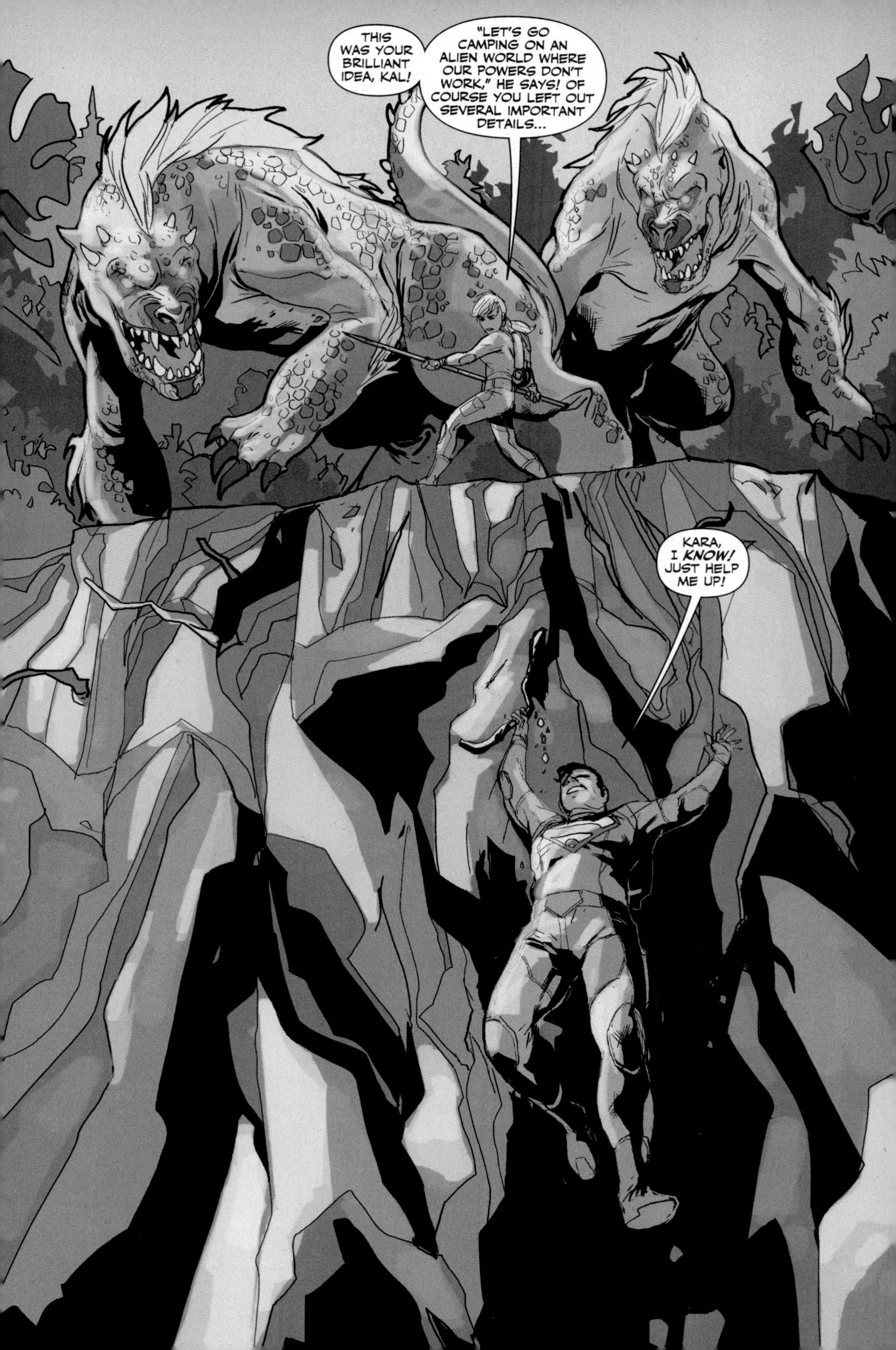
THIS WAS YOUR BRILLIANT IDEA, KAL!
"LET'S GO CAMPING ON AN ALIEN WORLD WHERE OUR POWERS DON'T WORK," HE SAYS! OF COURSE YOU LEFT OUT SEVERAL IMPORTANT DETAILS...
KARA, I KNOW! JUST HELP ME UP!

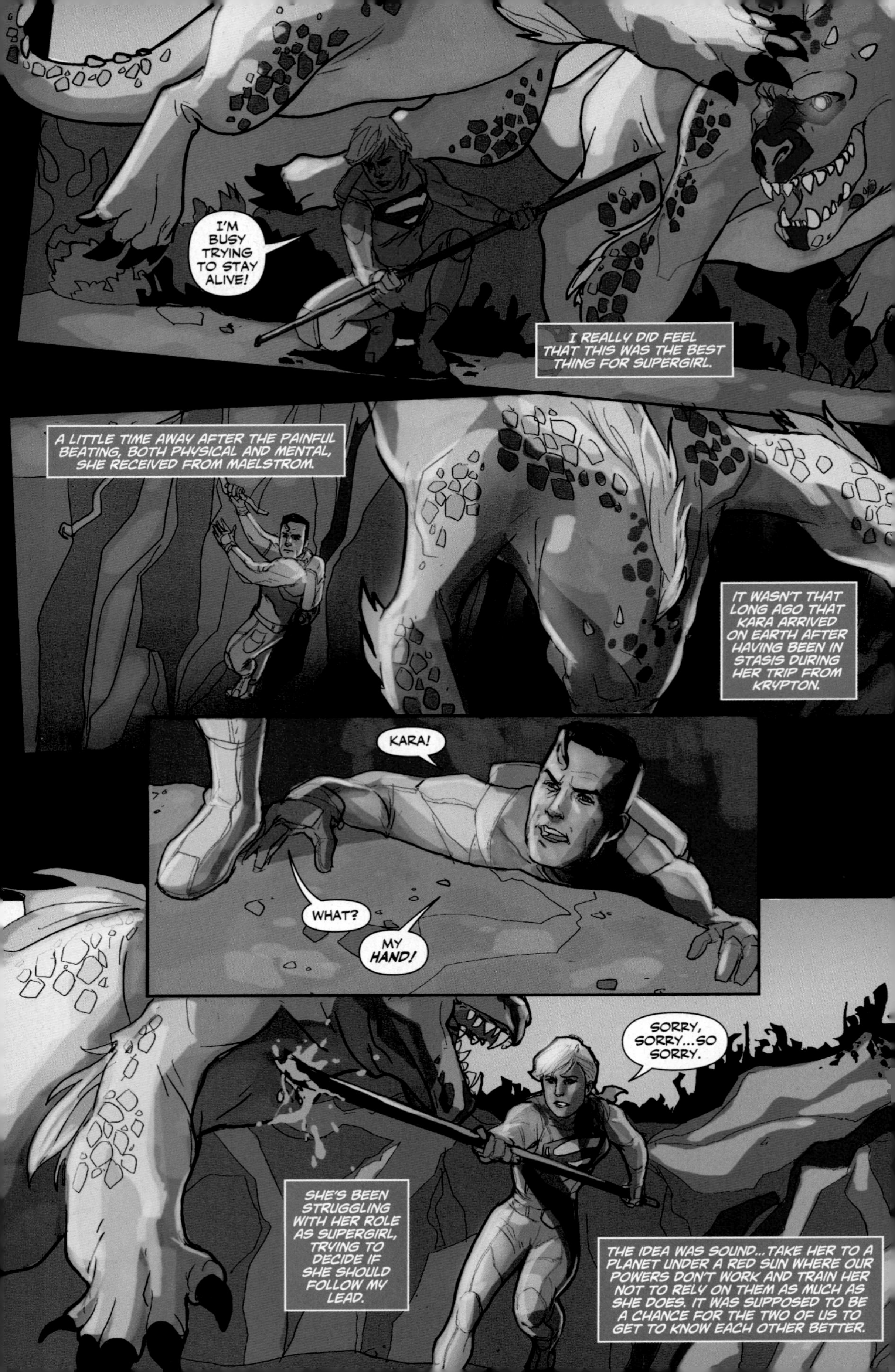
I'M BUSY TRYING TO STAY ALIVE!
I REALLY DID FEEL THAT THIS WAS THE BEST THING FOR SUPERGIRL.
A LITTLE TIME AWAY AFTER THE PAINFUL BEATING, BOTH PHYSICAL AND MENTAL, SHE RECEIVED FROM MAELSTROM.
IT WASN'T THAT LONG AGO THAT KARA ARRIVED ON EARTH AFTER HAVING BEEN IN STASIS DURING HER TRIP FROM KRYPTON.
KARA!
WHAT?
MY HAND!
SORRY, SORRY...SO SORRY.
SHE'S BEEN STRUGGLING WITH HER ROLE AS SUPERGIRL, TRYING TO DECIDE IF SHE SHOULD FOLLOW MY LEAD.
THE IDEA WAS SOUND...TAKE HER TO A PLANET UNDER A RED SUN WHERE OUR POWERS DON'T WORK AND TRAIN HER NOT TO RELY ON THEM AS MUCH AS SHE DOES. IT WAS SUPPOSED TO BE A CHANCE FOR THE TWO OF US TO GET TO KNOW EACH OTHER BETTER.

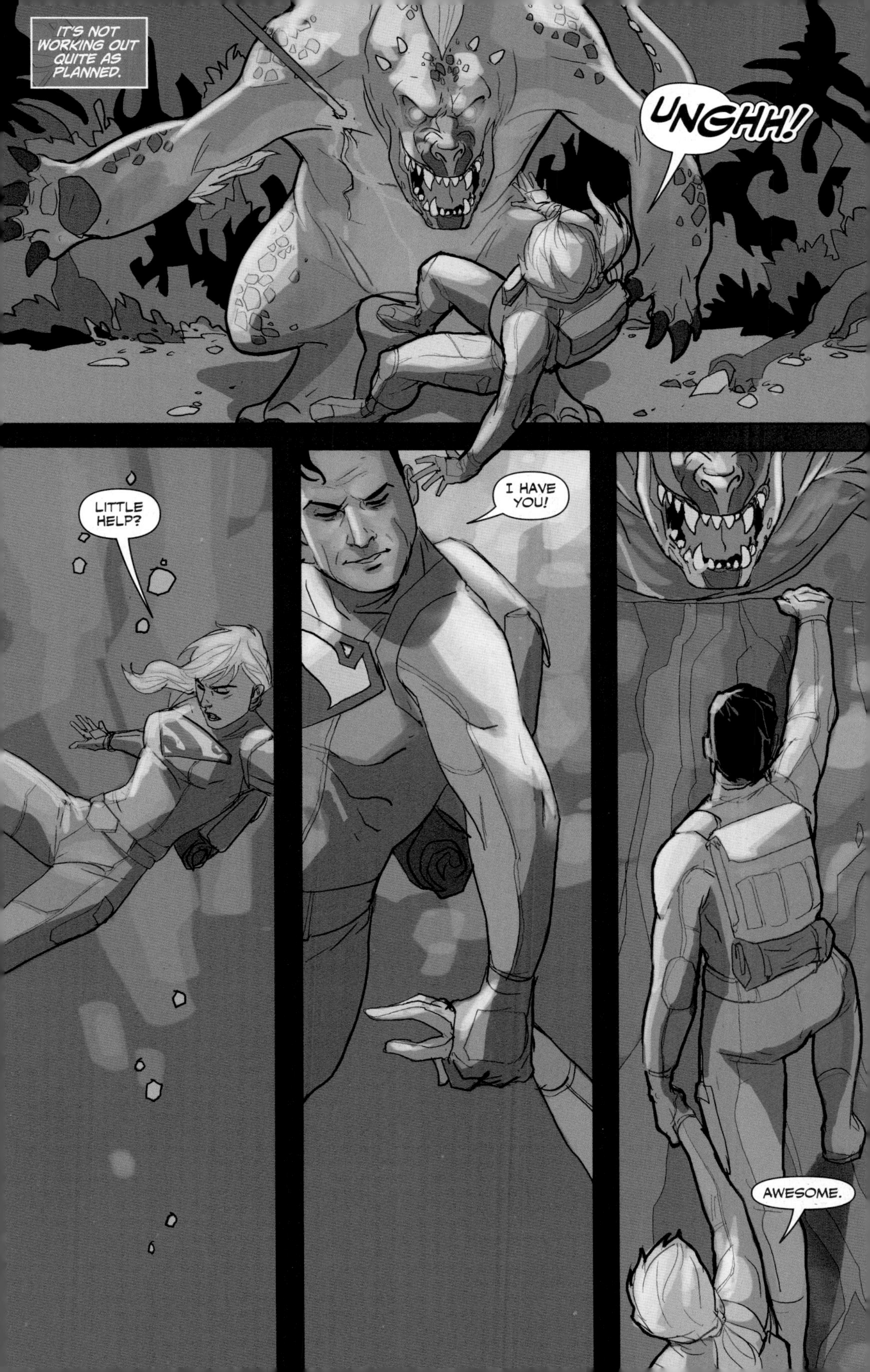
IT'S NOT WORKING OUT QUITE AS PLANNED.
UNGHH!
LITTLE HELP?
I HAVE YOU!
AWESOME.

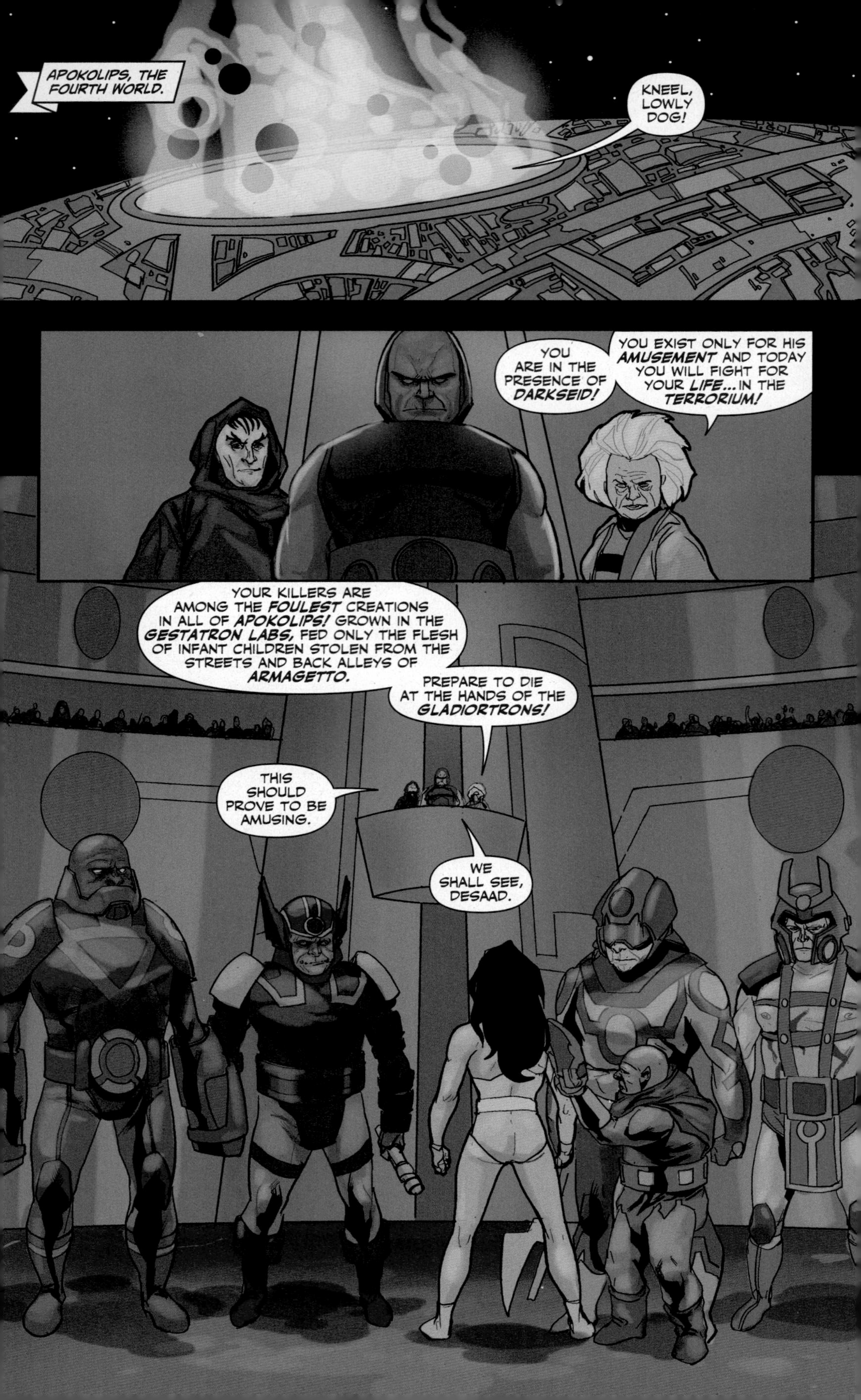
APOKOLIPS, THE FOURTH WORLD.
KNEEL, LOWLY DOG!
YOU ARE IN THE PRESENCE OF DARKSEID!
YOU EXIST ONLY FOR HIS AMUSEMENT AND TODAY YOU WILL FIGHT FOR YOUR LIFE... IN THE TERRORIUM!
YOUR KILLERS ARE AMONG THE FOULEST CREATIONS IN ALL OF APOKOLIPS! GROWN IN THE GESTATRON LABS, FED ONLY THE FLESH OF INFANT CHILDREN STOLEN FROM THE STREETS AND BACK ALLEYS OF ARMAGETTO.
PREPARE TO DIE AT THE HANDS OF THE GLADIORTRONS!
THIS SHOULD PROVE TO BE AMUSING.
WE SHALL SEE, DESAAD.

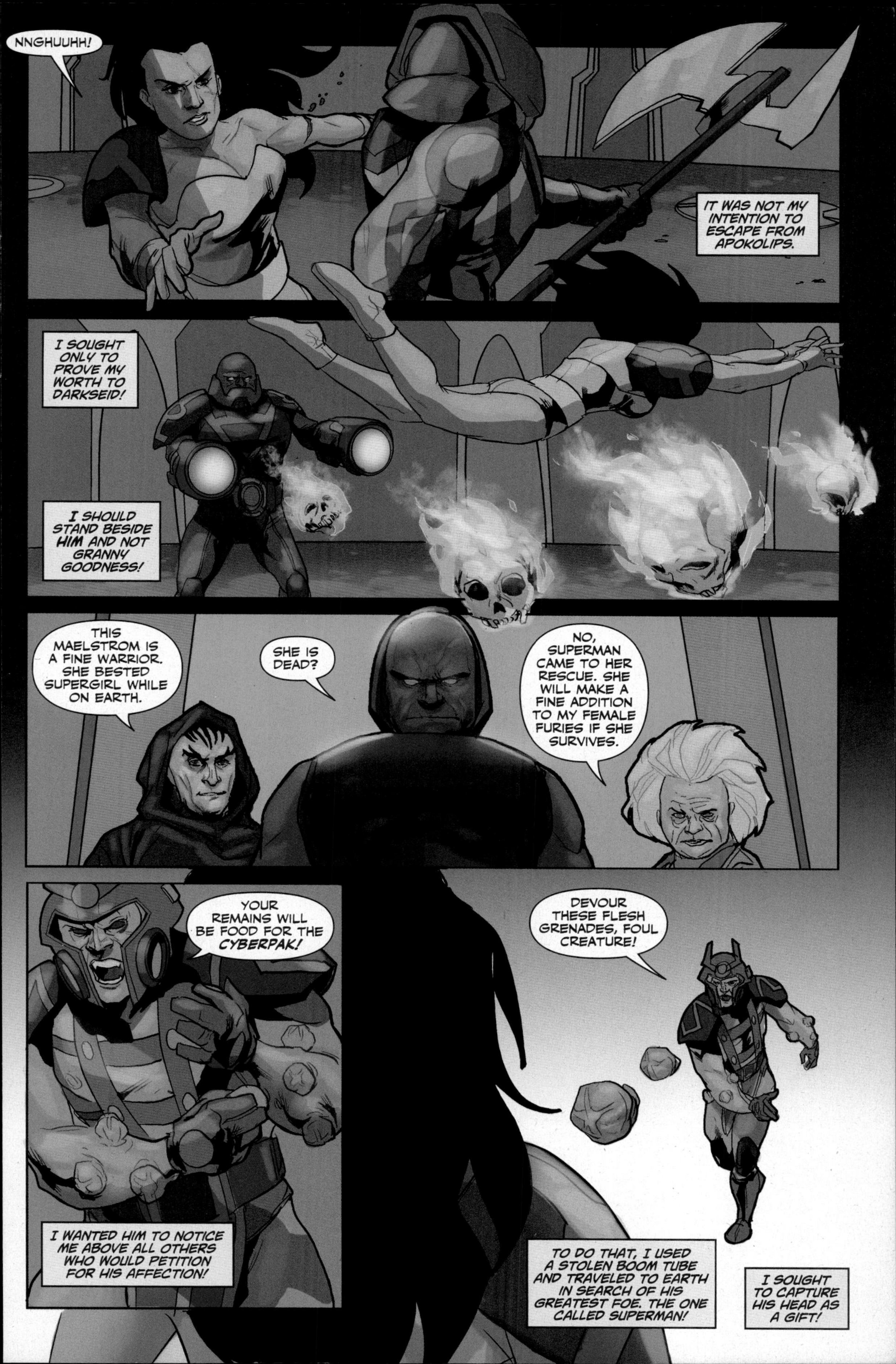
NNGHUUHH!
IT WAS NOT MY INTENTION TO ESCAPE FROM APOKOLIPS.
I SOUGHT ONLY TO PROVE MY WORTH TO DARKSEID!
I SHOULD STAND BESIDE HIM AND NOT GRANNY GOODNESS!
THIS MAELSTROM IS A FINE WARRIOR. SHE BESTED SUPERGIRL WHILE ON EARTH.
SHE IS DEAD?
NO, SUPERMAN CAME TO HER RESCUE. SHE WILL MAKE A FINE ADDITION TO MY FEMALE FURIES IF SHE SURVIVES.
YOUR REMAINS WILL BE FOOD FOR THE CYBERPAK!
DEVOUR THESE FLESH GRENADES, FOUL CREATURE!
I WANTED HIM TO NOTICE ME ABOVE ALL OTHERS WHO WOULD PETITION FOR HIS AFFECTION!
TO DO THAT, I USED A STOLEN BOOM TUBE AND TRAVELED TO EARTH IN SEARCH OF HIS GREATEST FOE. THE ONE CALLED SUPERMAN!
I SOUGHT TO CAPTURE HIS HEAD AS A GIFT!

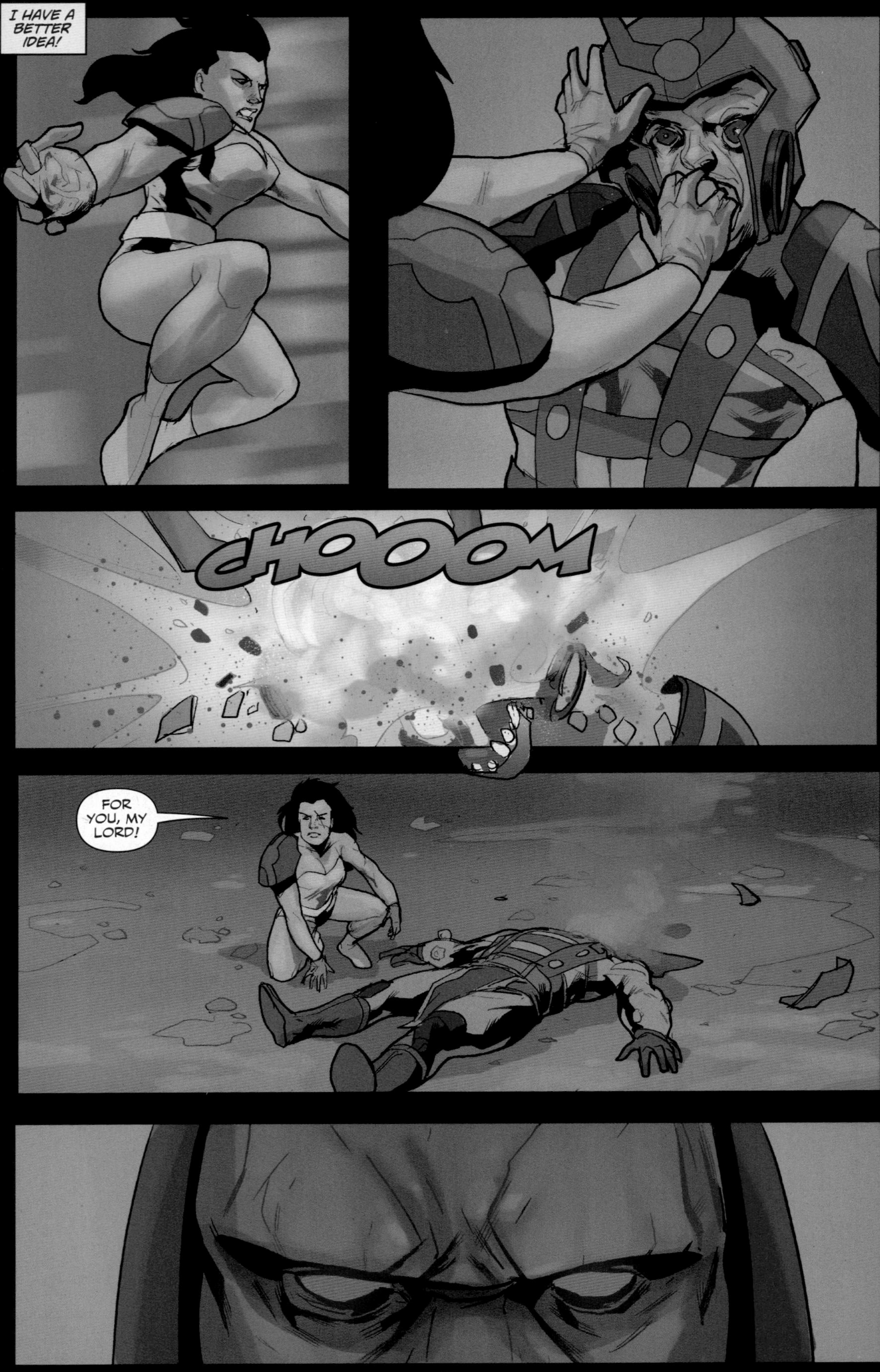
I HAVE A BETTER IDEA!
CHOOOM
FOR YOU, MY LORD!

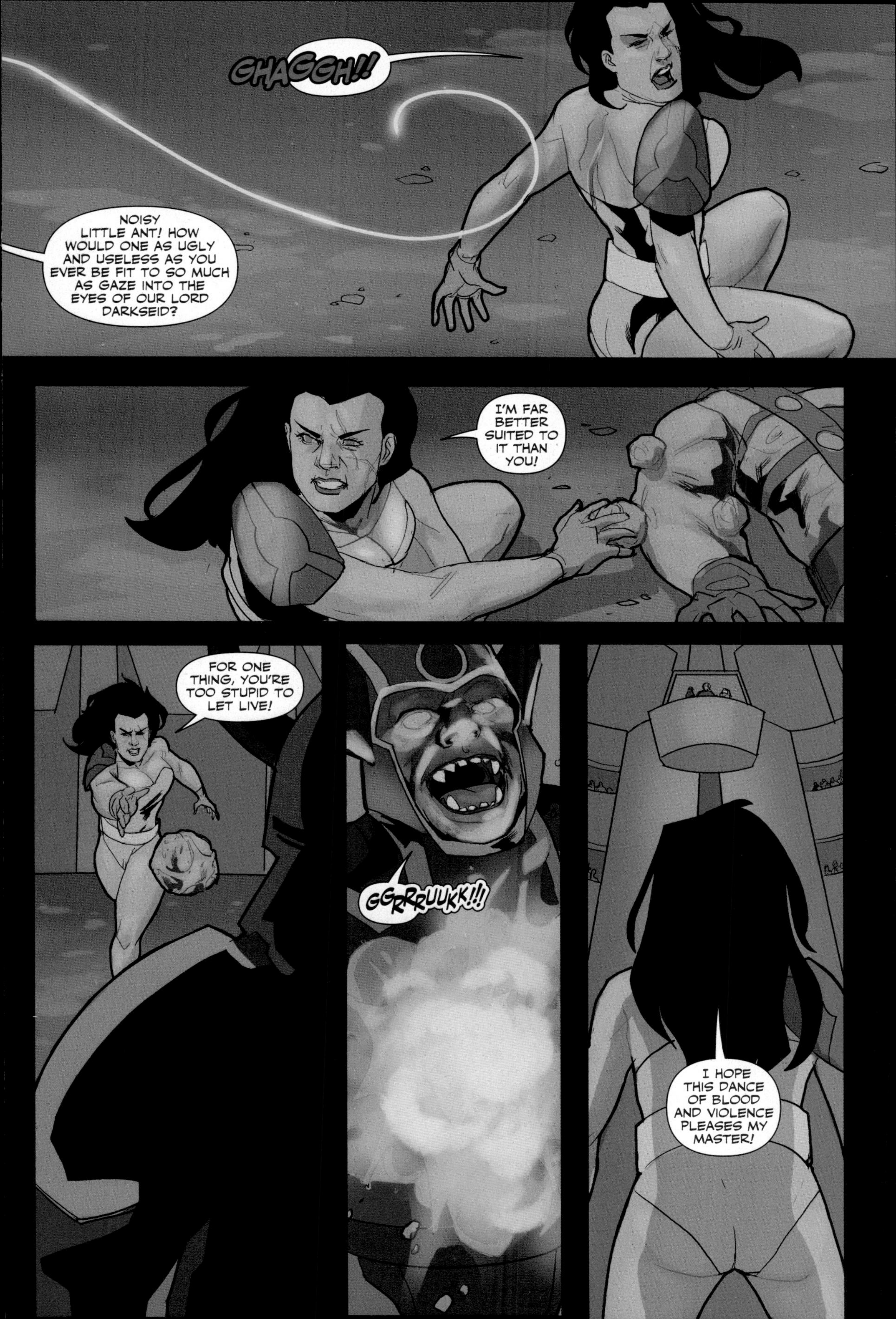
CHAGGH!!
NOISY LITTLE ANT! HOW WOULD ONE AS UGLY AND USELESS AS YOU EVER BE FIT TO SO MUCH AS GAZE INTO THE EYES OF OUR LORD DARKSEID?
I'M FAR BETTER SUITED TO IT THAN YOU!
FOR ONE THING, YOU'RE TOO STUPID TO LET LIVE!
GGRRRUUKK!!!
I HOPE THIS DANCE OF BLOOD AND VIOLENCE PLEASES MY MASTER!

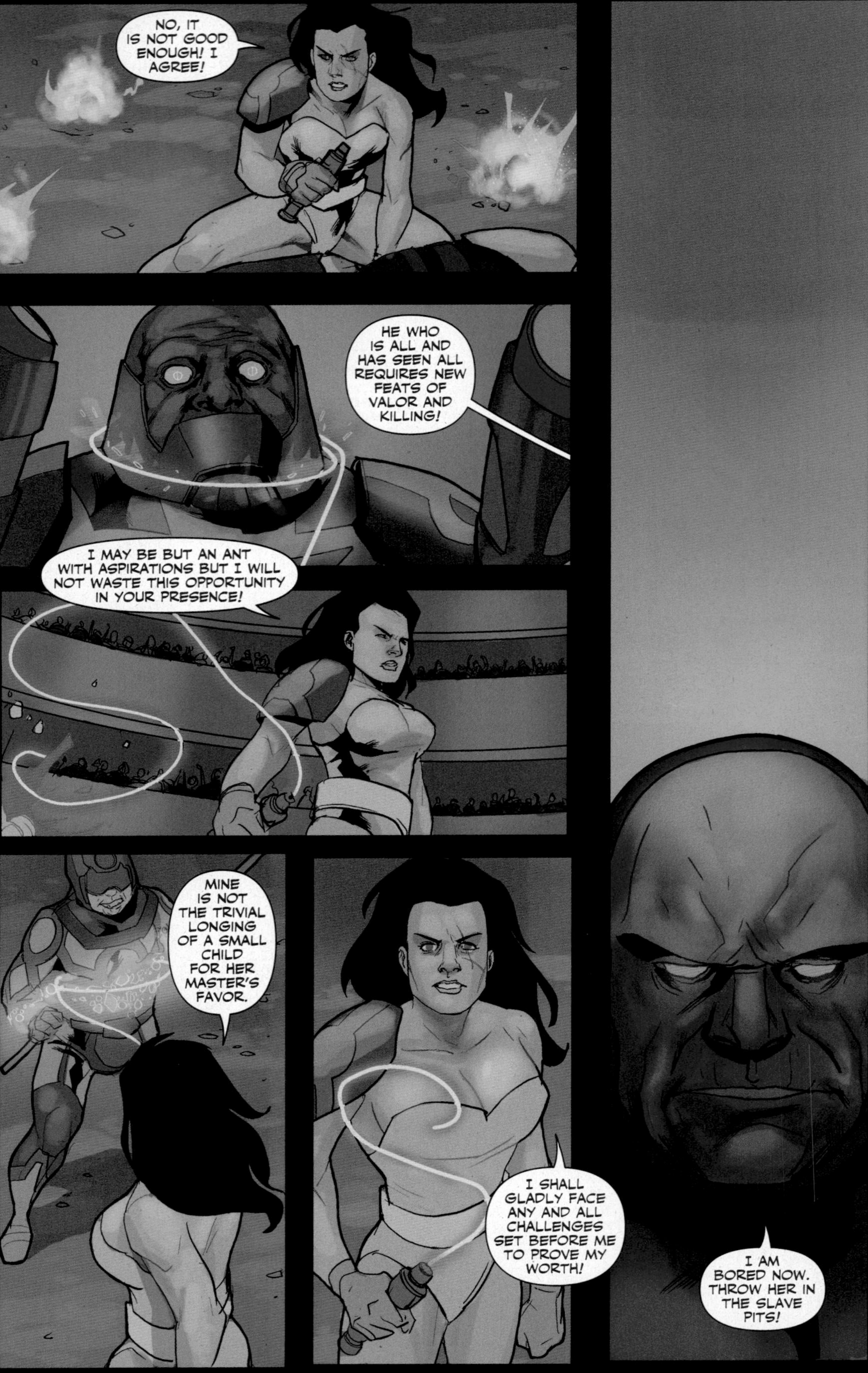
NO, IT IS NOT GOOD ENOUGH! I AGREE!
HE WHO IS ALL AND HAS SEEN ALL REQUIRES NEW FEATS OF VALOR AND KILLING!
I MAY BE BUT AN ANT WITH ASPIRATIONS BUT I WILL NOT WASTE THIS OPPORTUNITY IN YOUR PRESENCE!
MINE IS NOT THE TRIVIAL LONGING OF A SMALL CHILD FOR HER MASTER'S FAVOR.
I SHALL GLADLY FACE ANY AND ALL CHALLENGES SET BEFORE ME TO PROVE MY WORTH!
I AM BORED NOW. THROW HER IN THE SLAVE PITS!

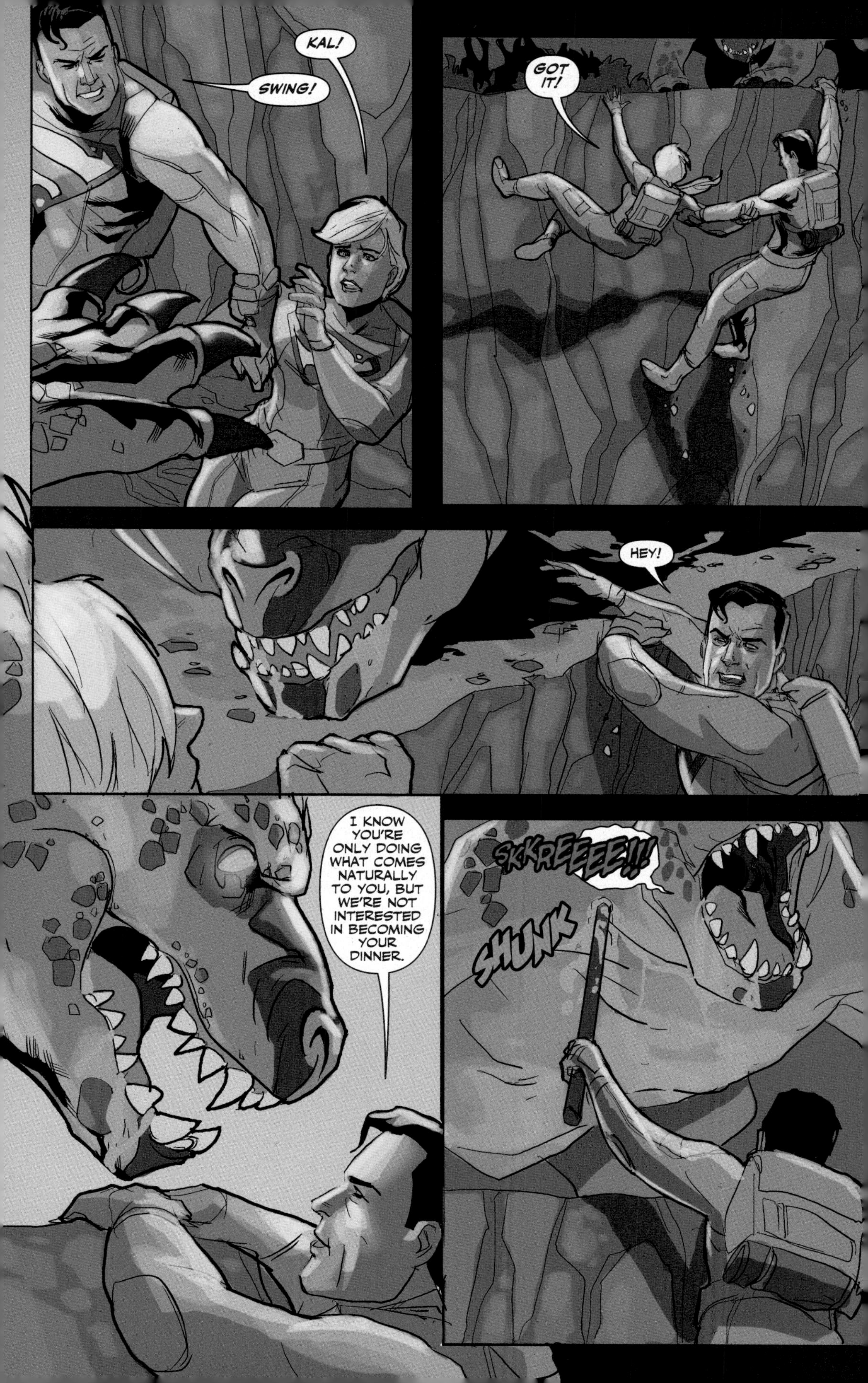
KAL!
SWING!
GOT IT!
HEY!
I KNOW YOU'RE ONLY DOING WHAT COMES NATURALLY TO YOU, BUT WE'RE NOT INTERESTED IN BECOMING YOUR DINNER.
SKKREEEEE!!!
SHUNK

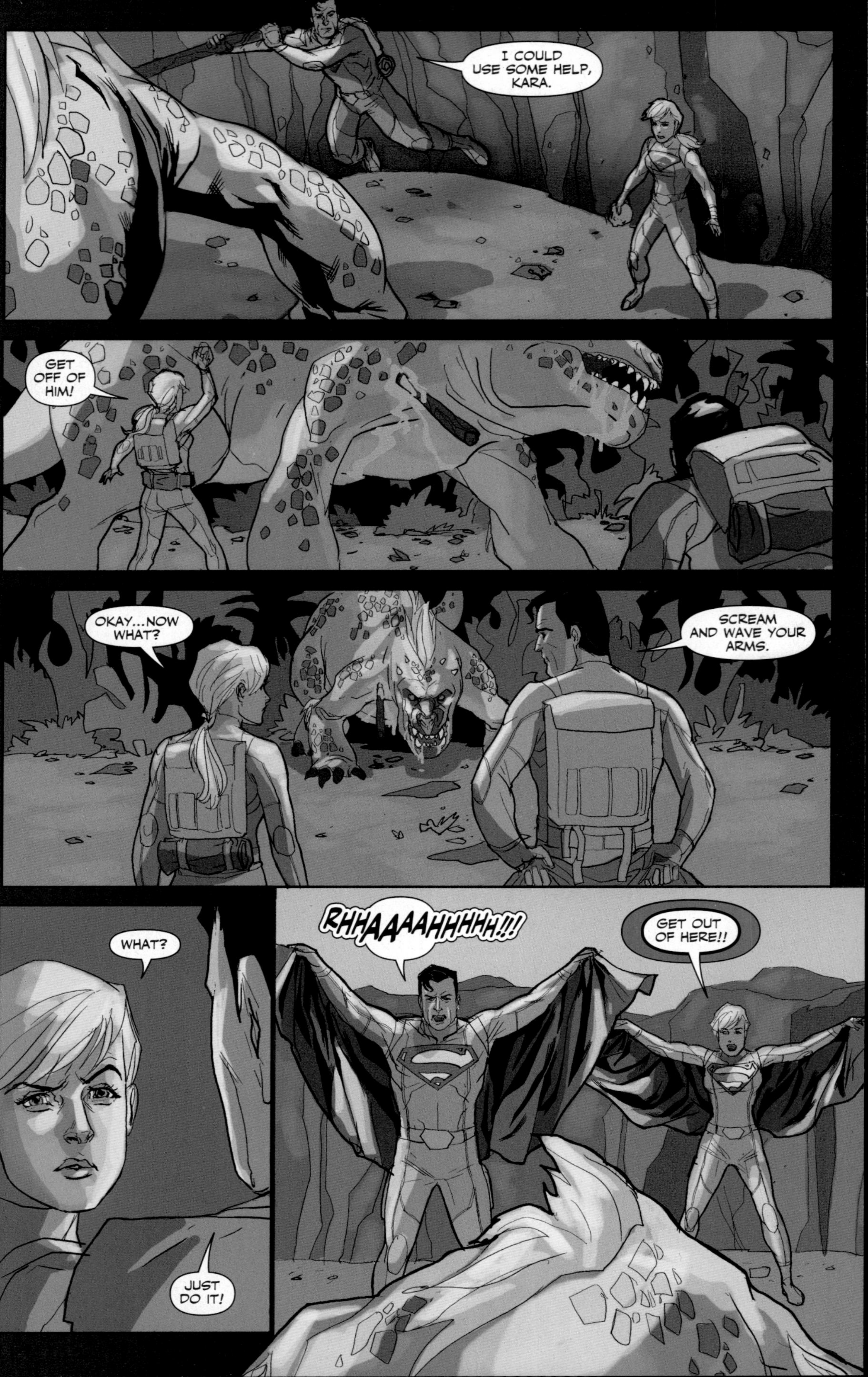
I COULD USE SOME HELP, KARA.
GET OFF OF HIM!
OKAY...NOW WHAT?
SCREAM AND WAVE YOUR ARMS.
WHAT?
JUST DO IT!
RHHAAAAHHHHH!!!
GET OUT OF HERE!!

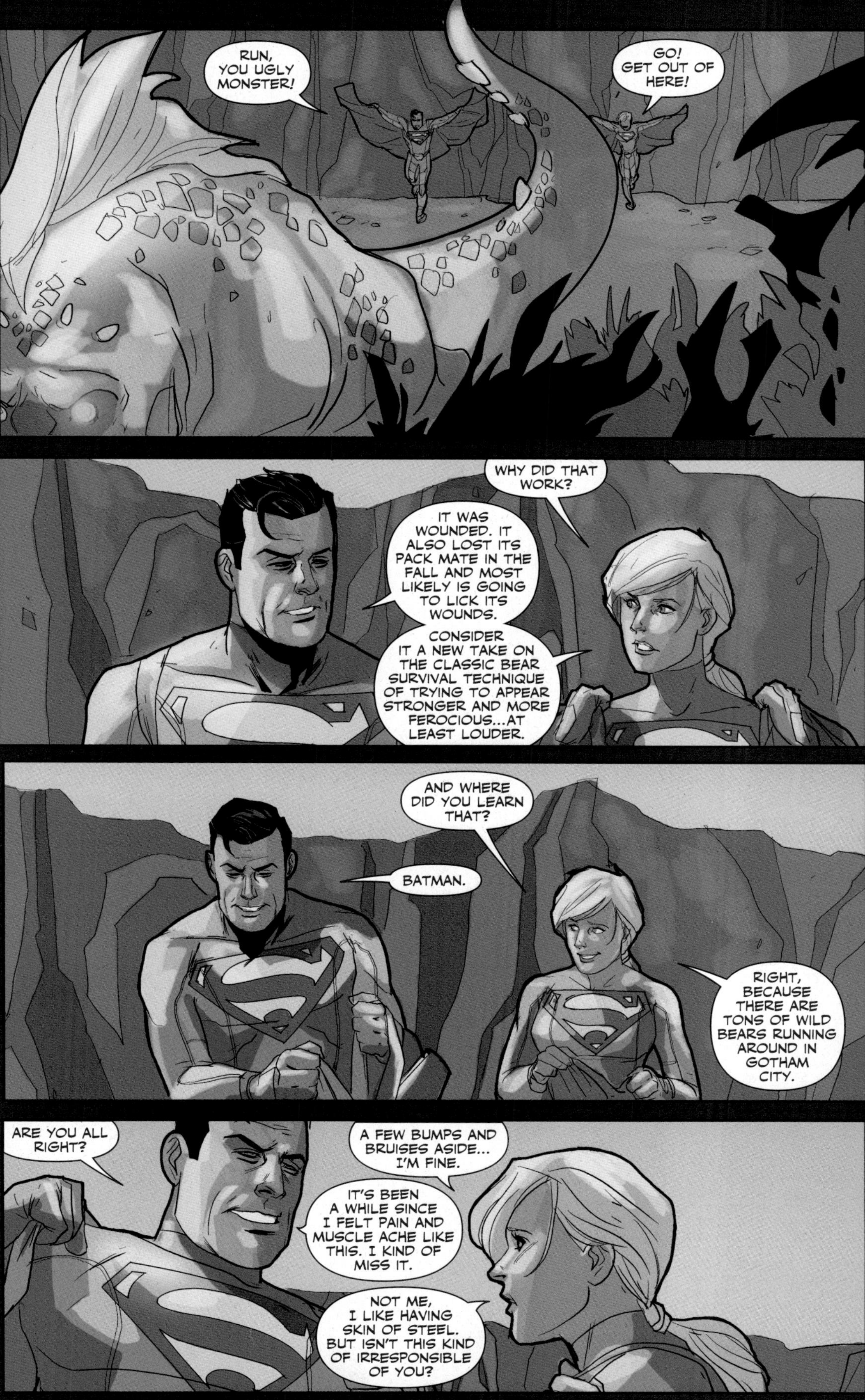
RUN, YOU UGLY MONSTER!
GO! GET OUT OF HERE!
WHY DID THAT WORK?
IT WAS WOUNDED. IT ALSO LOST ITS PACK MATE IN THE FALL AND MOST LIKELY IS GOING TO LICK ITS WOUNDS.
CONSIDER IT A NEW TAKE ON THE CLASSIC BEAR SURVIVAL TECHNIQUE OF TRYING TO APPEAR STRONGER AND MORE FEROCIOUS...AT LEAST LOUDER.
AND WHERE DID YOU LEARN THAT?
BATMAN.
RIGHT, BECAUSE THERE ARE TONS OF WILD BEARS RUNNING AROUND IN GOTHAM CITY.
ARE YOU ALL RIGHT?
A FEW BUMPS AND BRUISES ASIDE... I'M FINE.
IT'S BEEN A WHILE SINCE I FELT PAIN AND MUSCLE ACHE LIKE THIS. I KIND OF MISS IT.
NOT ME, I LIKE HAVING SKIN OF STEEL. BUT ISN'T THIS KIND OF IRRESPONSIBLE OF YOU?

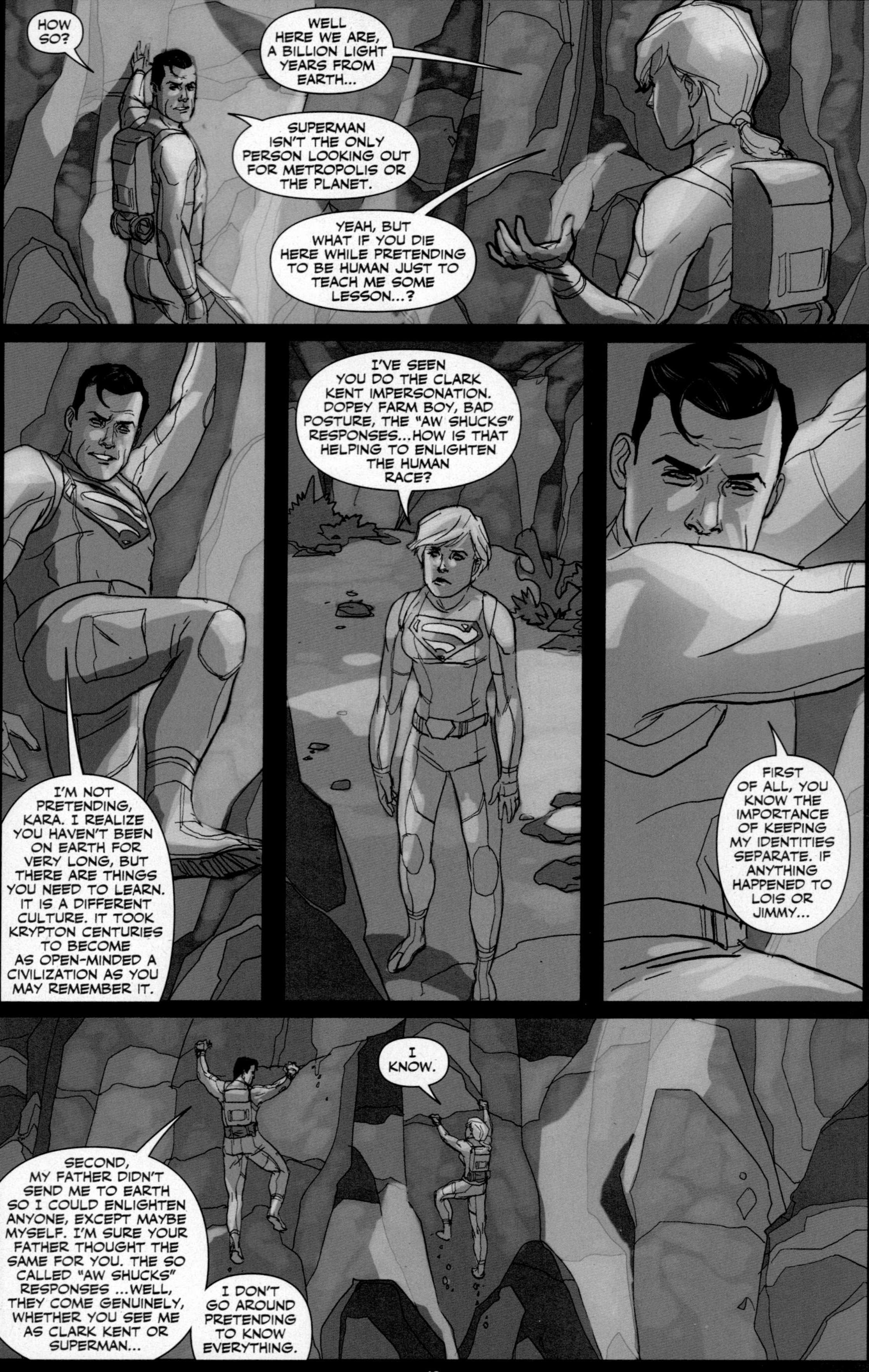
HOW SO?
WELL HERE WE ARE, A BILLION LIGHT YEARS FROM EARTH...
SUPERMAN ISN'T THE ONLY PERSON LOOKING OUT FOR METROPOLIS OR THE PLANET.
YEAH, BUT WHAT IF YOU DIE HERE WHILE PRETENDING TO BE HUMAN JUST TO TEACH ME SOME LESSON...?
I'VE SEEN YOU DO THE CLARK KENT IMPERSONATION. DOPEY FARM BOY, BAD POSTURE, THE "AW SHUCKS" RESPONSES...HOW IS THAT HELPING TO ENLIGHTEN THE HUMAN RACE?
I'M NOT PRETENDING, KARA. I REALIZE YOU HAVEN'T BEEN ON EARTH FOR VERY LONG, BUT THERE ARE THINGS YOU NEED TO LEARN. IT IS A DIFFERENT CULTURE. IT TOOK KRYPTON CENTURIES TO BECOME AS OPEN-MINDED A CIVILIZATION AS YOU MAY REMEMBER IT.
FIRST OF ALL, YOU KNOW THE IMPORTANCE OF KEEPING MY IDENTITIES SEPARATE. IF ANYTHING HAPPENED TO LOIS OR JIMMY...
I KNOW.
SECOND, MY FATHER DIDN'T SEND ME TO EARTH SO I COULD ENLIGHTEN ANYONE, EXCEPT MAYBE MYSELF. I'M SURE YOUR FATHER THOUGHT THE SAME FOR YOU. THE SO CALLED "AW SHUCKS" RESPONSES ...WELL, THEY COME GENUINELY, WHETHER YOU SEE ME AS CLARK KENT OR SUPERMAN...
I DON'T GO AROUND PRETENDING TO KNOW EVERYTHING.

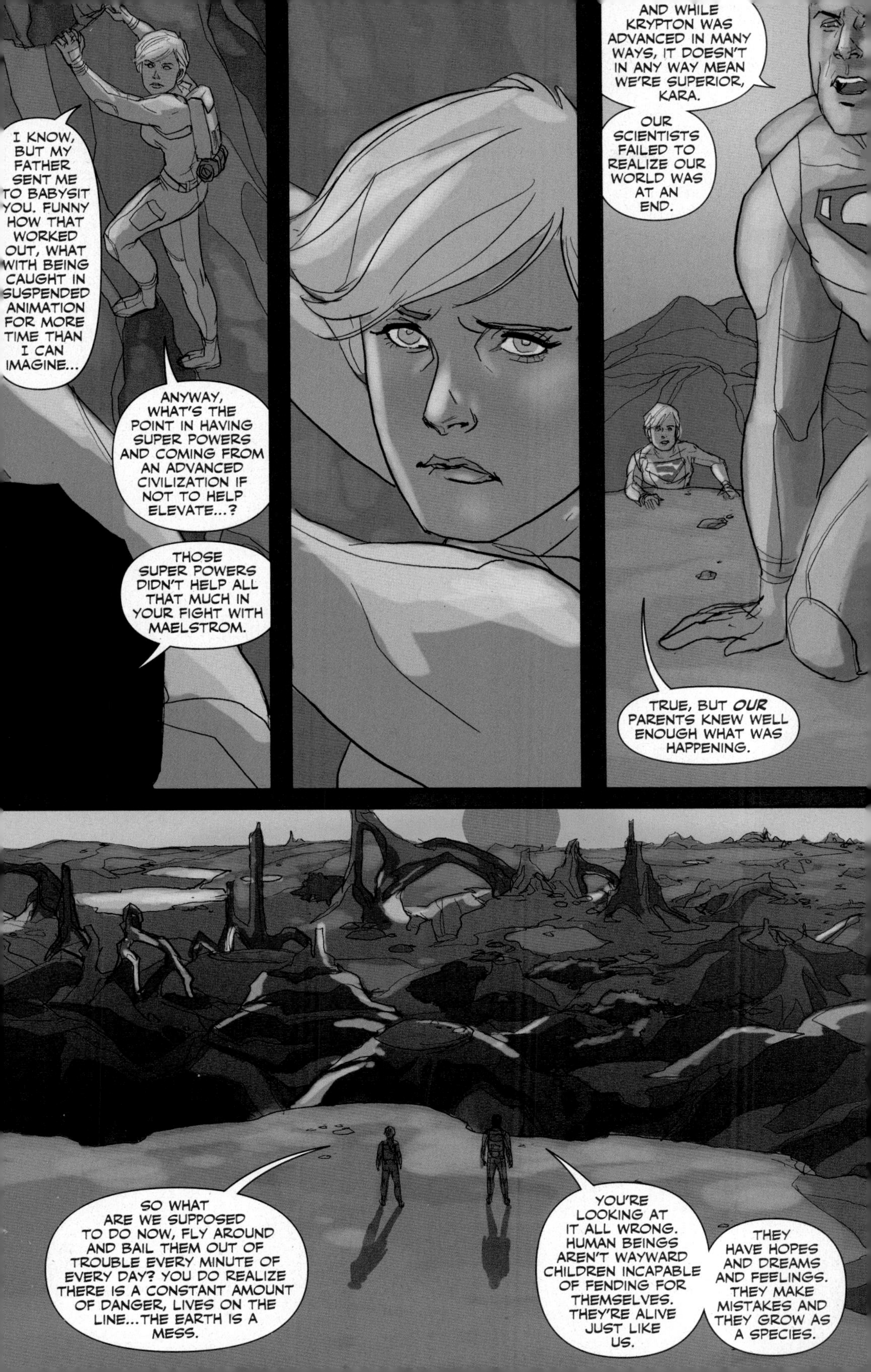
I KNOW, BUT MY FATHER SENT ME TO BABYSIT YOU. FUNNY HOW THAT WORKED OUT, WHAT WITH BEING CAUGHT IN SUSPENDED ANIMATION FOR MORE TIME THAN I CAN IMAGINE...
ANYWAY, WHAT'S THE POINT IN HAVING SUPER POWERS AND COMING FROM AN ADVANCED CIVILIZATION IF NOT TO HELP ELEVATE...?
THOSE SUPER POWERS DIDN'T HELP ALL THAT MUCH IN YOUR FIGHT WITH MAELSTROM.
AND WHILE KRYPTON WAS ADVANCED IN MANY WAYS, IT DOESN'T IN ANY WAY MEAN WE'RE SUPERIOR, KARA.
OUR SCIENTISTS FAILED TO REALIZE OUR WORLD WAS AT AN END.
TRUE, BUT *OUR* PARENTS KNEW WELL ENOUGH WHAT WAS HAPPENING.
SO WHAT ARE WE SUPPOSED TO DO NOW, FLY AROUND AND BAIL THEM OUT OF TROUBLE EVERY MINUTE OF EVERY DAY? YOU DO REALIZE THERE IS A CONSTANT AMOUNT OF DANGER, LIVES ON THE LINE...THE EARTH IS A MESS.
YOU'RE LOOKING AT IT ALL WRONG. HUMAN BEINGS AREN'T WAYWARD CHILDREN INCAPABLE OF FENDING FOR THEMSELVES. THEY'RE ALIVE JUST LIKE US.
THEY HAVE HOPES AND DREAMS AND FEELINGS. THEY MAKE MISTAKES AND THEY GROW AS A SPECIES.

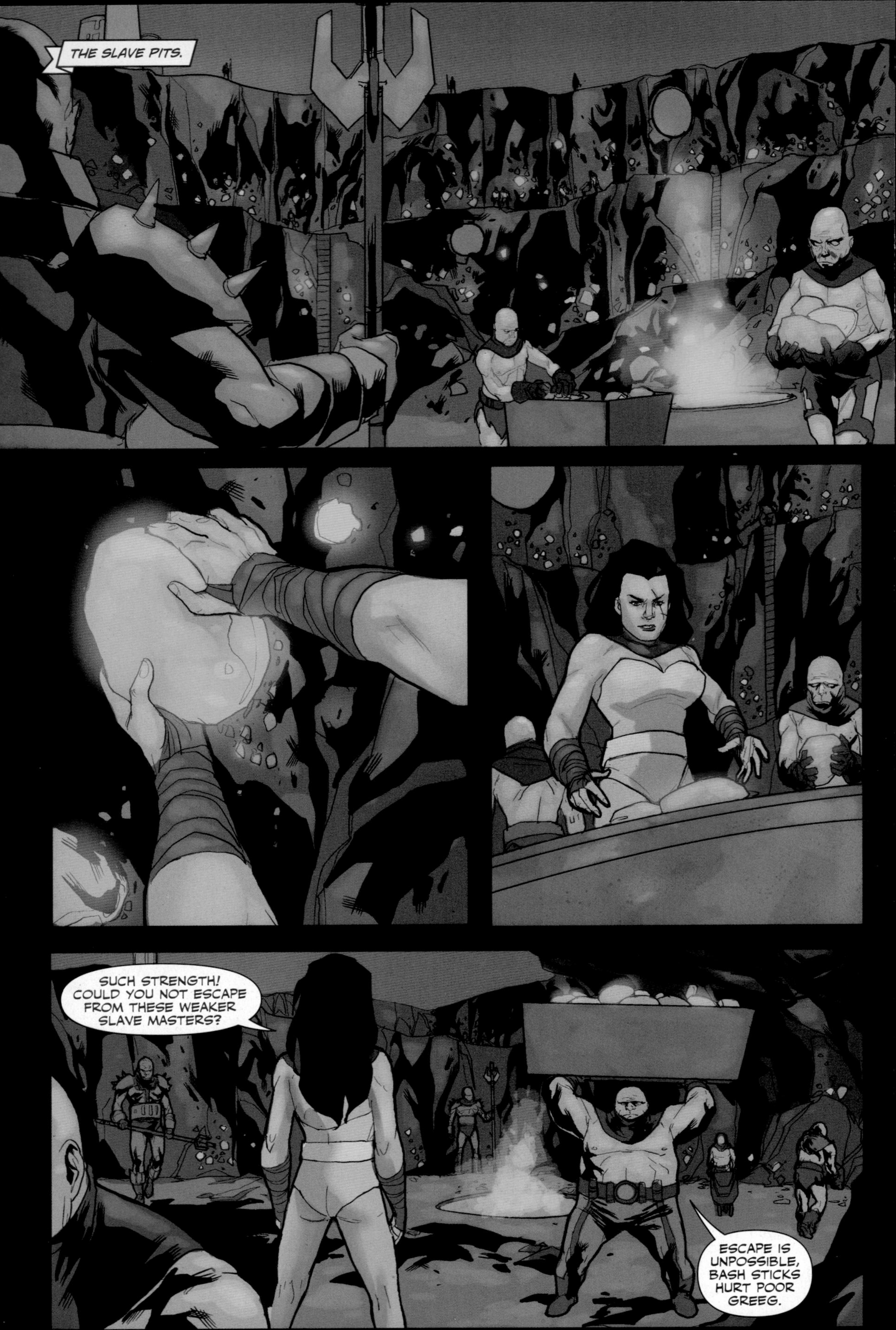
THE SLAVE PITS.
SUCH STRENGTH! COULD YOU NOT ESCAPE FROM THESE WEAKER SLAVE MASTERS?
ESCAPE IS UNPOSSIBLE, BASH STICKS HURT POOR GREEG.

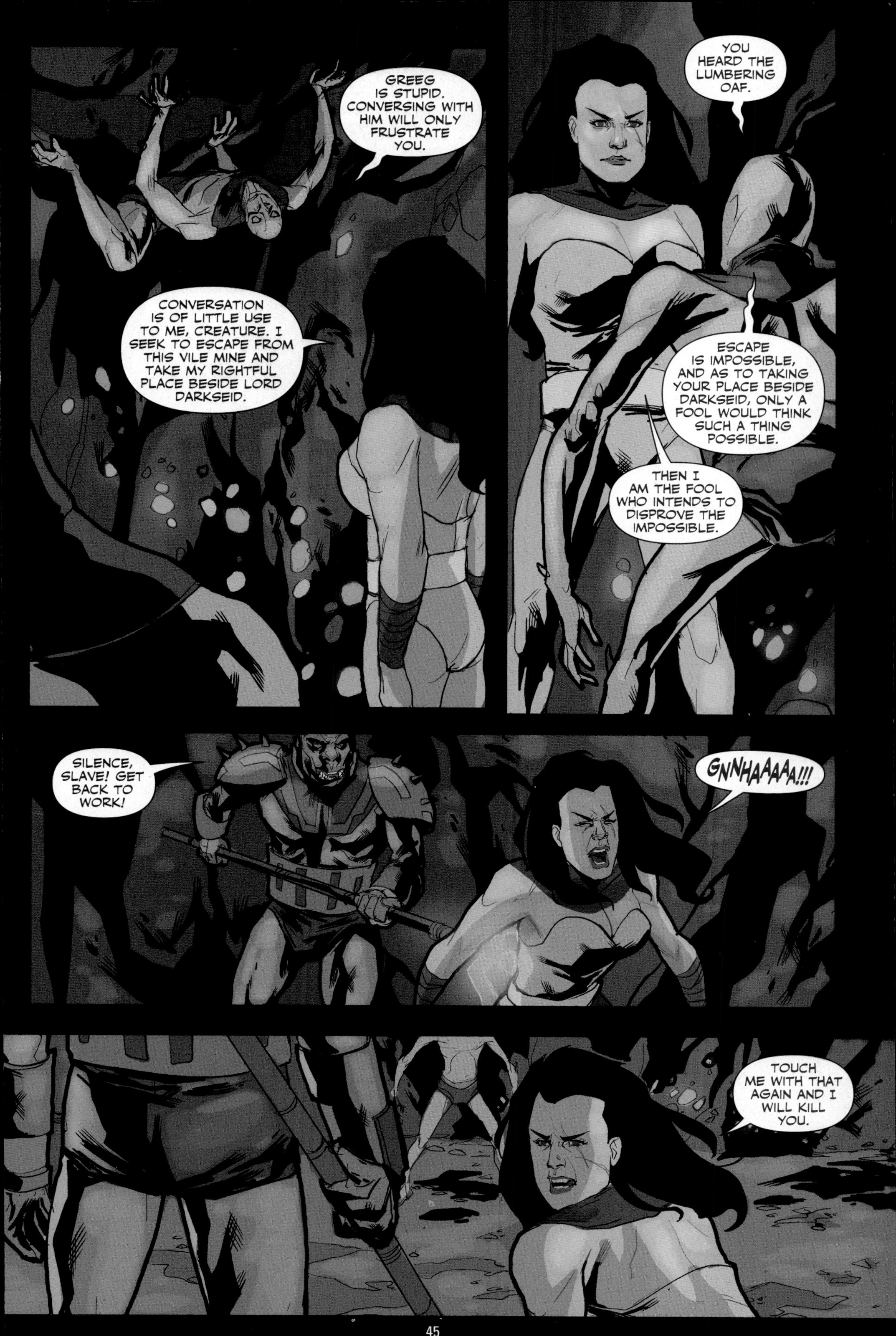
GREEG IS STUPID. CONVERSING WITH HIM WILL ONLY FRUSTRATE YOU.
CONVERSATION IS OF LITTLE USE TO ME, CREATURE. I SEEK TO ESCAPE FROM THIS VILE MINE AND TAKE MY RIGHTFUL PLACE BESIDE LORD DARKSEID.
YOU HEARD THE LUMBERING OAF.
ESCAPE IS IMPOSSIBLE, AND AS TO TAKING YOUR PLACE BESIDE DARKSEID, ONLY A FOOL WOULD THINK SUCH A THING POSSIBLE.
THEN I AM THE FOOL WHO INTENDS TO DISPROVE THE IMPOSSIBLE.
SILENCE, SLAVE! GET BACK TO WORK!
GNNHAAAAA!!!
TOUCH ME WITH THAT AGAIN AND I WILL KILL YOU.

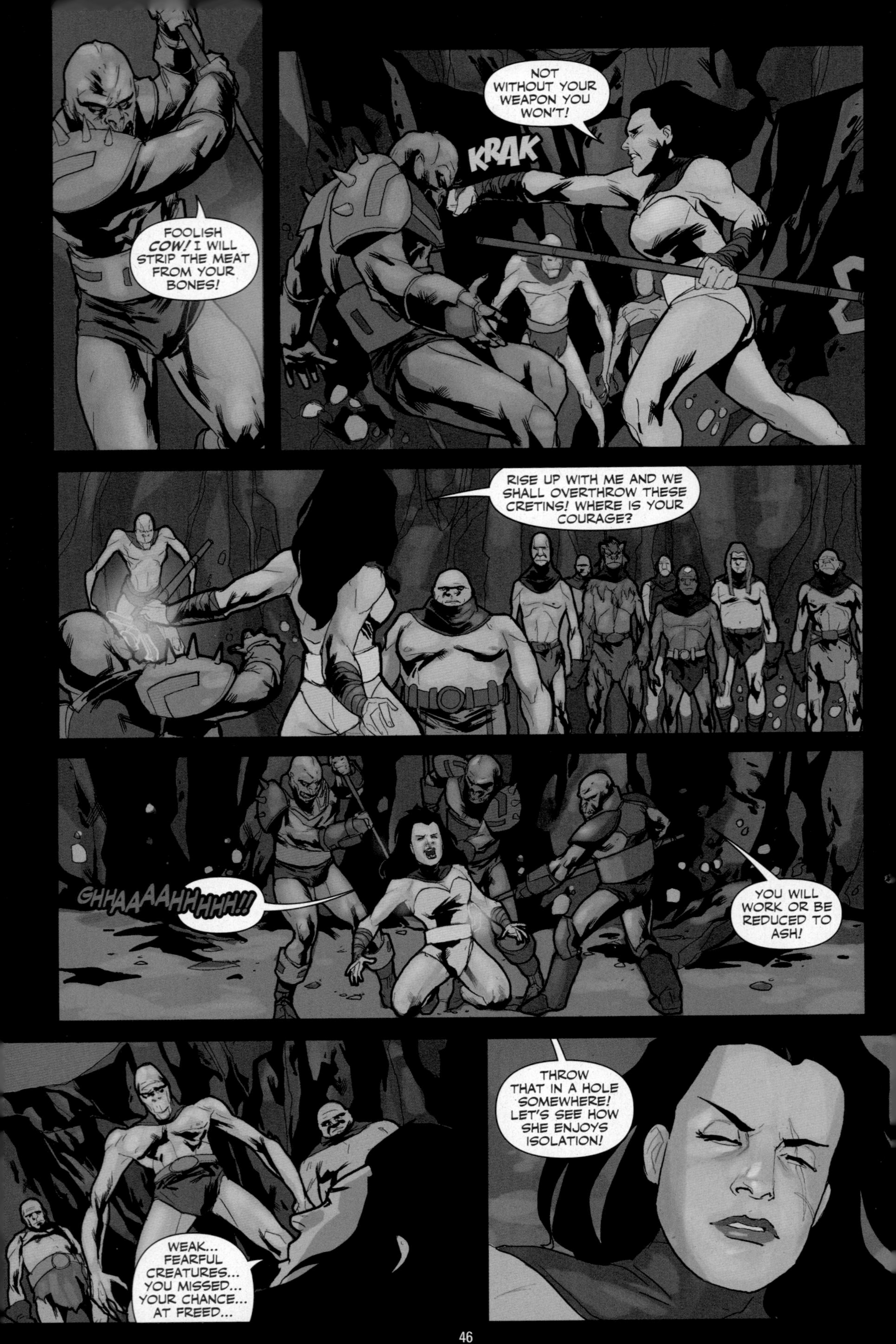
FOOLISH COW! I WILL STRIP THE MEAT FROM YOUR BONES!
NOT WITHOUT YOUR WEAPON YOU WON'T!
KRAK
RISE UP WITH ME AND WE SHALL OVERTHROW THESE CRETINS! WHERE IS YOUR COURAGE?
GHHAAAAHHHHH!!
YOU WILL WORK OR BE REDUCED TO ASH!
WEAK... FEARFUL CREATURES... YOU MISSED... YOUR CHANCE... AT FREED...
THROW THAT IN A HOLE SOMEWHERE! LET'S SEE HOW SHE ENJOYS ISOLATION!

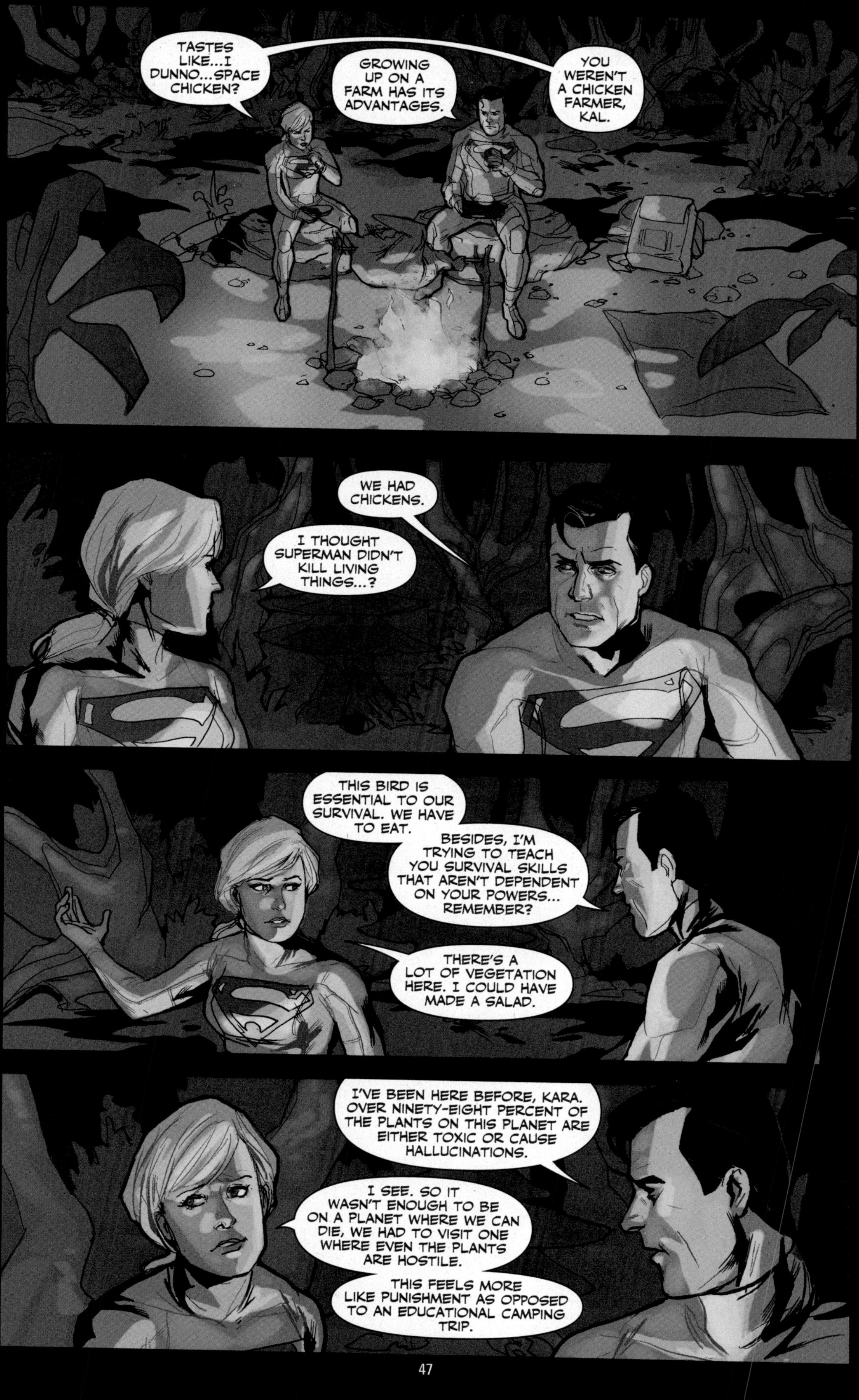
TASTES LIKE...I DUNNO...SPACE CHICKEN?
GROWING UP ON A FARM HAS ITS ADVANTAGES.
YOU WEREN'T A CHICKEN FARMER, KAL.
WE HAD CHICKENS.
I THOUGHT SUPERMAN DIDN'T KILL LIVING THINGS...?
THIS BIRD IS ESSENTIAL TO OUR SURVIVAL. WE HAVE TO EAT.
BESIDES, I'M TRYING TO TEACH YOU SURVIVAL SKILLS THAT AREN'T DEPENDENT ON YOUR POWERS... REMEMBER?
THERE'S A LOT OF VEGETATION HERE. I COULD HAVE MADE A SALAD.
I'VE BEEN HERE BEFORE, KARA. OVER NINETY-EIGHT PERCENT OF THE PLANTS ON THIS PLANET ARE EITHER TOXIC OR CAUSE HALLUCINATIONS.
I SEE. SO IT WASN'T ENOUGH TO BE ON A PLANET WHERE WE CAN DIE, WE HAD TO VISIT ONE WHERE EVEN THE PLANTS ARE HOSTILE.
THIS FEELS MORE LIKE PUNISHMENT AS OPPOSED TO AN EDUCATIONAL CAMPING TRIP.

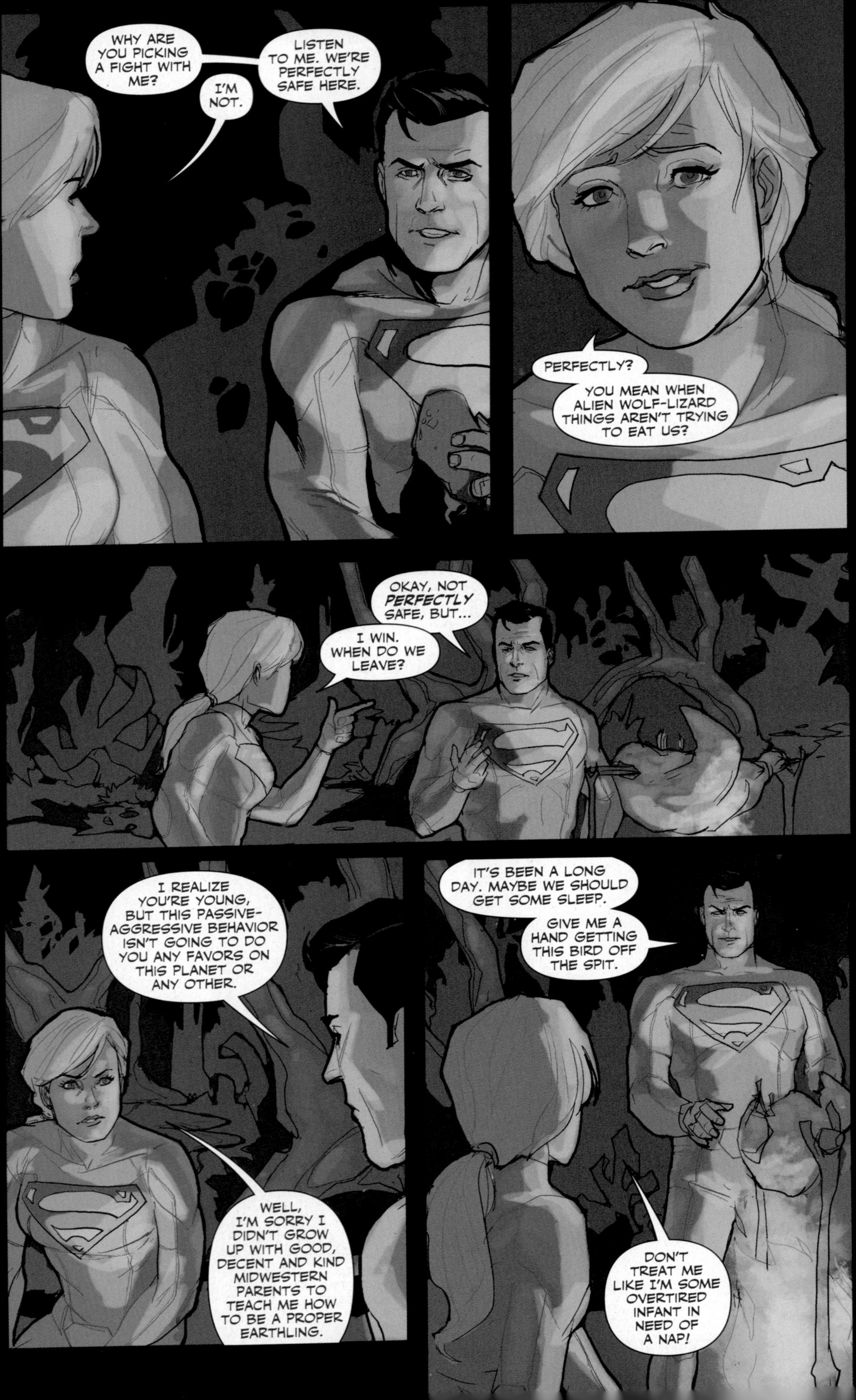

WHY ARE YOU PICKING A FIGHT WITH ME?
LISTEN TO ME. WE'RE PERFECTLY SAFE HERE.
I'M NOT.
PERFECTLY?
YOU MEAN WHEN ALIEN WOLF-LIZARD THINGS AREN'T TRYING TO EAT US?
OKAY, NOT *PERFECTLY* SAFE, BUT...
I WIN. WHEN DO WE LEAVE?
I REALIZE YOU'RE YOUNG, BUT THIS PASSIVE-AGGRESSIVE BEHAVIOR ISN'T GOING TO DO YOU ANY FAVORS ON THIS PLANET OR ANY OTHER.
WELL, I'M SORRY I DIDN'T GROW UP WITH GOOD, DECENT AND KIND MIDWESTERN PARENTS TO TEACH ME HOW TO BE A PROPER EARTHLING.
IT'S BEEN A LONG DAY. MAYBE WE SHOULD GET SOME SLEEP.
GIVE ME A HAND GETTING THIS BIRD OFF THE SPIT.
DON'T TREAT ME LIKE I'M SOME OVERTIRED INFANT IN NEED OF A NAP!

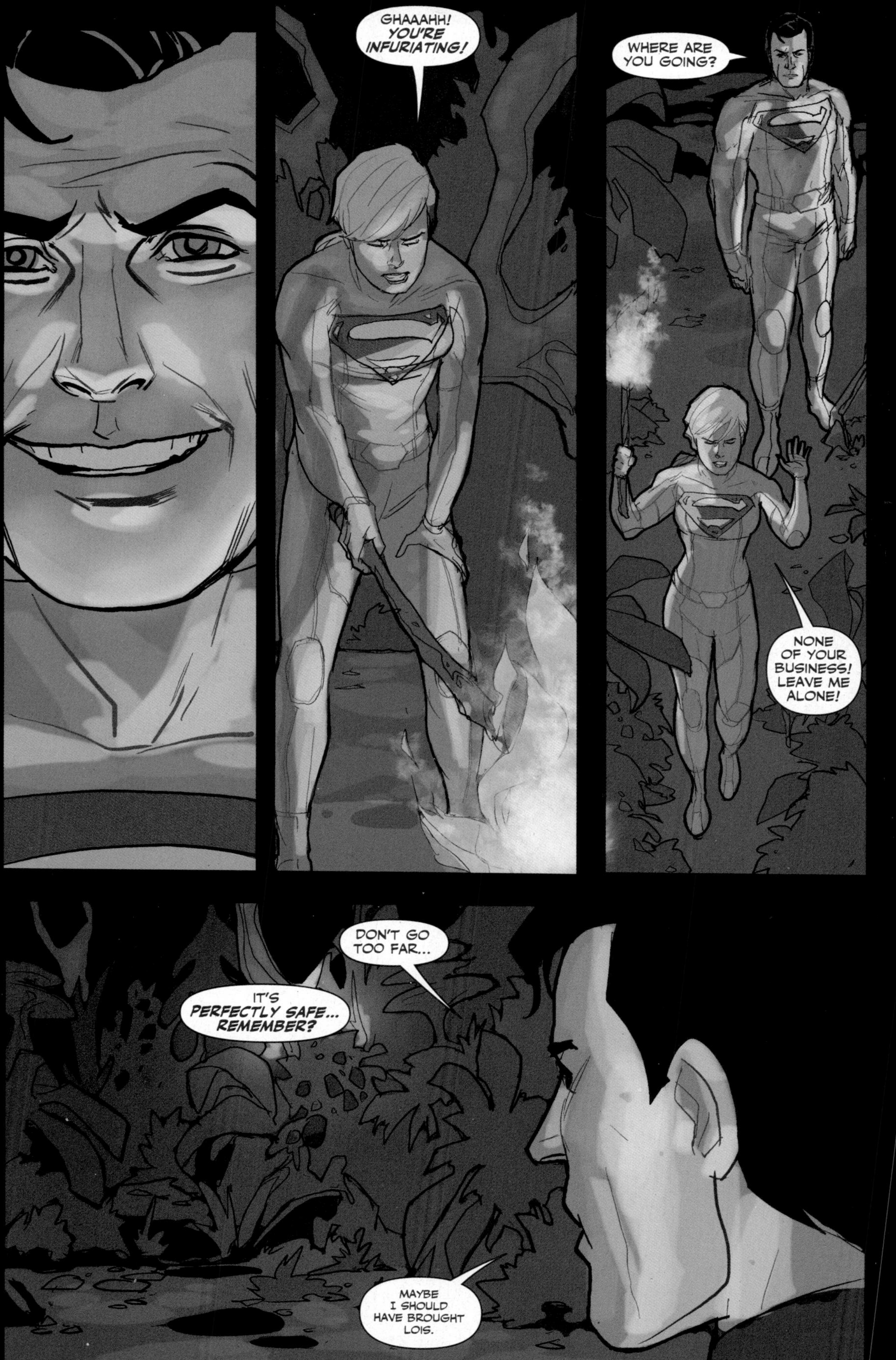

GHAAAHH! YOU'RE INFURIATING!
WHERE ARE YOU GOING?
NONE OF YOUR BUSINESS! LEAVE ME ALONE!
DON'T GO TOO FAR...
IT'S PERFECTLY SAFE... REMEMBER?
MAYBE I SHOULD HAVE BROUGHT LOIS.

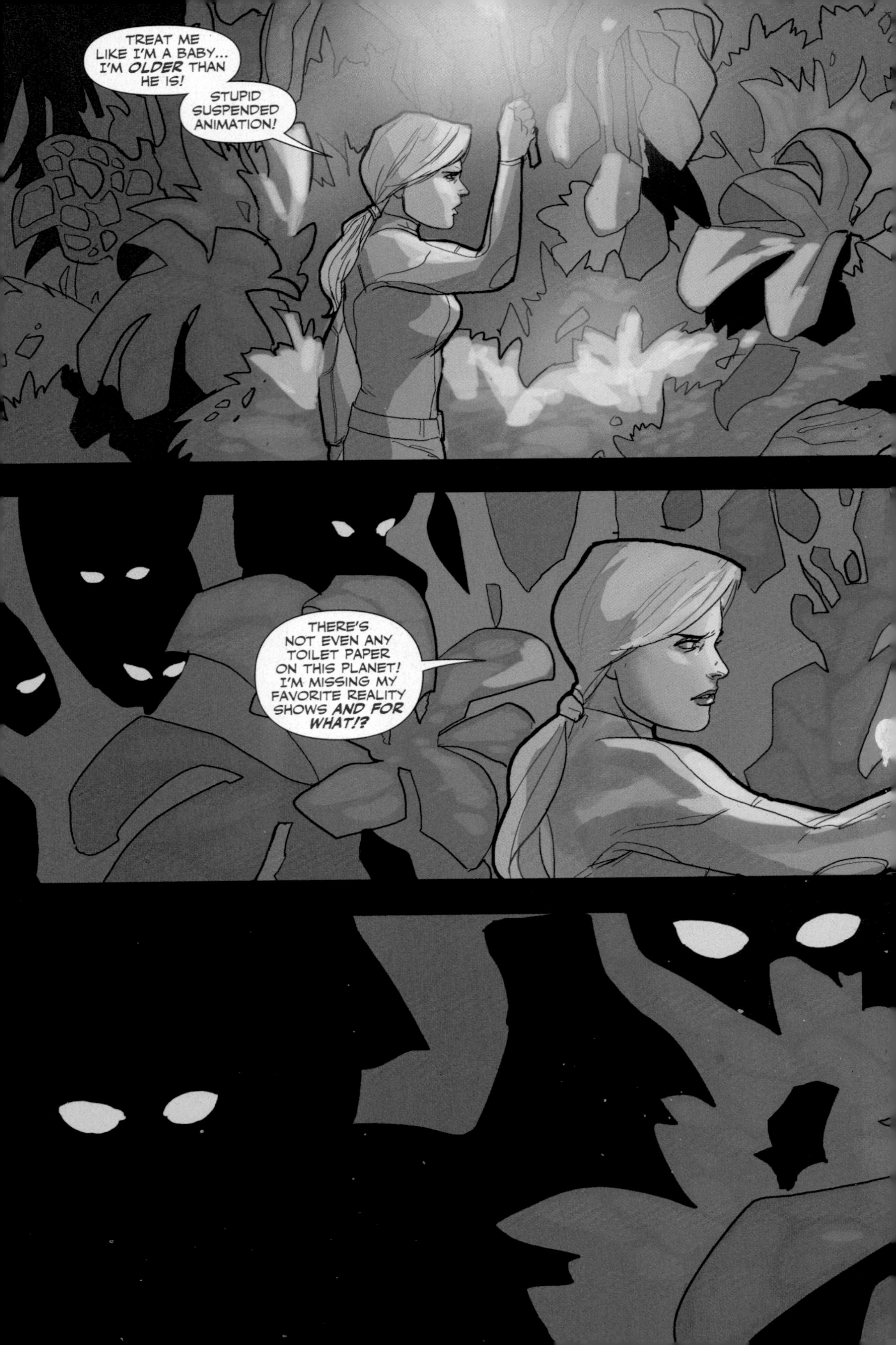
TREAT ME LIKE I'M A BABY... I'M *OLDER* THAN HE IS!
STUPID SUSPENDED ANIMATION!
THERE'S NOT EVEN ANY TOILET PAPER ON THIS PLANET! I'M MISSING MY FAVORITE REALITY SHOWS *AND FOR WHAT!?*

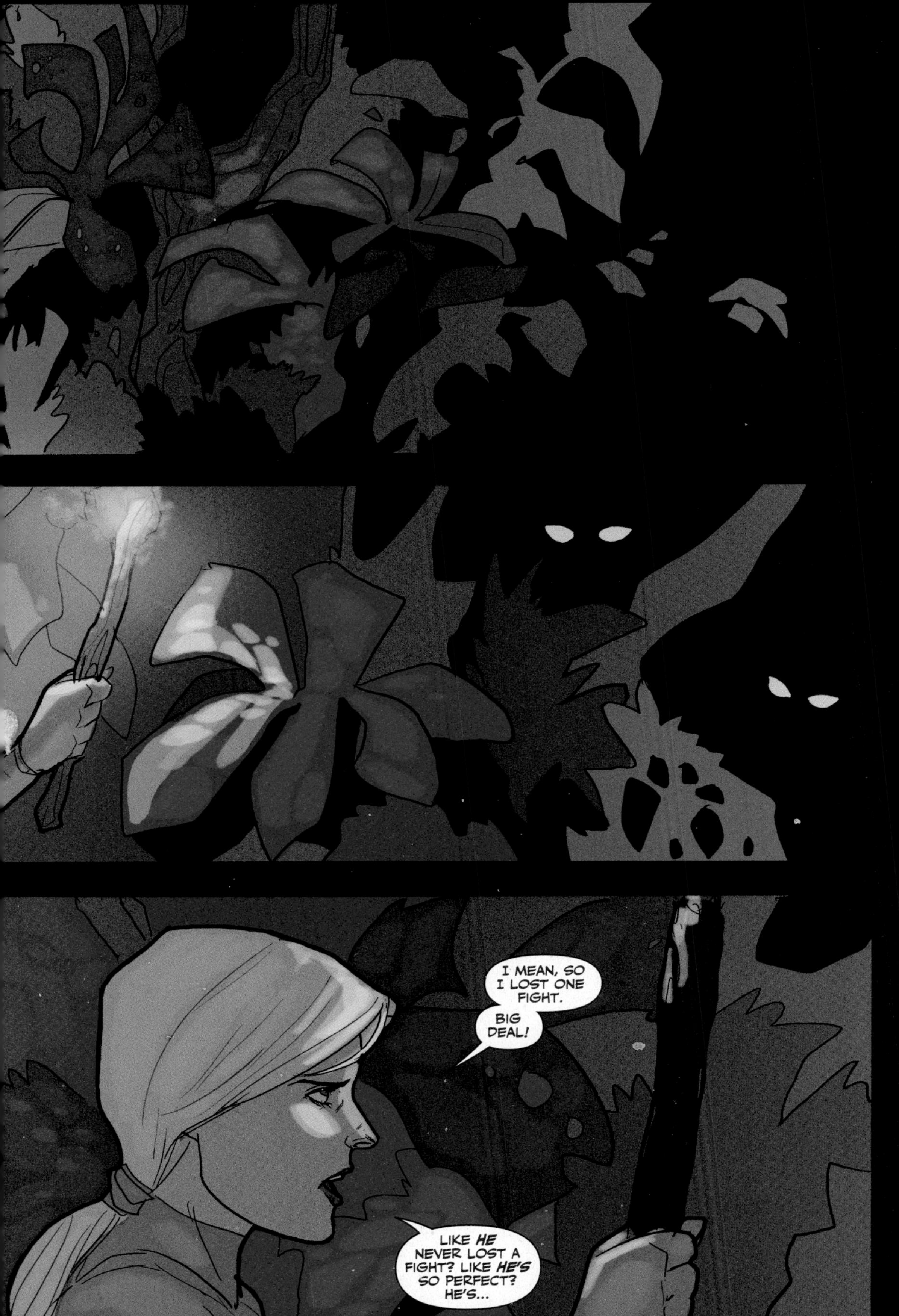
I MEAN, SO I LOST ONE FIGHT.
BIG DEAL!
LIKE HE NEVER LOST A FIGHT? LIKE HE'S SO PERFECT? HE'S...

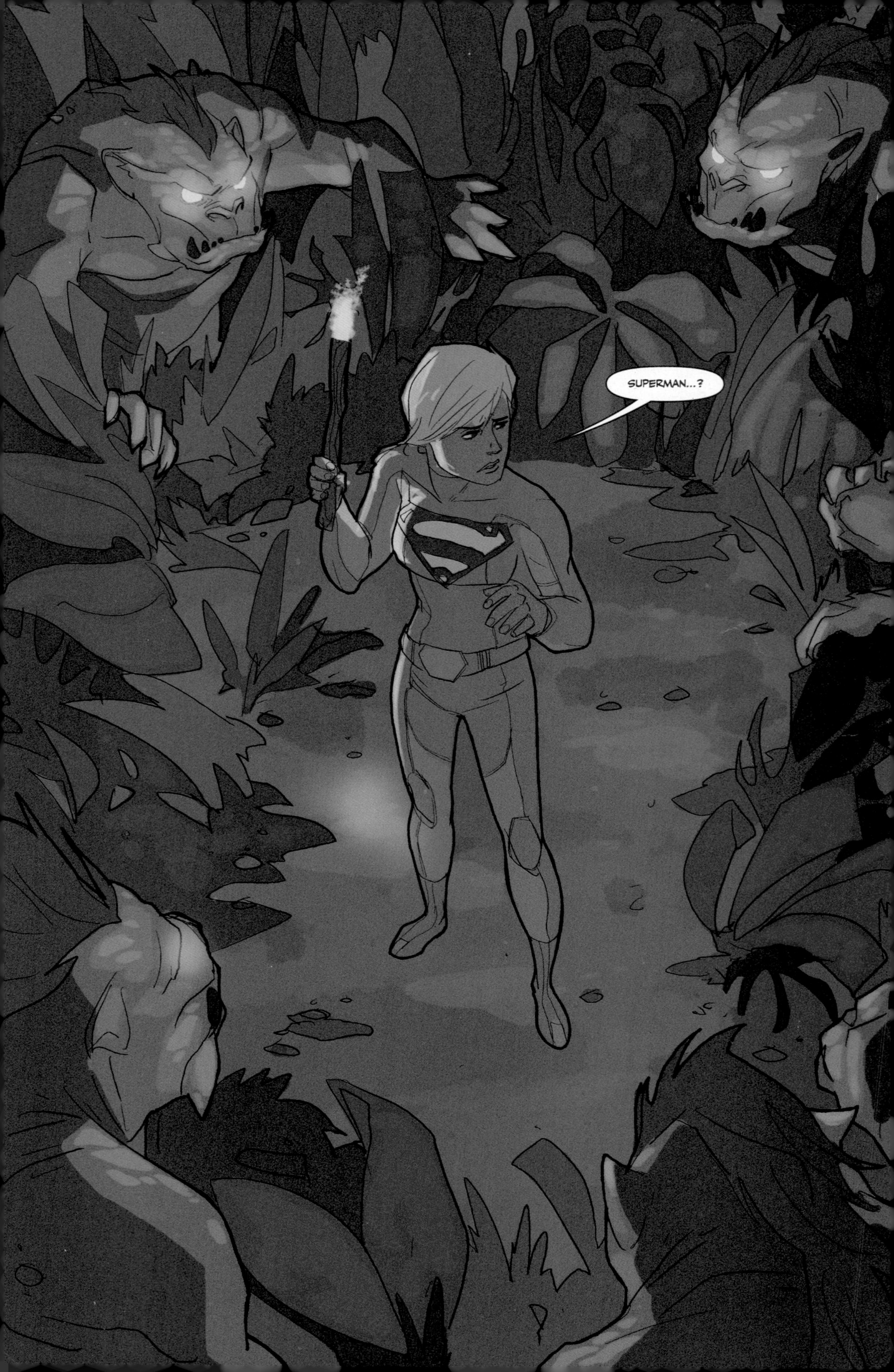
SUPERMAN...?

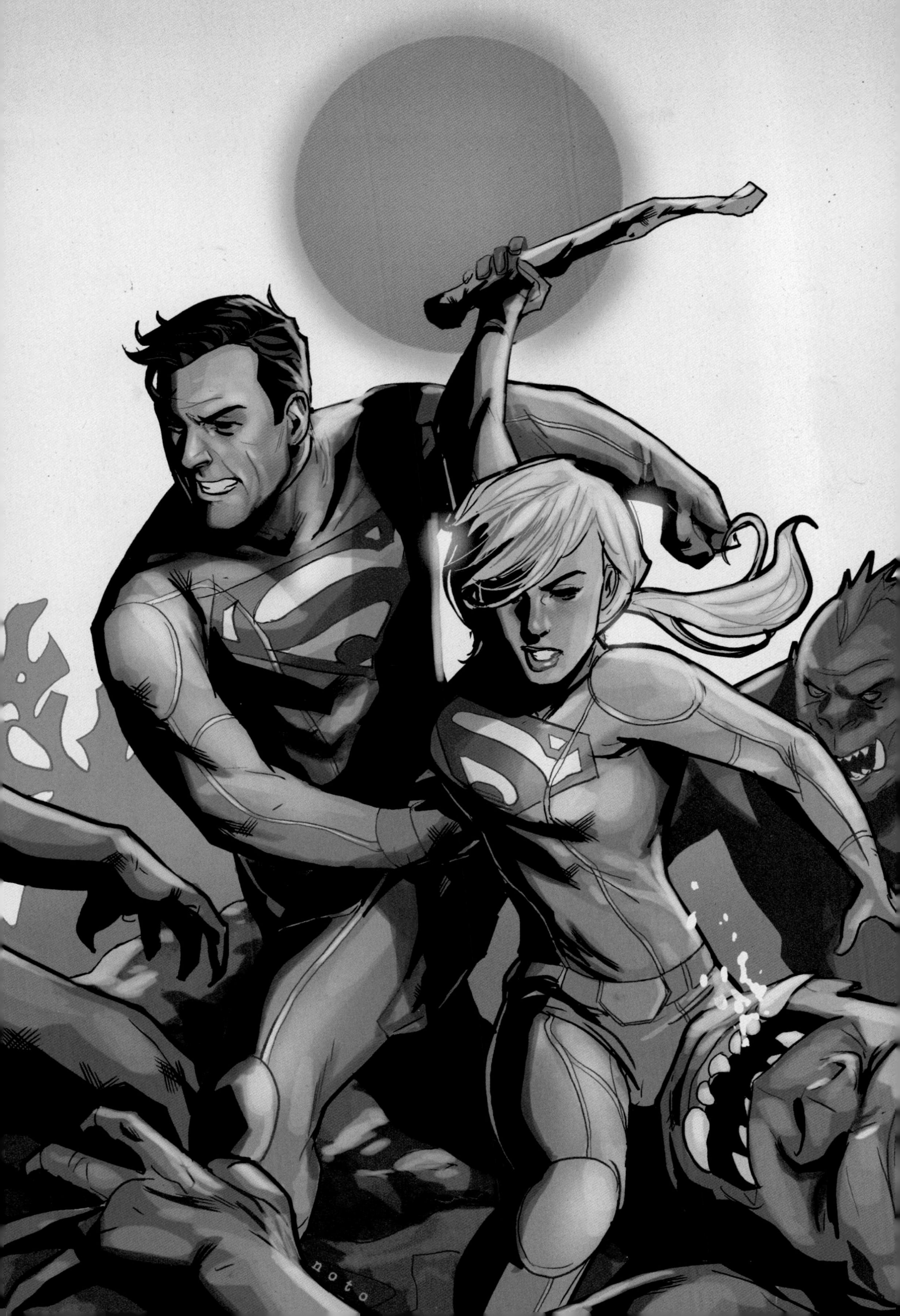
noto

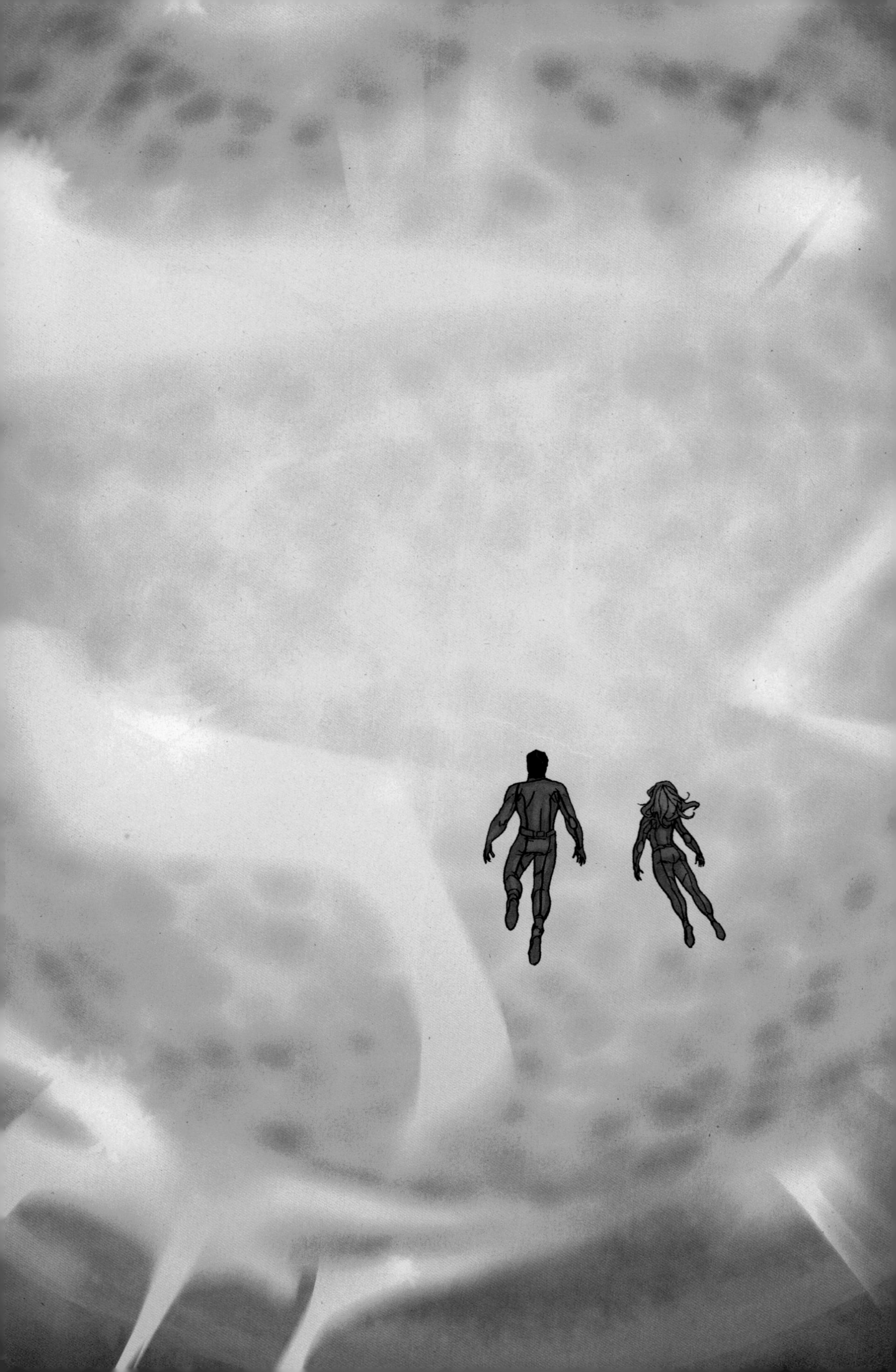

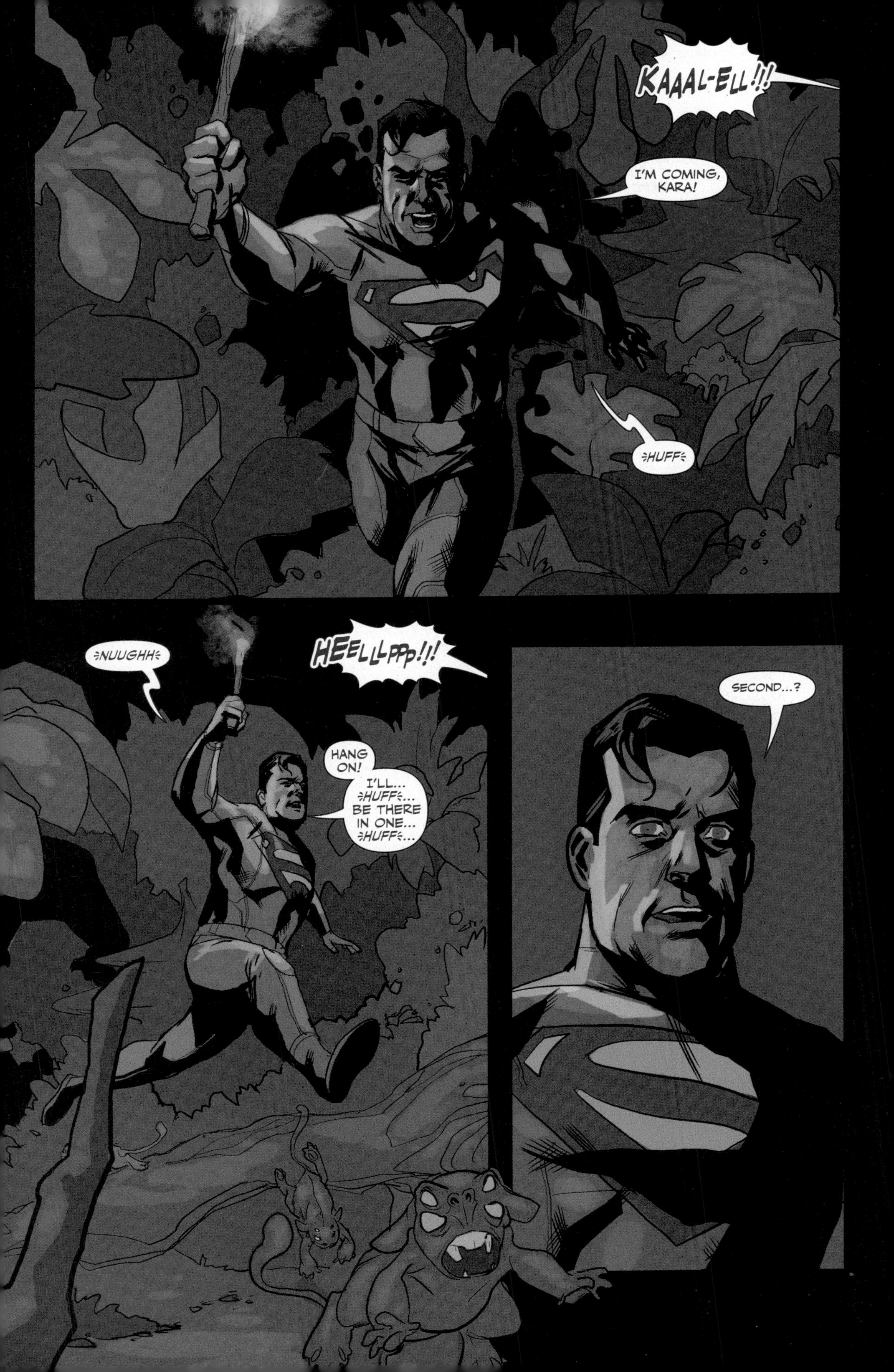
KAAAL-ELL!!!
I'M COMING, KARA!
HUFF
NUUGHH
HEELLLPPP!!!
HANG ON!
I'LL... HUFF... BE THERE IN ONE... HUFF...
SECOND...?

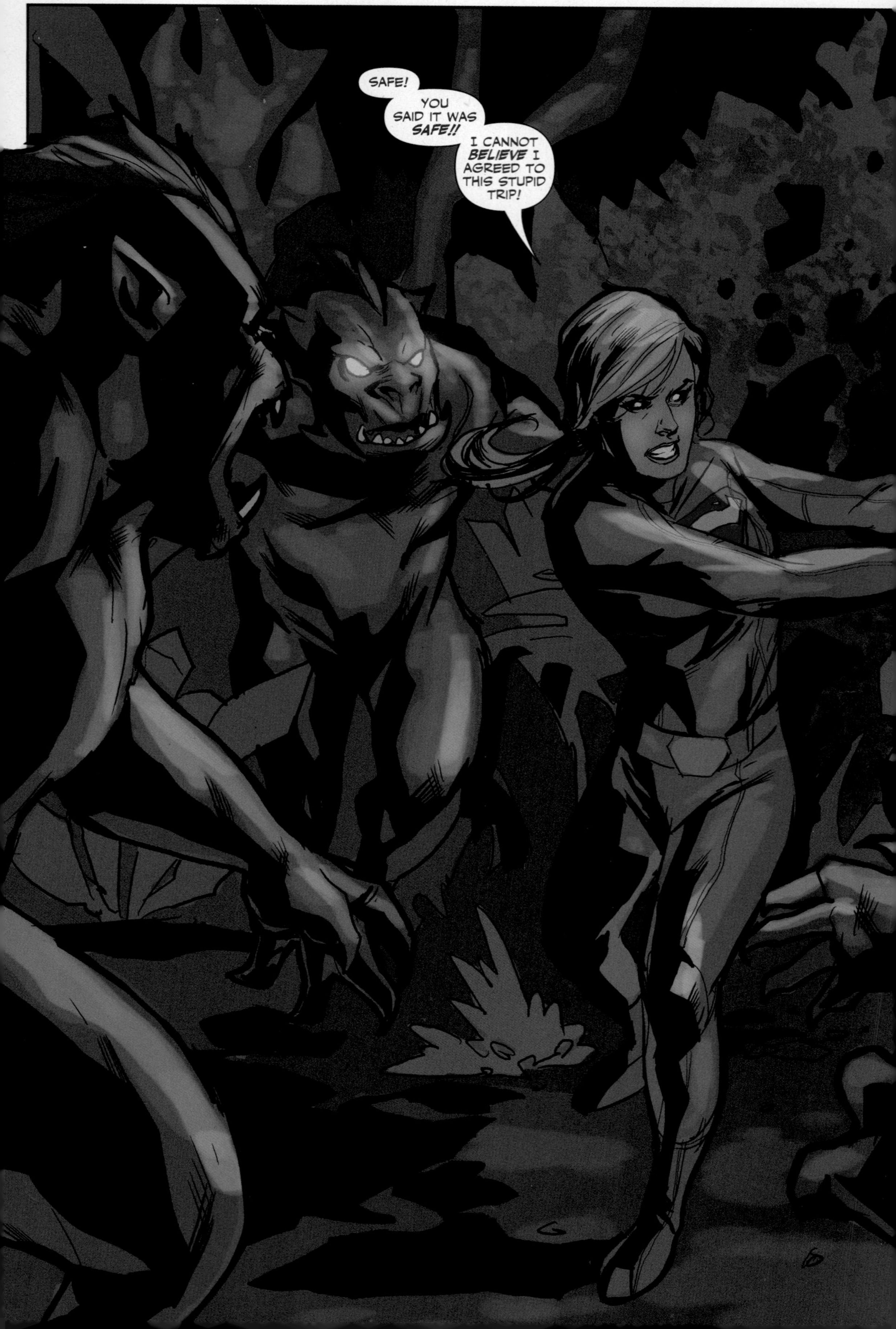
SAFE!
YOU SAID IT WAS SAFE!!
I CANNOT BELIEVE I AGREED TO THIS STUPID TRIP!

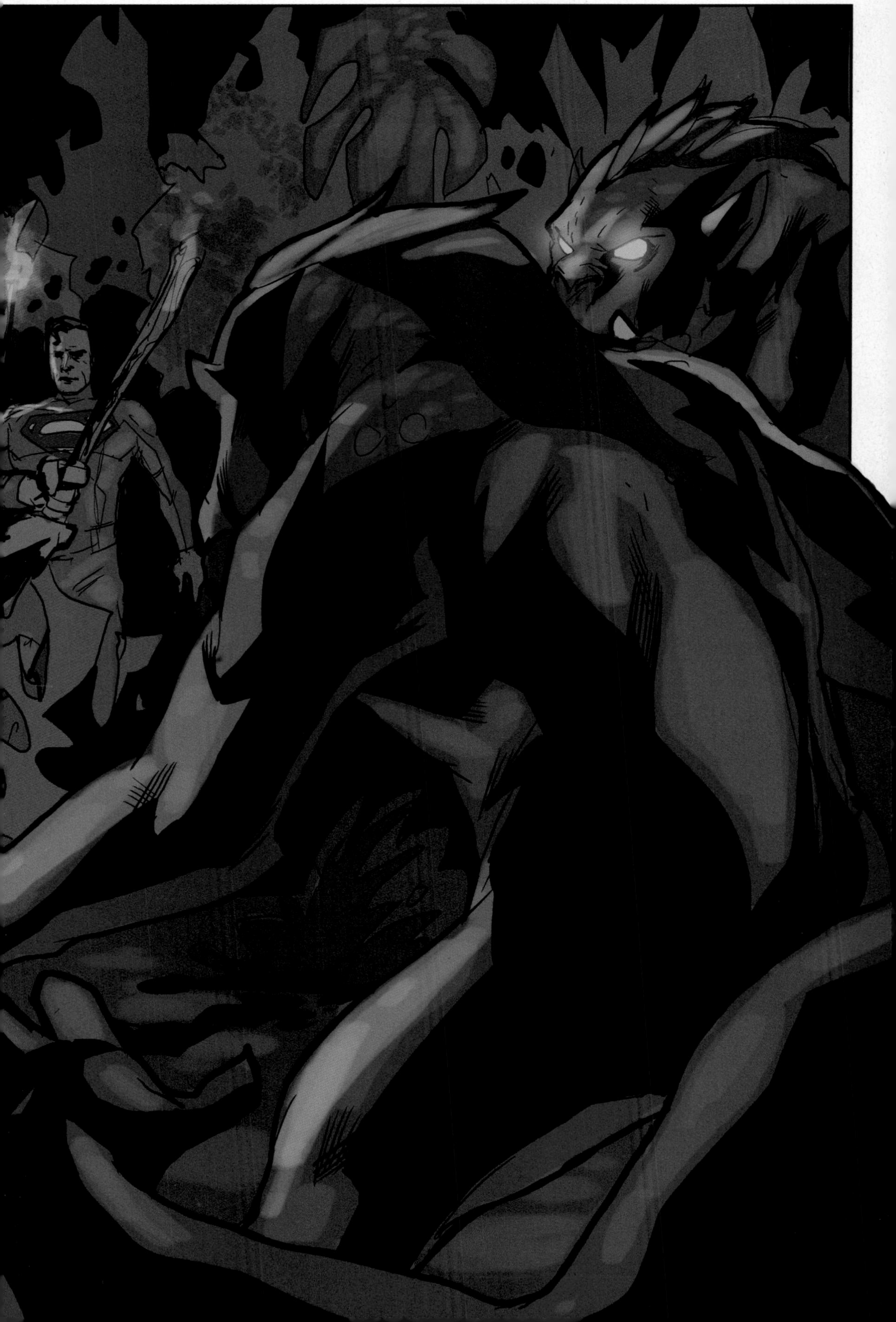

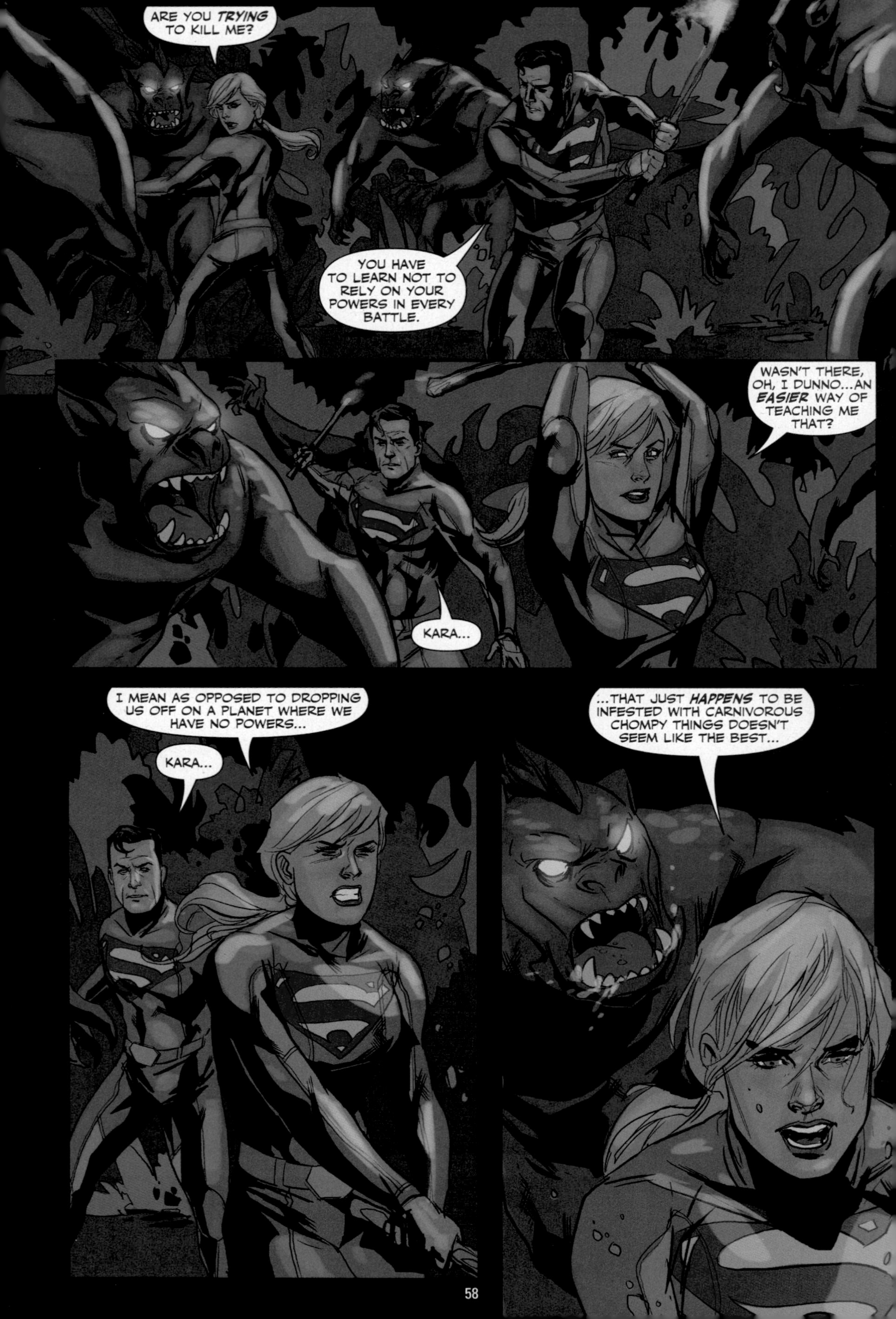
ARE YOU *TRYING* TO KILL ME?
YOU HAVE TO LEARN NOT TO RELY ON YOUR POWERS IN EVERY BATTLE.
WASN'T THERE, OH, I DUNNO...AN *EASIER* WAY OF TEACHING ME THAT?
KARA...
I MEAN AS OPPOSED TO DROPPING US OFF ON A PLANET WHERE WE HAVE NO POWERS...
KARA...
...THAT JUST *HAPPENS* TO BE INFESTED WITH CARNIVOROUS CHOMPY THINGS DOESN'T SEEM LIKE THE BEST...

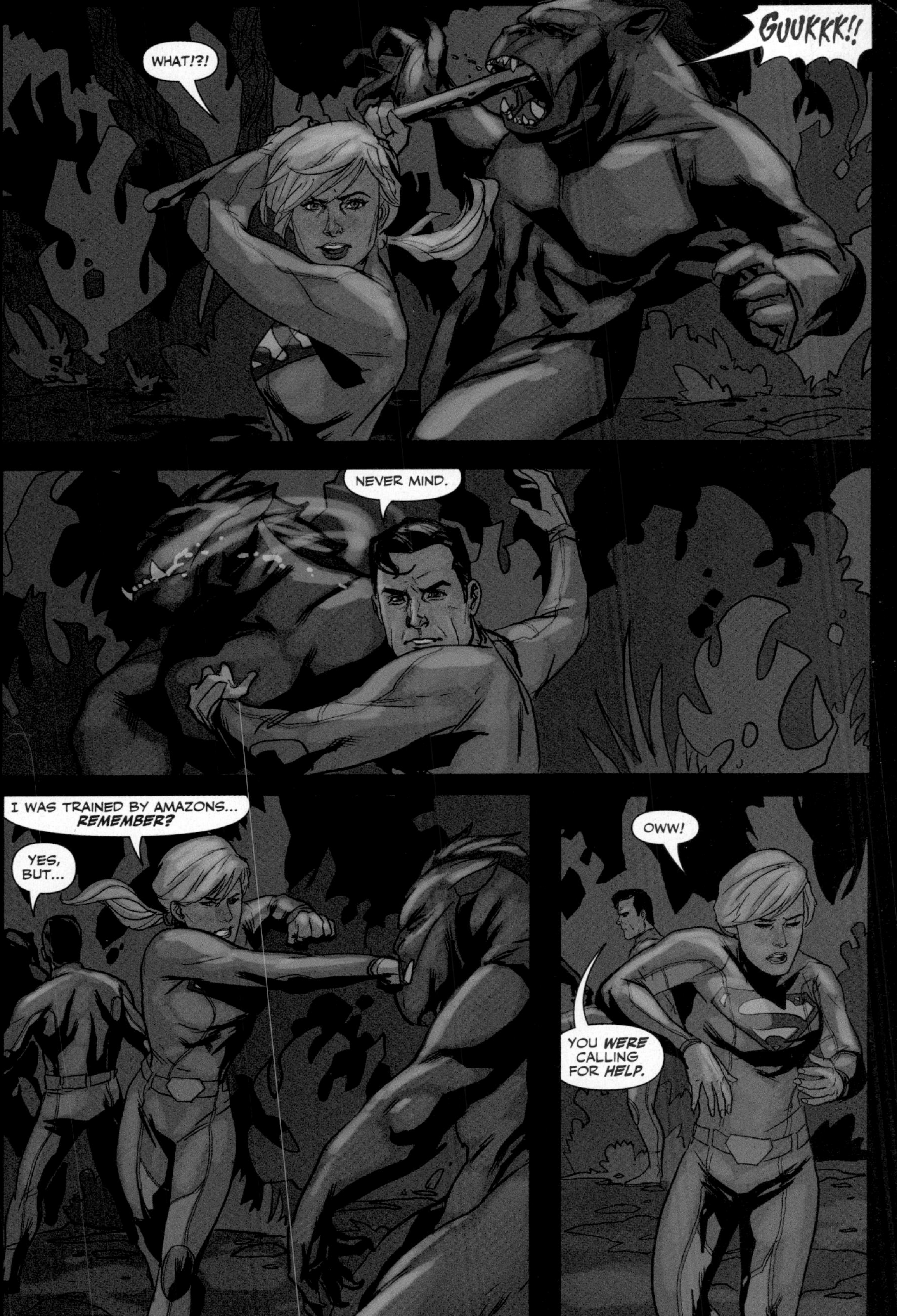
WHAT!?!
GUUKKK!!
NEVER MIND.
I WAS TRAINED BY AMAZONS... REMEMBER?
YES, BUT...
OWW!
YOU WERE CALLING FOR HELP.

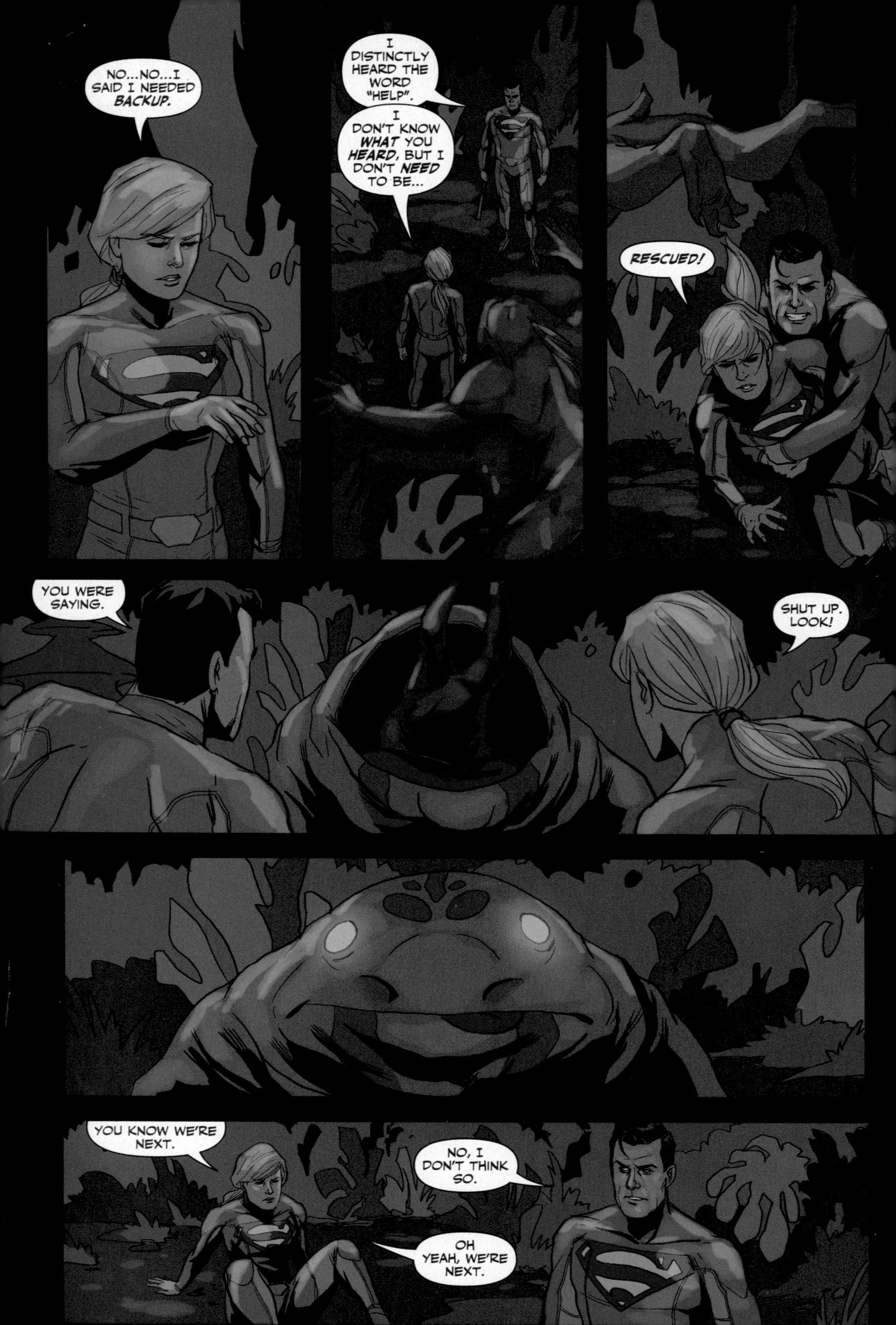
NO...NO...I SAID I NEEDED *BACKUP.*
I DISTINCTLY HEARD THE WORD "HELP".
I DON'T KNOW *WHAT* YOU *HEARD*, BUT I DON'T *NEED* TO BE...
RESCUED!
YOU WERE SAYING.
SHUT UP. LOOK!
YOU KNOW WE'RE NEXT.
NO, I DON'T THINK SO.
OH YEAH, WE'RE NEXT.

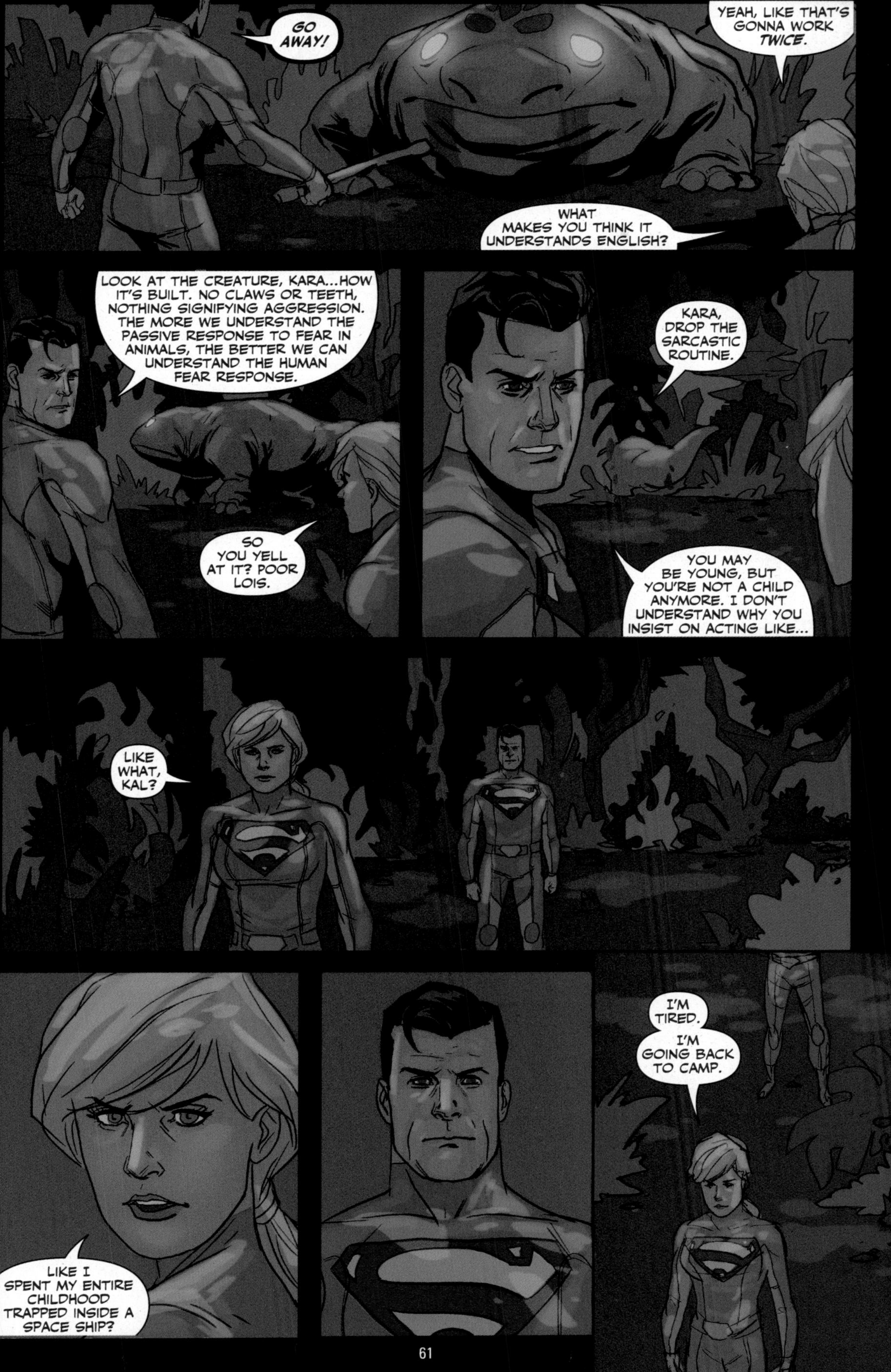
GO AWAY!
YEAH, LIKE THAT'S GONNA WORK TWICE.
WHAT MAKES YOU THINK IT UNDERSTANDS ENGLISH?
LOOK AT THE CREATURE, KARA...HOW IT'S BUILT. NO CLAWS OR TEETH, NOTHING SIGNIFYING AGGRESSION. THE MORE WE UNDERSTAND THE PASSIVE RESPONSE TO FEAR IN ANIMALS, THE BETTER WE CAN UNDERSTAND THE HUMAN FEAR RESPONSE.
SO YOU YELL AT IT? POOR LOIS.
KARA, DROP THE SARCASTIC ROUTINE.
YOU MAY BE YOUNG, BUT YOU'RE NOT A CHILD ANYMORE. I DON'T UNDERSTAND WHY YOU INSIST ON ACTING LIKE...
LIKE WHAT, KAL?
LIKE I SPENT MY ENTIRE CHILDHOOD TRAPPED INSIDE A SPACE SHIP?
I'M TIRED.
I'M GOING BACK TO CAMP.

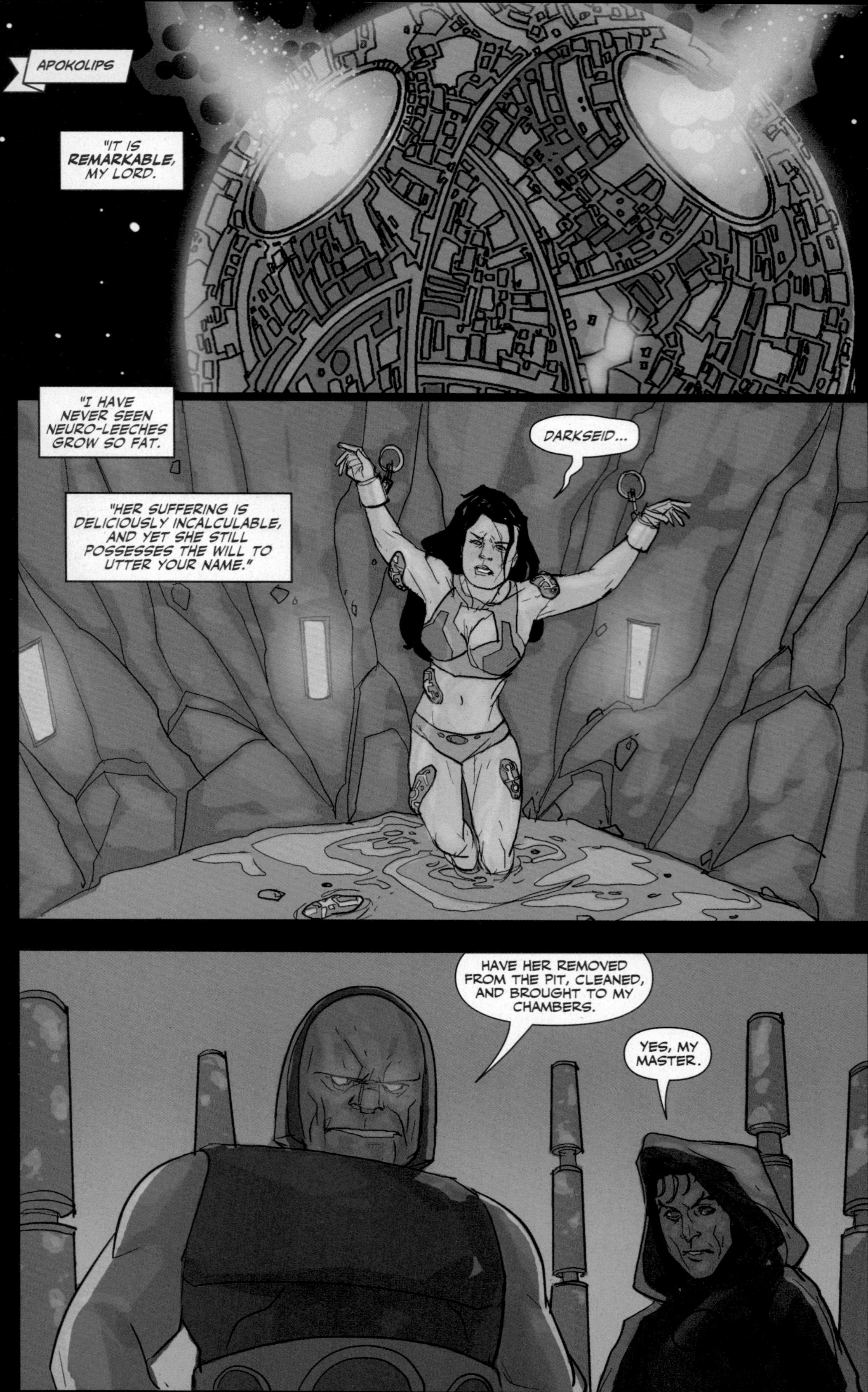
APOKOLIPS
"IT IS REMARKABLE, MY LORD.
"I HAVE NEVER SEEN NEURO-LEECHES GROW SO FAT.
DARKSEID...
"HER SUFFERING IS DELICIOUSLY INCALCULABLE, AND YET SHE STILL POSSESSES THE WILL TO UTTER YOUR NAME."
HAVE HER REMOVED FROM THE PIT, CLEANED, AND BROUGHT TO MY CHAMBERS.
YES, MY MASTER.

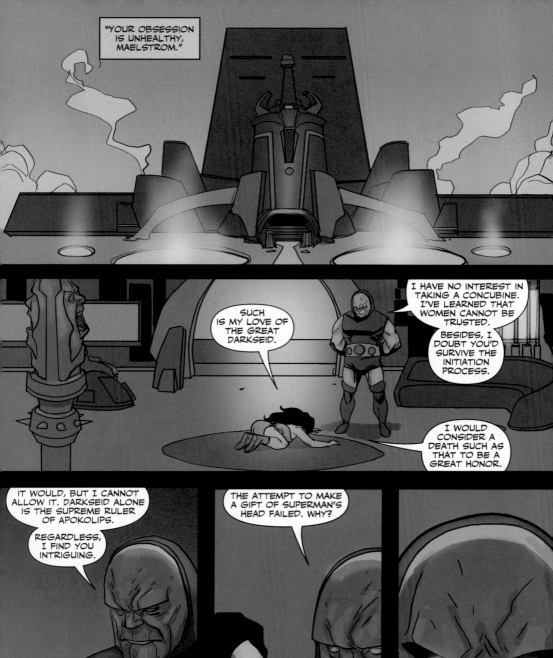

"YOUR OBSESSION IS UNHEALTHY, MAELSTROM."

SUCH IS MY LOVE OF THE GREAT DARKSEID.

I HAVE NO INTEREST IN TAKING A CONCUBINE. I'VE LEARNED THAT WOMEN CANNOT BE TRUSTED.

BESIDES, I DOUBT YOU'D SURVIVE THE INITIATION PROCESS.

I WOULD CONSIDER A DEATH SUCH AS THAT TO BE A GREAT HONOR.

IT WOULD, BUT I CANNOT ALLOW IT. DARKSEID ALONE IS THE SUPREME RULER OF APOKOLIPS.

REGARDLESS, I FIND YOU INTRIGUING.

THE ATTEMPT TO MAKE A GIFT OF SUPERMAN'S HEAD FAILED. WHY?

THERE WAS ANOTHER KRYPTONIAN, A FEMALE. WHEN I WAS ABOUT TO KILL HER, HE ATTACKED. SUCH IS HIS COWARDICE.

COWARDICE? SUPERMAN IS NO COWARD.

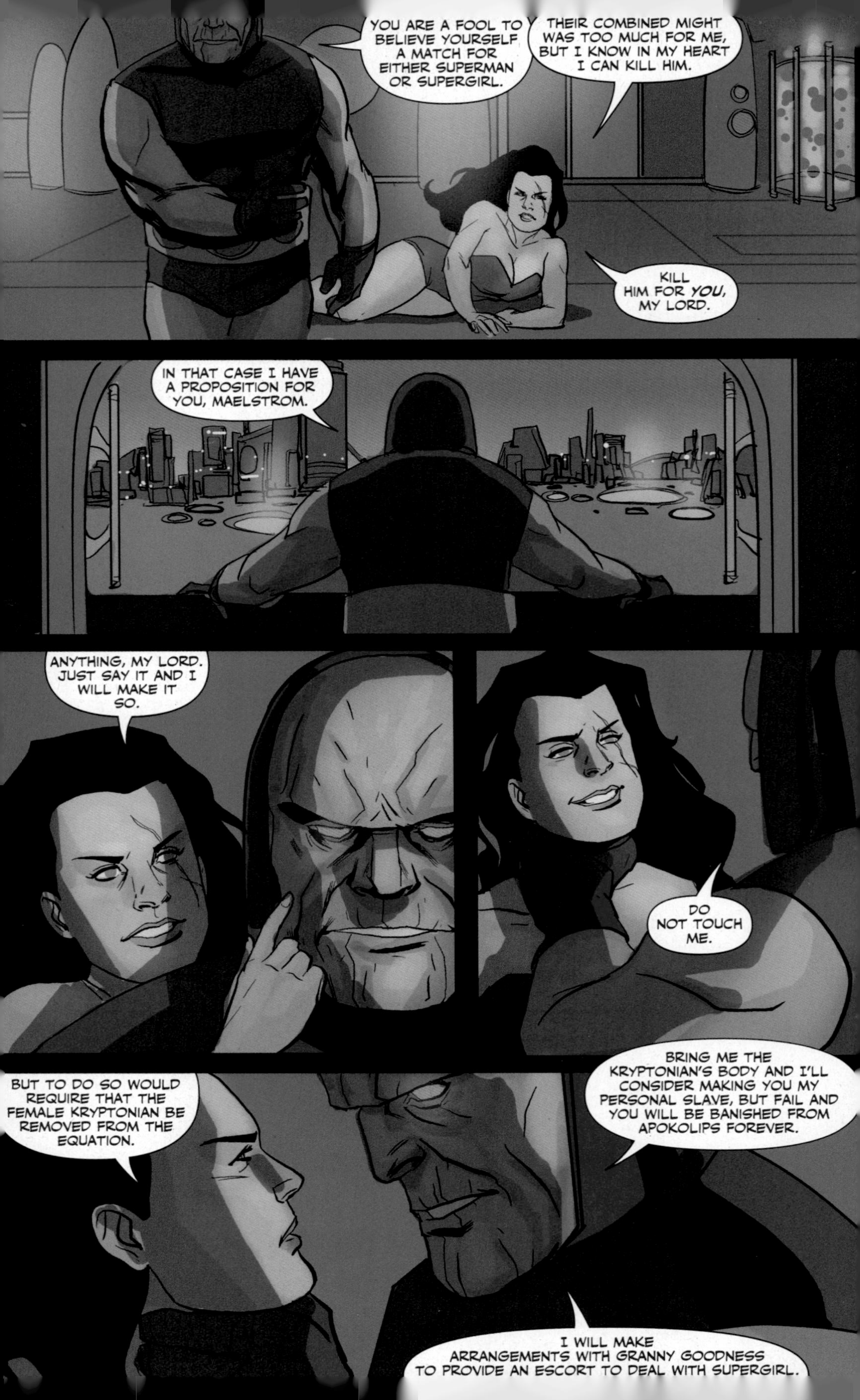
YOU ARE A FOOL TO BELIEVE YOURSELF A MATCH FOR EITHER SUPERMAN OR SUPERGIRL.
THEIR COMBINED MIGHT WAS TOO MUCH FOR ME, BUT I KNOW IN MY HEART I CAN KILL HIM.
KILL HIM FOR *YOU*, MY LORD.
IN THAT CASE I HAVE A PROPOSITION FOR YOU, MAELSTROM.
ANYTHING, MY LORD. JUST SAY IT AND I WILL MAKE IT SO.
DO NOT TOUCH ME.
BUT TO DO SO WOULD REQUIRE THAT THE FEMALE KRYPTONIAN BE REMOVED FROM THE EQUATION.
BRING ME THE KRYPTONIAN'S BODY AND I'LL CONSIDER MAKING YOU MY PERSONAL SLAVE, BUT FAIL AND YOU WILL BE BANISHED FROM APOKOLIPS FOREVER.
I WILL MAKE ARRANGEMENTS WITH GRANNY GOODNESS TO PROVIDE AN ESCORT TO DEAL WITH SUPERGIRL.

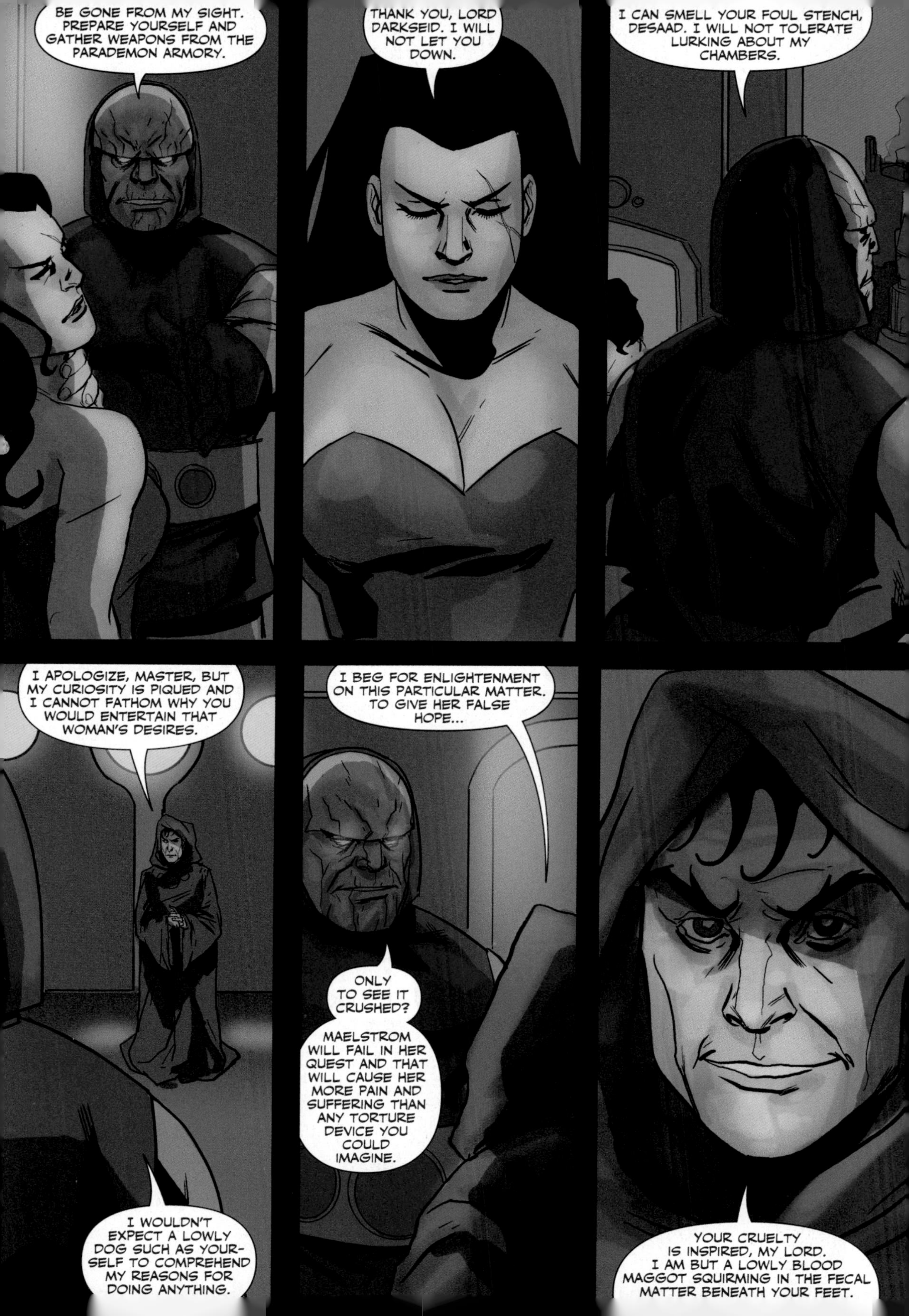
BE GONE FROM MY SIGHT. PREPARE YOURSELF AND GATHER WEAPONS FROM THE PARADEMON ARMORY.
THANK YOU, LORD DARKSEID. I WILL NOT LET YOU DOWN.
I CAN SMELL YOUR FOUL STENCH, DESAAD. I WILL NOT TOLERATE LURKING ABOUT MY CHAMBERS.
I APOLOGIZE, MASTER, BUT MY CURIOSITY IS PIQUED AND I CANNOT FATHOM WHY YOU WOULD ENTERTAIN THAT WOMAN'S DESIRES.
I BEG FOR ENLIGHTENMENT ON THIS PARTICULAR MATTER. TO GIVE HER FALSE HOPE...
ONLY TO SEE IT CRUSHED?
MAELSTROM WILL FAIL IN HER QUEST AND THAT WILL CAUSE HER MORE PAIN AND SUFFERING THAN ANY TORTURE DEVICE YOU COULD IMAGINE.
I WOULDN'T EXPECT A LOWLY DOG SUCH AS YOUR-SELF TO COMPREHEND MY REASONS FOR DOING ANYTHING.
YOUR CRUELTY IS INSPIRED, MY LORD. I AM BUT A LOWLY BLOOD MAGGOT SQUIRMING IN THE FECAL MATTER BENEATH YOUR FEET.

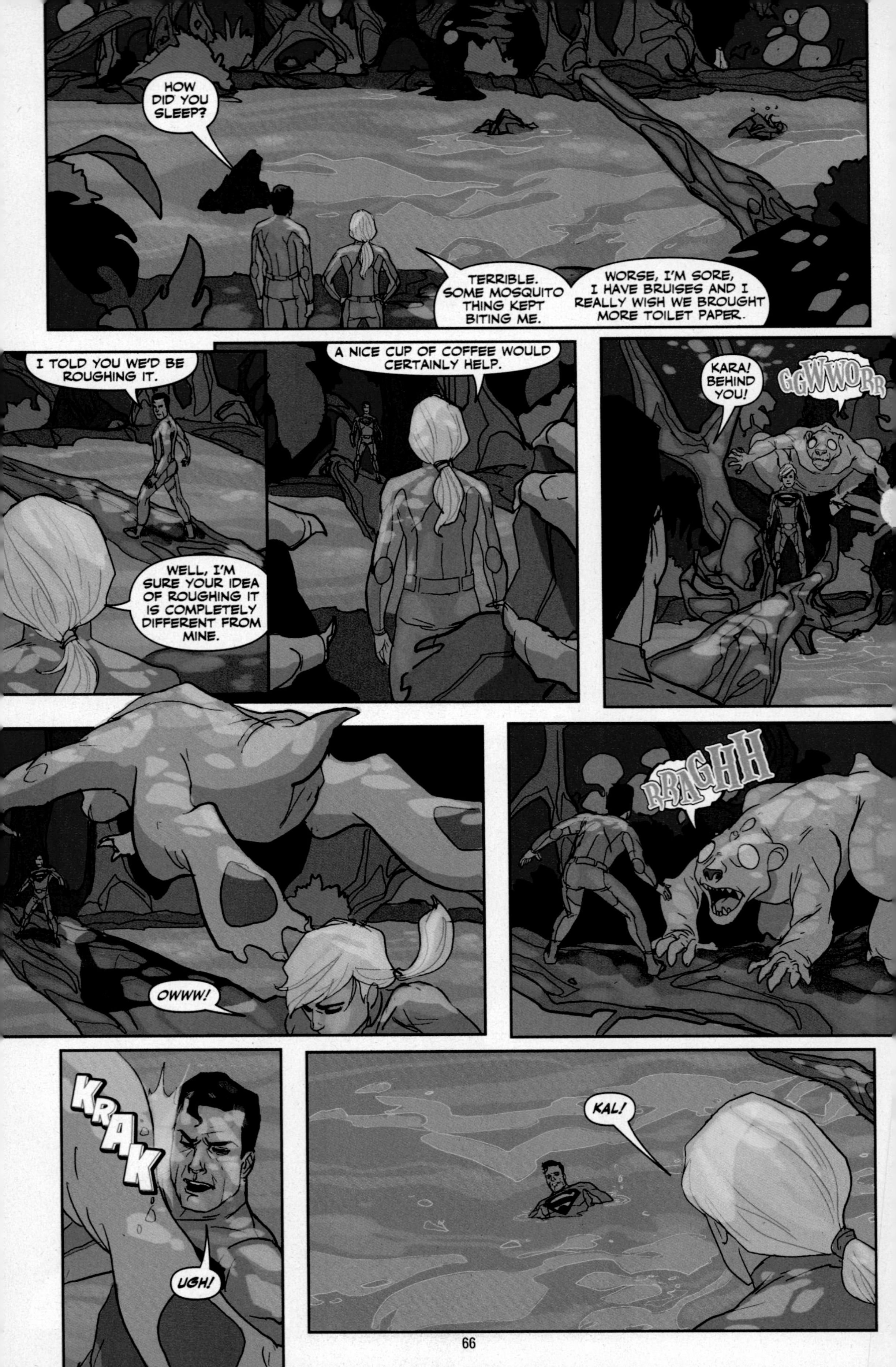
HOW DID YOU SLEEP?
TERRIBLE. SOME MOSQUITO THING KEPT BITING ME.
WORSE, I'M SORE, I HAVE BRUISES AND I REALLY WISH WE BROUGHT MORE TOILET PAPER.
I TOLD YOU WE'D BE ROUGHING IT.
WELL, I'M SURE YOUR IDEA OF ROUGHING IT IS COMPLETELY DIFFERENT FROM MINE.
A NICE CUP OF COFFEE WOULD CERTAINLY HELP.
KARA! BEHIND YOU!
GGWWORR
OWWW!
RRAGHH
KRAK
UGH!
KAL!

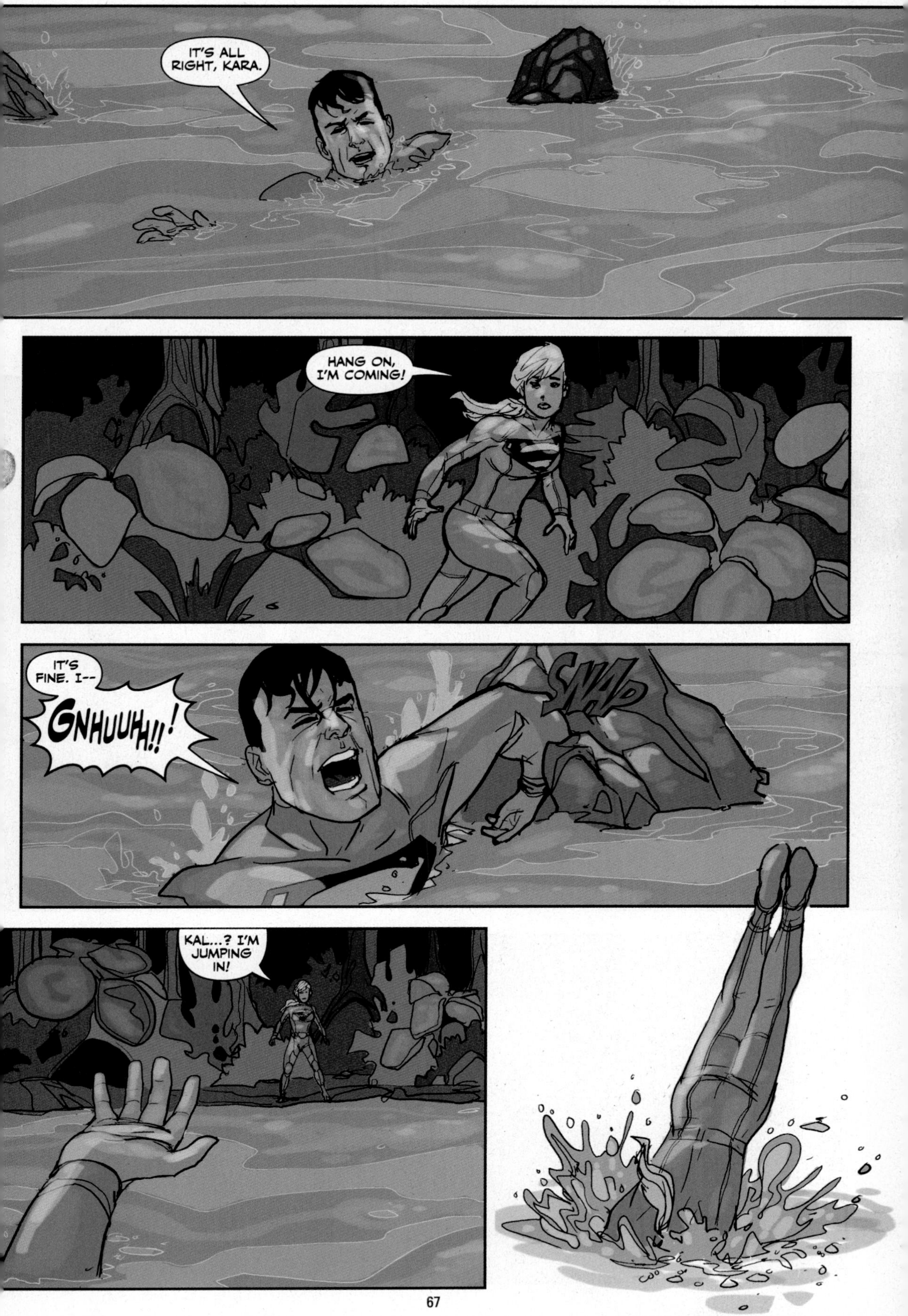
IT'S ALL RIGHT, KARA.
HANG ON, I'M COMING!
IT'S FINE. I--
GNHUUHH!!!
SNAP
KAL...? I'M JUMPING IN!

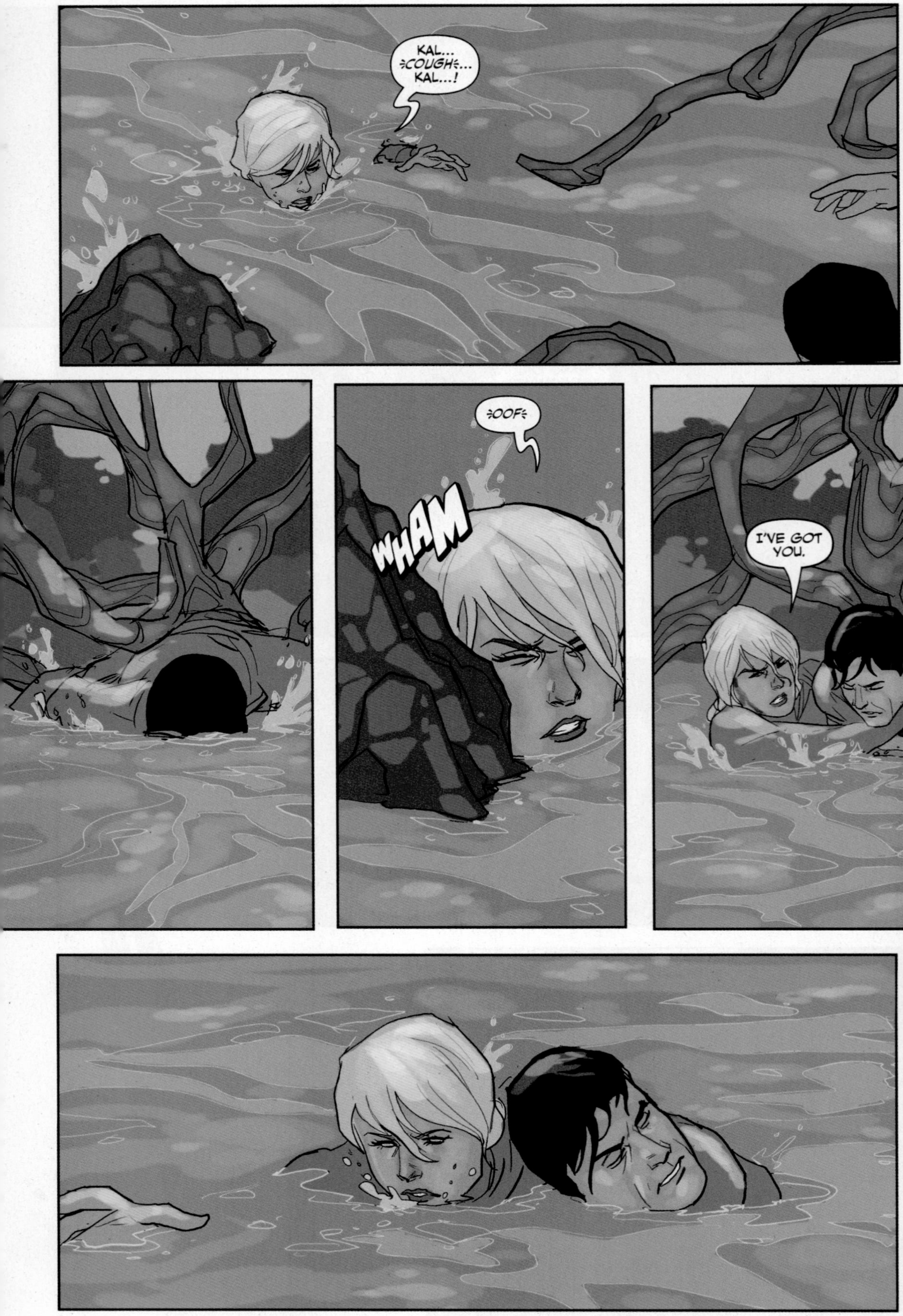
KAL... ≈COUGH≈... KAL...!
≈OOF≈
WHAM
I'VE GOT YOU.

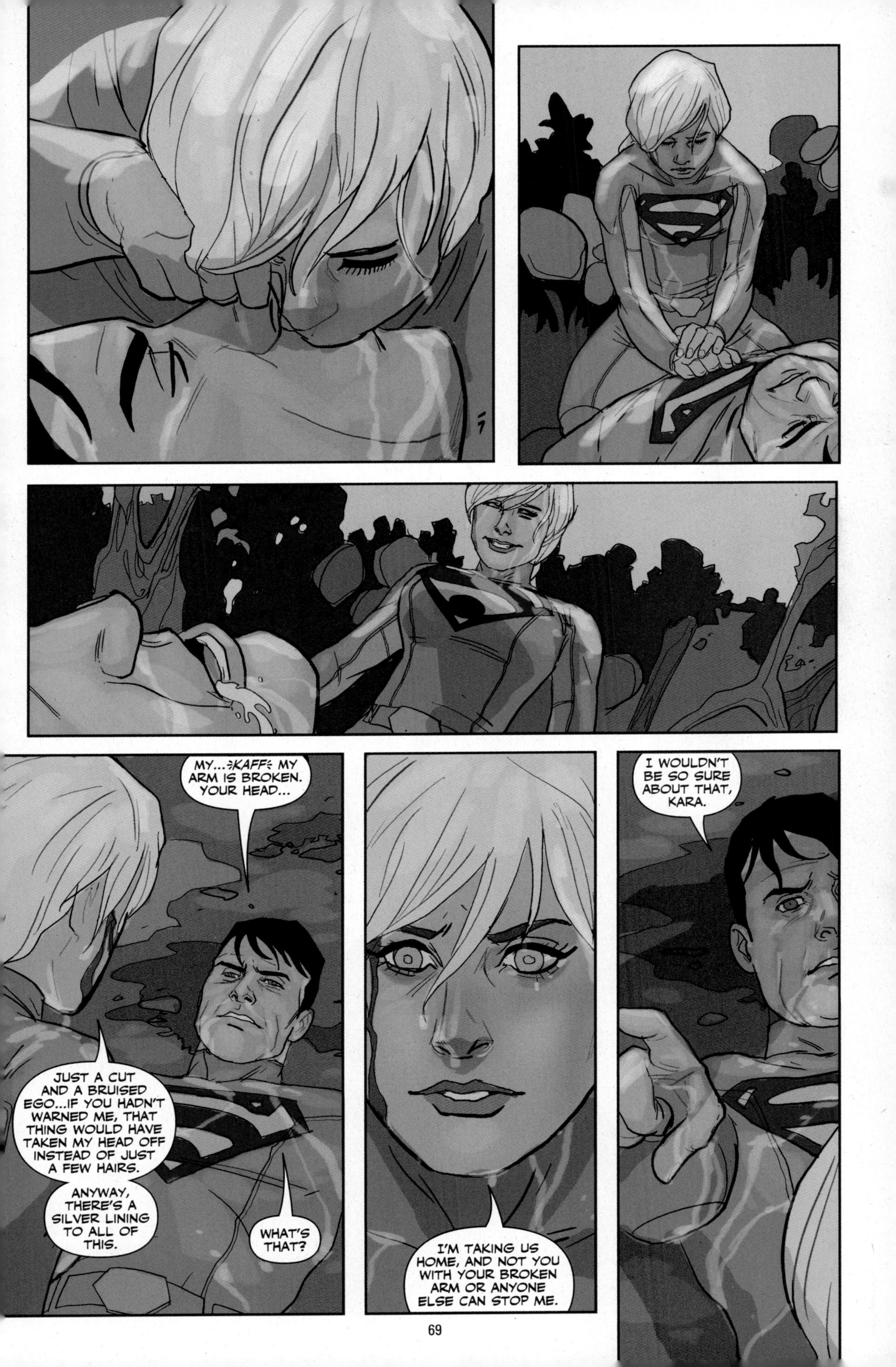
MY...⁂KAFF⁂ MY ARM IS BROKEN. YOUR HEAD...
JUST A CUT AND A BRUISED EGO...IF YOU HADN'T WARNED ME, THAT THING WOULD HAVE TAKEN MY HEAD OFF INSTEAD OF JUST A FEW HAIRS.
ANYWAY, THERE'S A SILVER LINING TO ALL OF THIS.
WHAT'S THAT?
I'M TAKING US HOME, AND NOT YOU WITH YOUR BROKEN ARM OR ANYONE ELSE CAN STOP ME.
I WOULDN'T BE SO SURE ABOUT THAT, KARA.

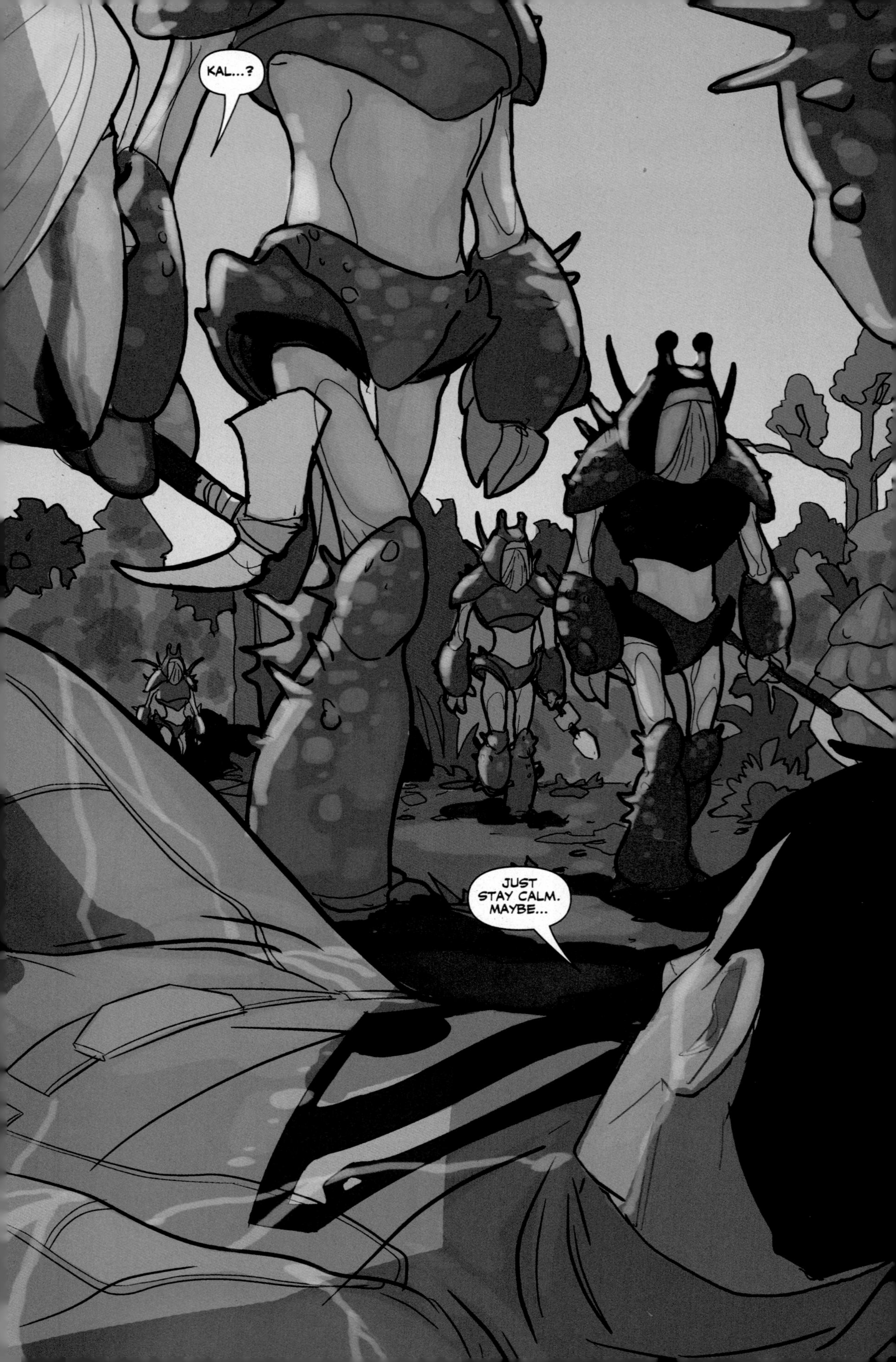
KAL...?
JUST STAY CALM. MAYBE...

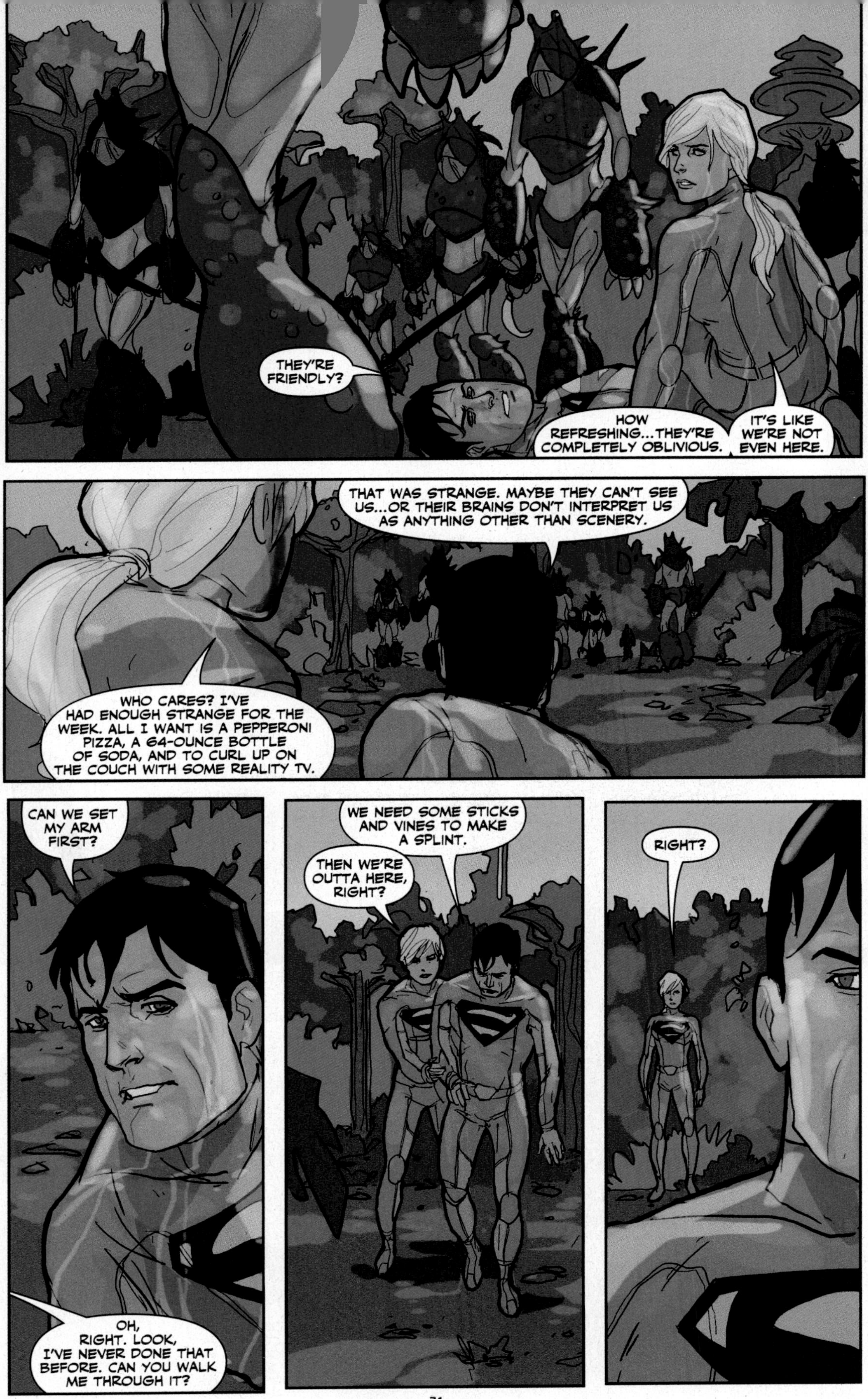
THEY'RE FRIENDLY?
HOW REFRESHING...THEY'RE COMPLETELY OBLIVIOUS.
IT'S LIKE WE'RE NOT EVEN HERE.
THAT WAS STRANGE. MAYBE THEY CAN'T SEE US...OR THEIR BRAINS DON'T INTERPRET US AS ANYTHING OTHER THAN SCENERY.
WHO CARES? I'VE HAD ENOUGH STRANGE FOR THE WEEK. ALL I WANT IS A PEPPERONI PIZZA, A 64-OUNCE BOTTLE OF SODA, AND TO CURL UP ON THE COUCH WITH SOME REALITY TV.
CAN WE SET MY ARM FIRST?
OH, RIGHT. LOOK, I'VE NEVER DONE THAT BEFORE. CAN YOU WALK ME THROUGH IT?
WE NEED SOME STICKS AND VINES TO MAKE A SPLINT.
THEN WE'RE OUTTA HERE, RIGHT?
RIGHT?

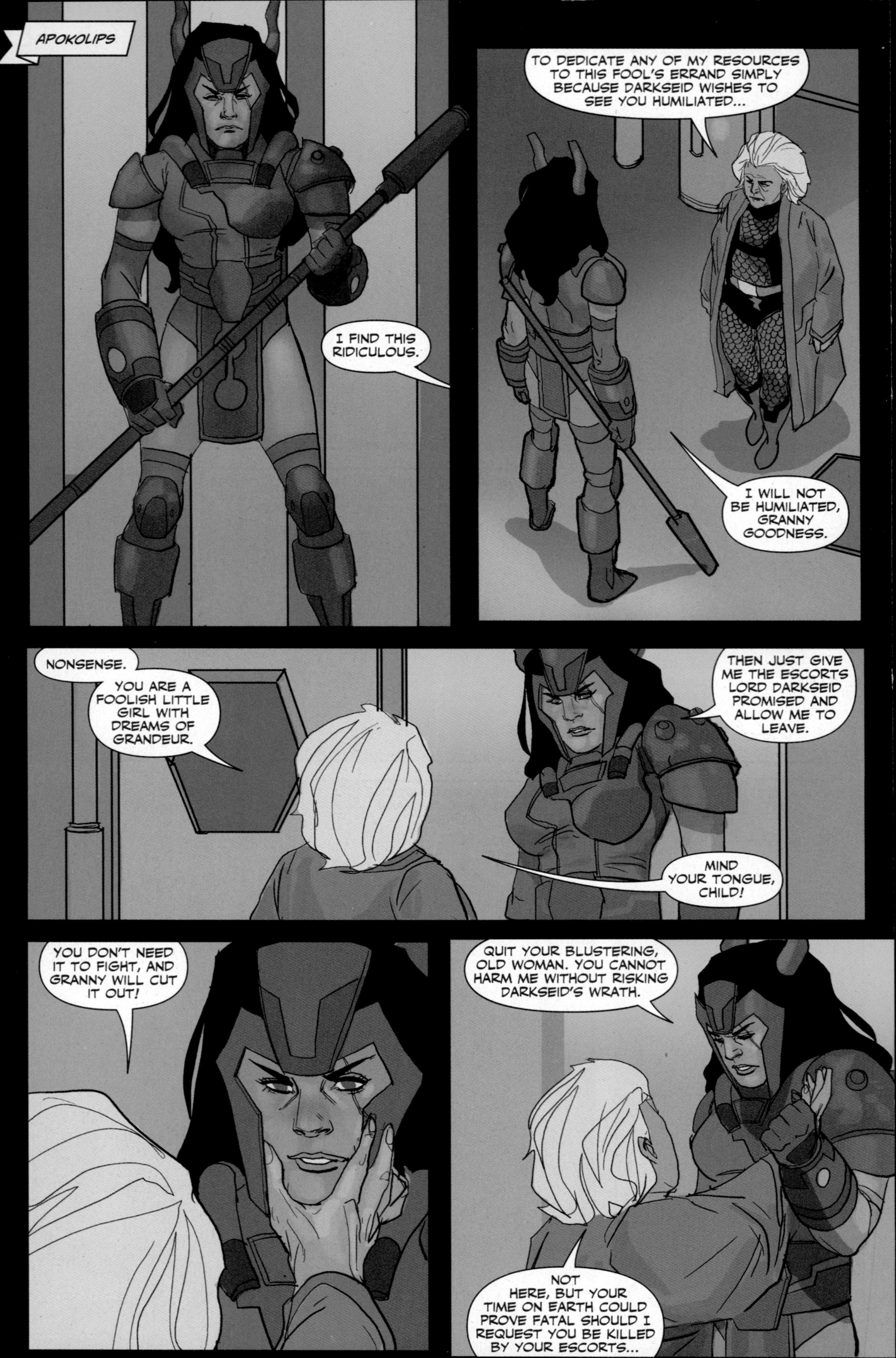

APOKOLIPS
I FIND THIS RIDICULOUS.
TO DEDICATE ANY OF MY RESOURCES TO THIS FOOL'S ERRAND SIMPLY BECAUSE DARKSEID WISHES TO SEE YOU HUMILIATED...
I WILL NOT BE HUMILIATED, GRANNY GOODNESS.
NONSENSE.
YOU ARE A FOOLISH LITTLE GIRL WITH DREAMS OF GRANDEUR.
THEN JUST GIVE ME THE ESCORTS LORD DARKSEID PROMISED AND ALLOW ME TO LEAVE.
MIND YOUR TONGUE, CHILD!
YOU DON'T NEED IT TO FIGHT, AND GRANNY WILL CUT IT OUT!
QUIT YOUR BLUSTERING, OLD WOMAN. YOU CANNOT HARM ME WITHOUT RISKING DARKSEID'S WRATH.
NOT HERE, BUT YOUR TIME ON EARTH COULD PROVE FATAL SHOULD I REQUEST YOU BE KILLED BY YOUR ESCORTS...

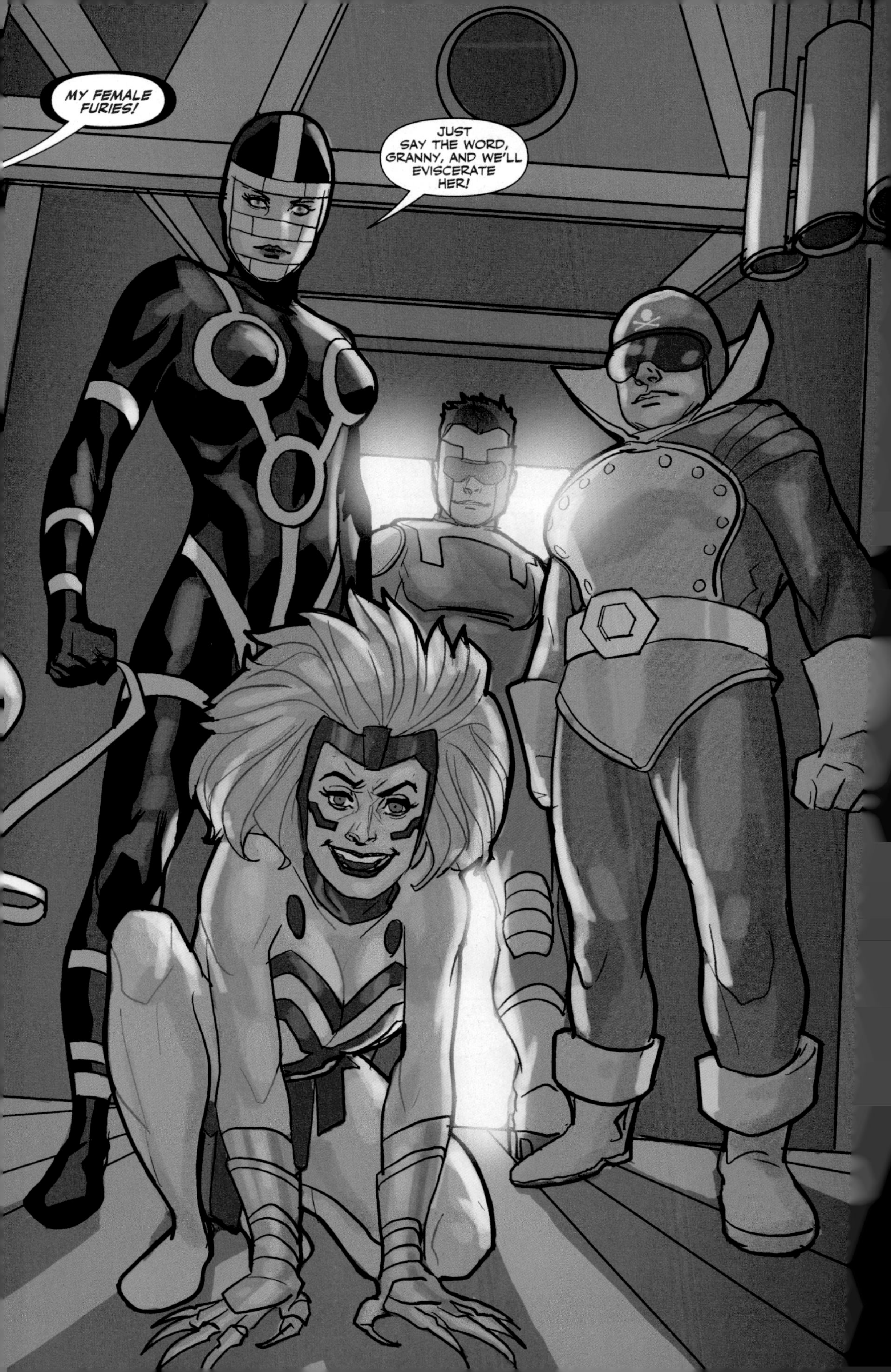
MY FEMALE FURIES!
JUST SAY THE WORD, GRANNY, AND WE'LL EVISCERATE HER!

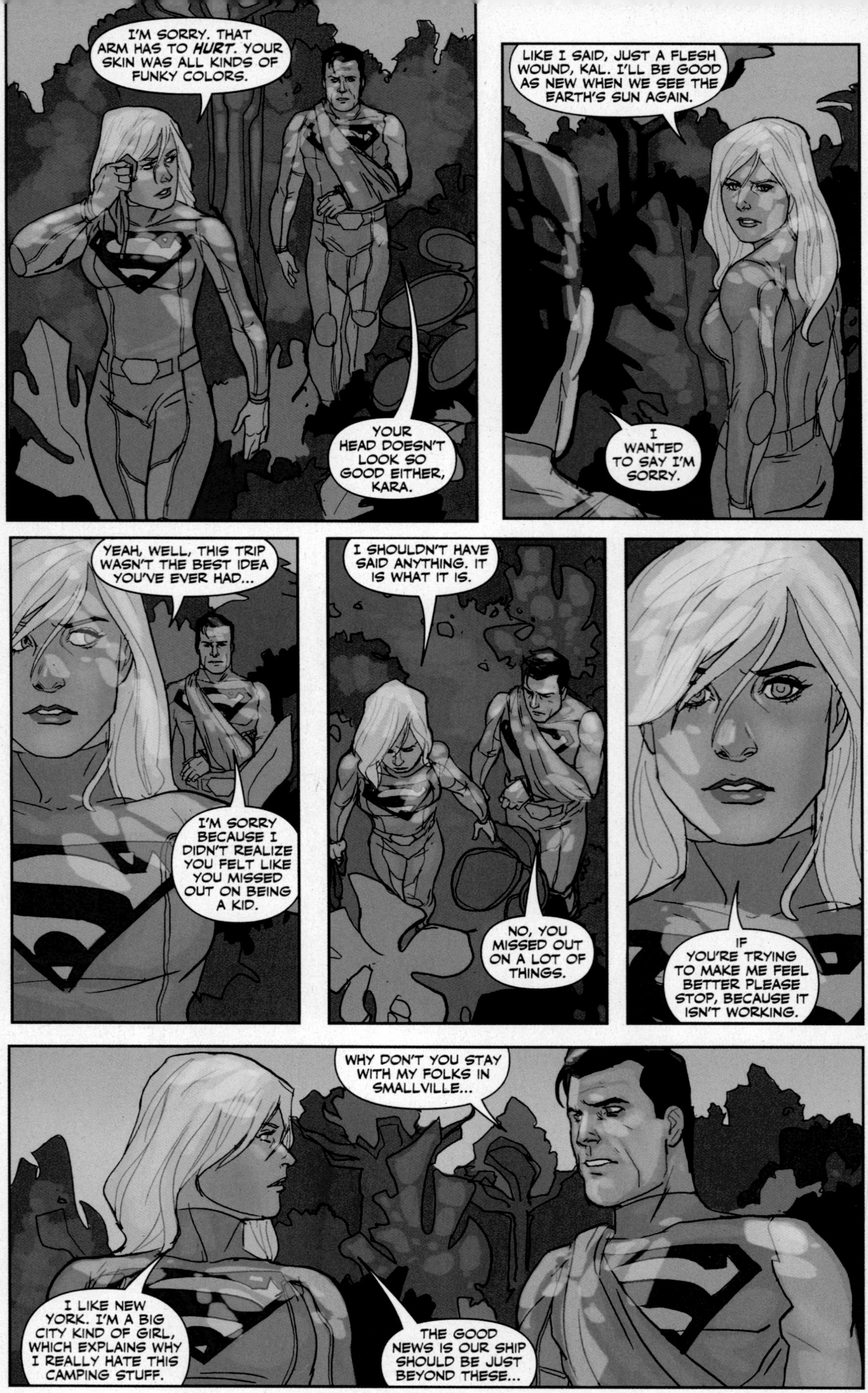

I'M SORRY. THAT ARM HAS TO *HURT*. YOUR SKIN WAS ALL KINDS OF FUNKY COLORS.
YOUR HEAD DOESN'T LOOK SO GOOD EITHER, KARA.
LIKE I SAID, JUST A FLESH WOUND, KAL. I'LL BE GOOD AS NEW WHEN WE SEE THE EARTH'S SUN AGAIN.
I WANTED TO SAY I'M SORRY.
YEAH, WELL, THIS TRIP WASN'T THE BEST IDEA YOU'VE EVER HAD...
I'M SORRY BECAUSE I DIDN'T REALIZE YOU FELT LIKE YOU MISSED OUT ON BEING A KID.
I SHOULDN'T HAVE SAID ANYTHING. IT IS WHAT IT IS.
NO, YOU MISSED OUT ON A LOT OF THINGS.
IF YOU'RE TRYING TO MAKE ME FEEL BETTER PLEASE STOP, BECAUSE IT ISN'T WORKING.
WHY DON'T YOU STAY WITH MY FOLKS IN SMALLVILLE...
I LIKE NEW YORK. I'M A BIG CITY KIND OF GIRL, WHICH EXPLAINS WHY I REALLY HATE THIS CAMPING STUFF.
THE GOOD NEWS IS OUR SHIP SHOULD BE JUST BEYOND THESE...

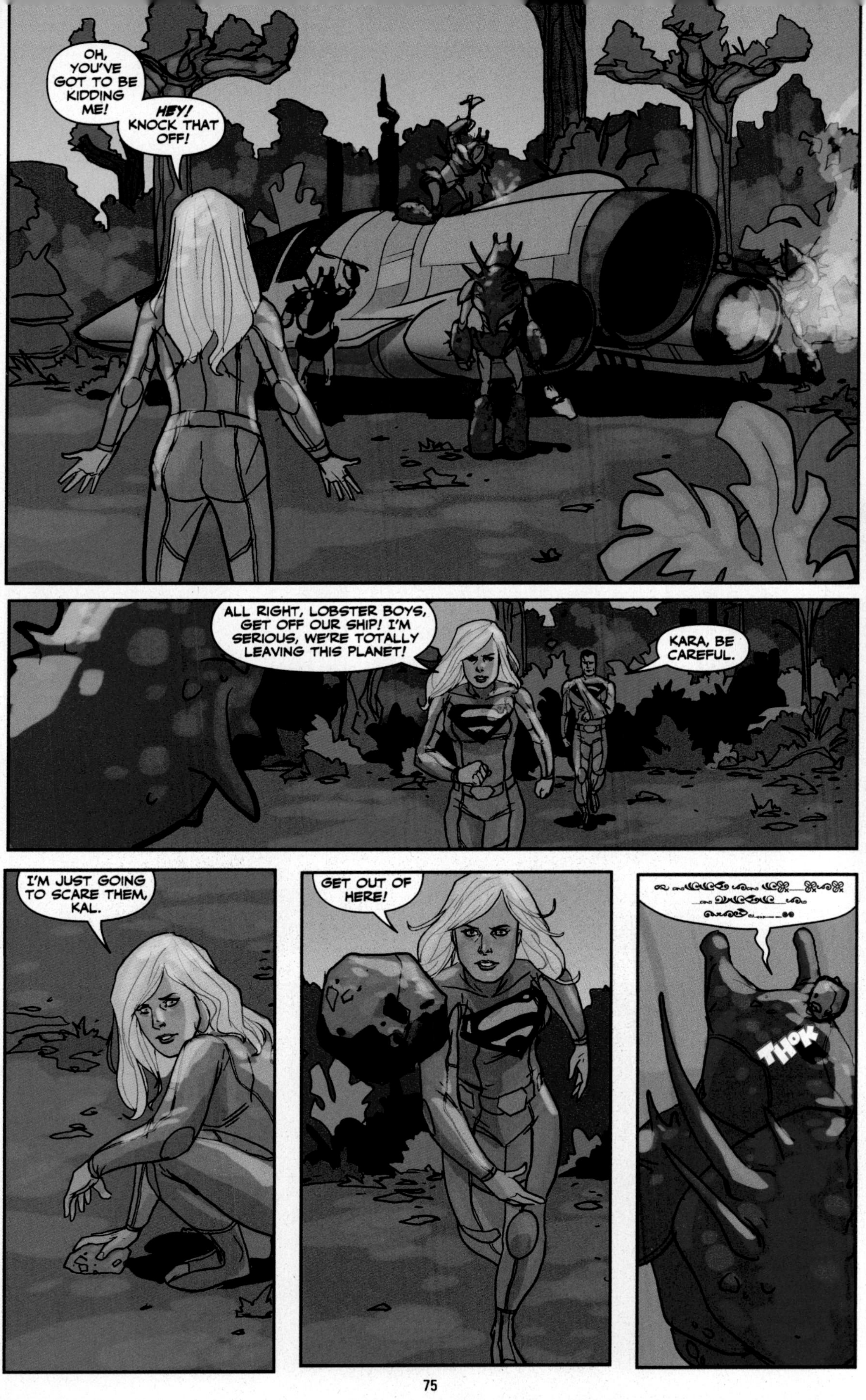
OH, YOU'VE GOT TO BE KIDDING ME!
HEY! KNOCK THAT OFF!
ALL RIGHT, LOBSTER BOYS, GET OFF OUR SHIP! I'M SERIOUS, WE'RE TOTALLY LEAVING THIS PLANET!
KARA, BE CAREFUL.
I'M JUST GOING TO SCARE THEM, KAL.
GET OUT OF HERE!
THOK

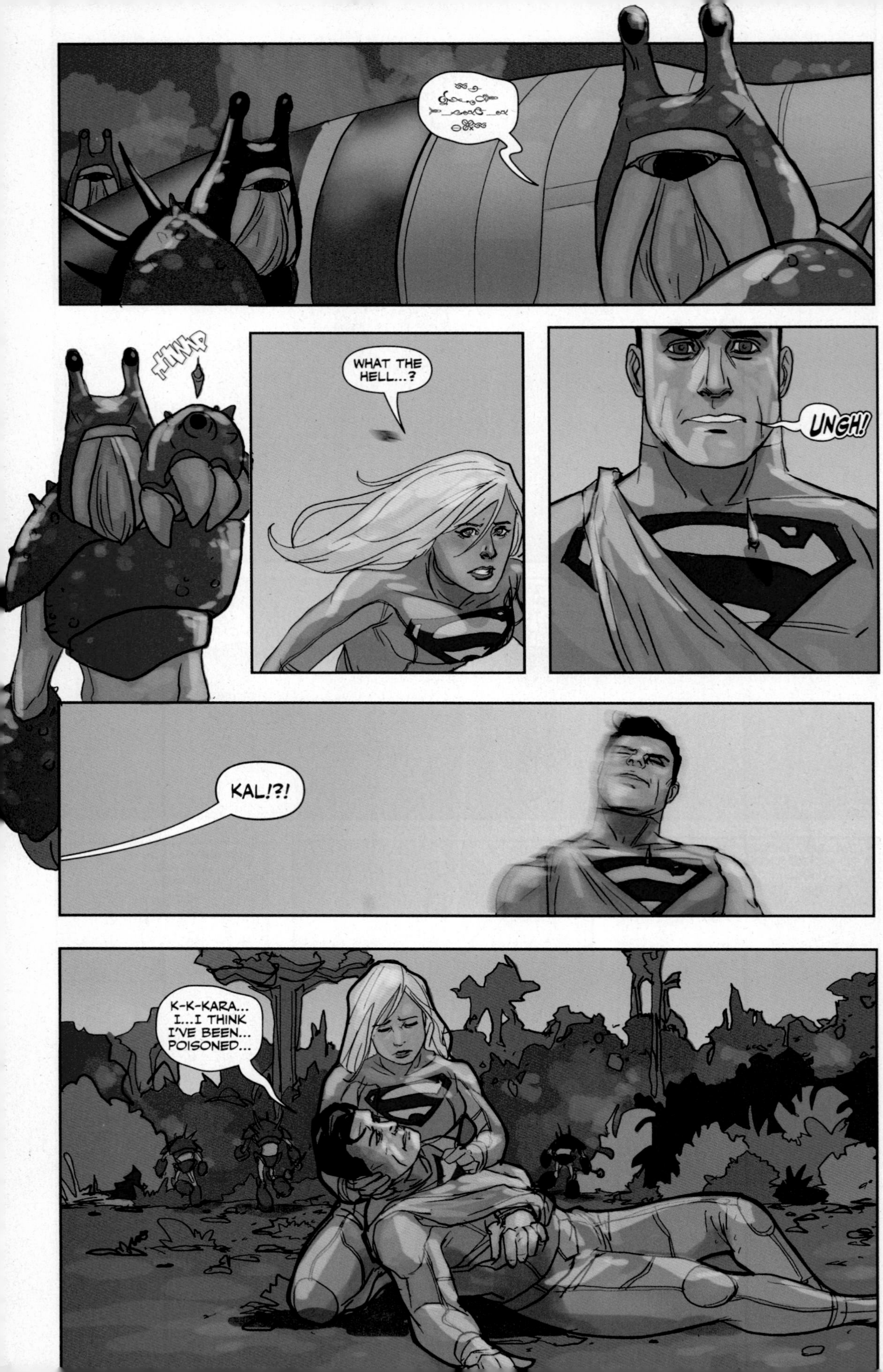
THWAP
WHAT THE HELL...?
UNGH!
KAL!?!
K-K-KARA... I...I THINK I'VE BEEN... POISONED...

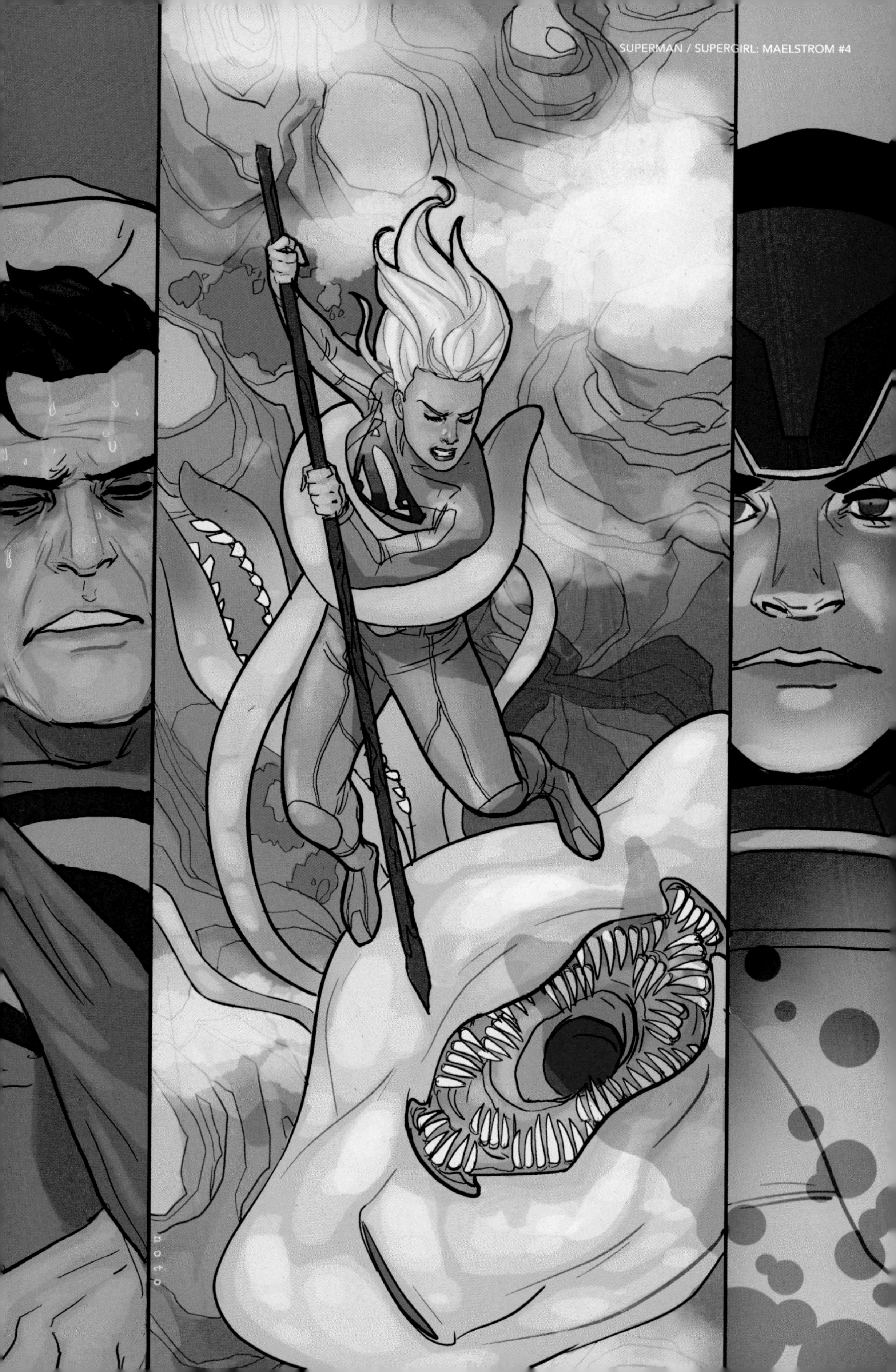

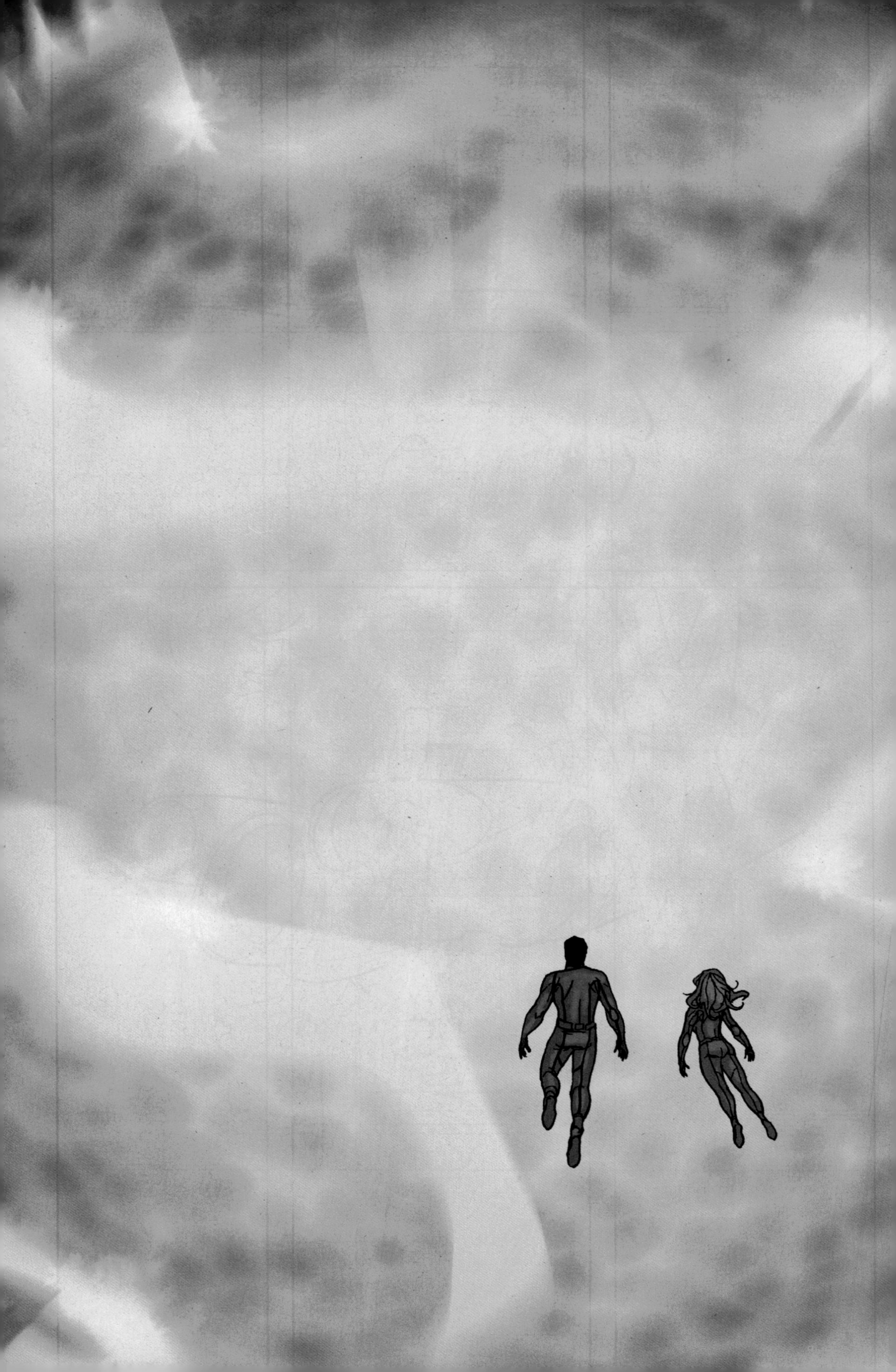

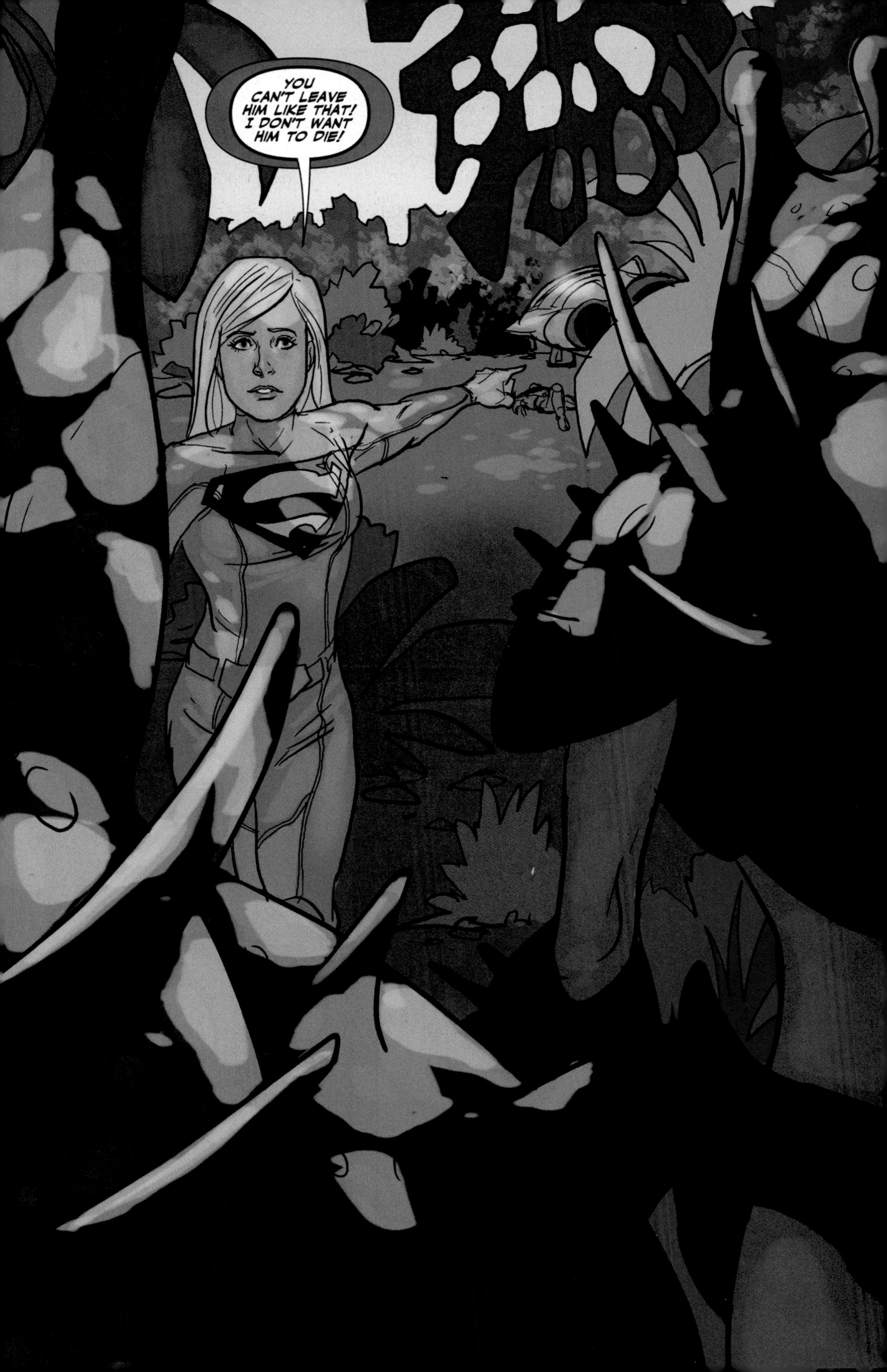
YOU CAN'T LEAVE HIM LIKE THAT! I DON'T WANT HIM TO DIE!

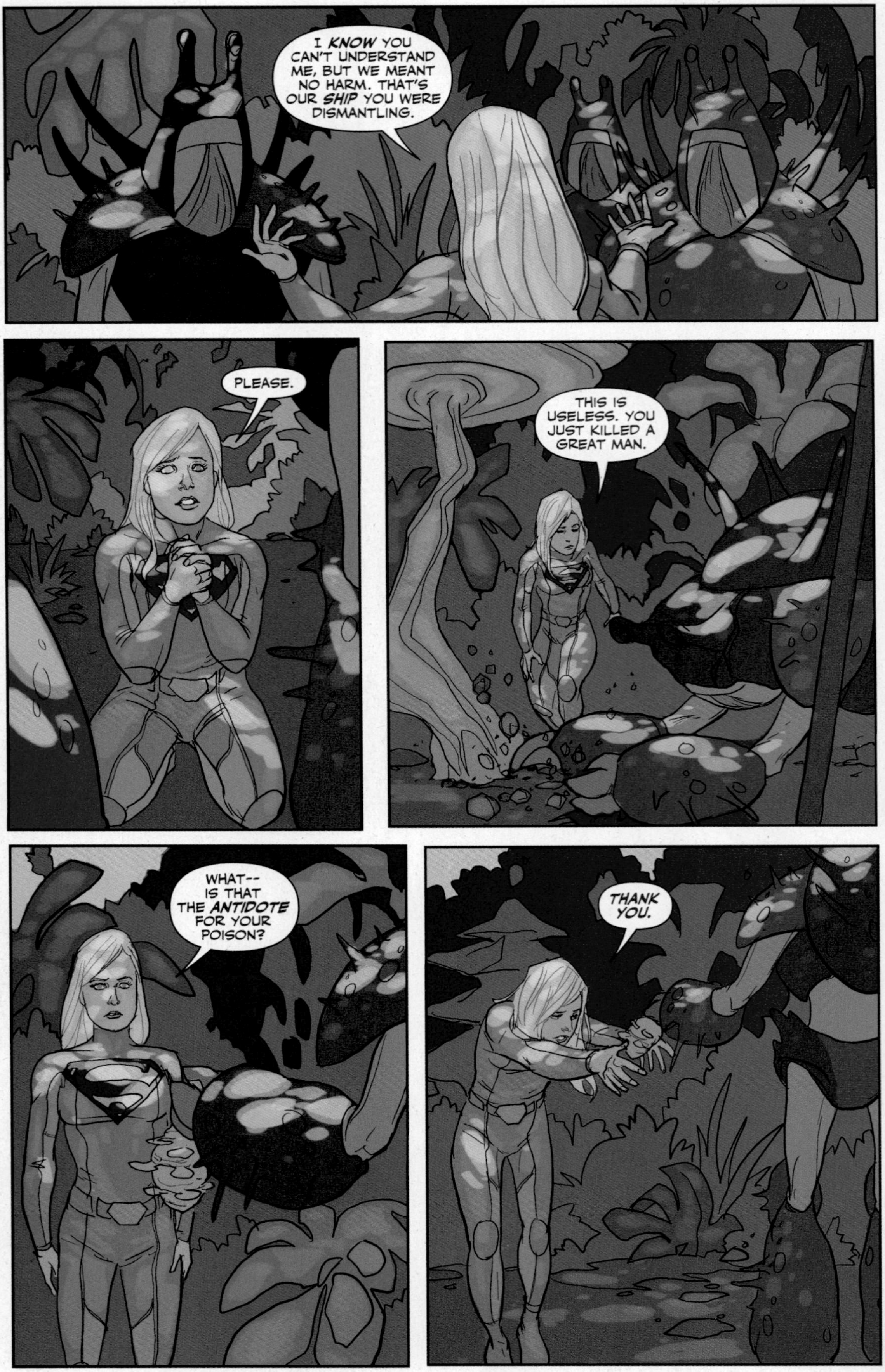
I KNOW YOU CAN'T UNDERSTAND ME, BUT WE MEANT NO HARM. THAT'S OUR SHIP YOU WERE DISMANTLING.
PLEASE.
THIS IS USELESS. YOU JUST KILLED A GREAT MAN.
WHAT-- IS THAT THE ANTIDOTE FOR YOUR POISON?
THANK YOU.

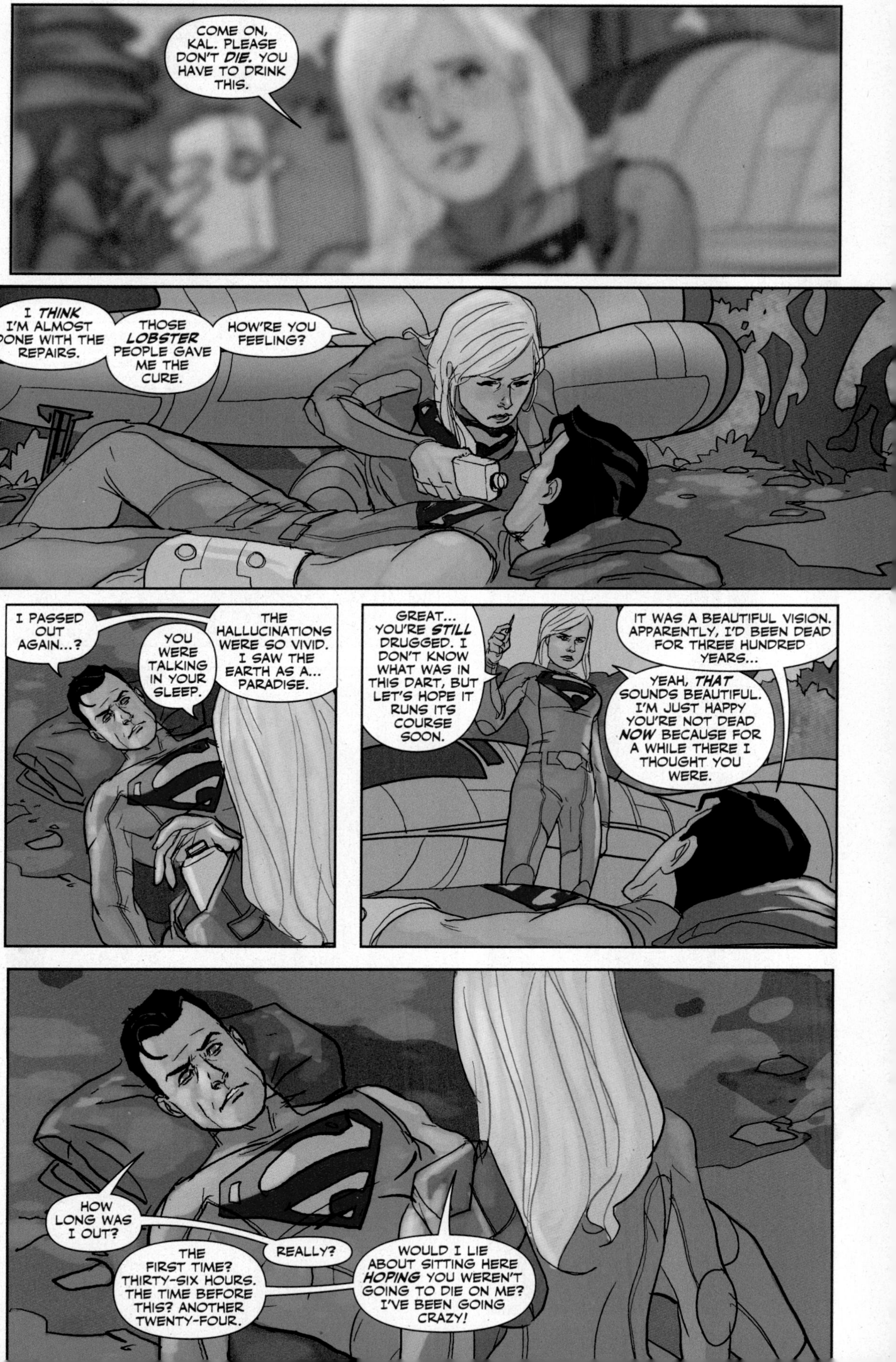
COME ON, KAL. PLEASE DON'T DIE. YOU HAVE TO DRINK THIS.
I THINK I'M ALMOST DONE WITH THE REPAIRS.
THOSE LOBSTER PEOPLE GAVE ME THE CURE.
HOW'RE YOU FEELING?
I PASSED OUT AGAIN...?
YOU WERE TALKING IN YOUR SLEEP.
THE HALLUCINATIONS WERE SO VIVID. I SAW THE EARTH AS A... PARADISE.
GREAT... YOU'RE STILL DRUGGED. I DON'T KNOW WHAT WAS IN THIS DART, BUT LET'S HOPE IT RUNS ITS COURSE SOON.
IT WAS A BEAUTIFUL VISION. APPARENTLY, I'D BEEN DEAD FOR THREE HUNDRED YEARS...
YEAH, THAT SOUNDS BEAUTIFUL. I'M JUST HAPPY YOU'RE NOT DEAD NOW BECAUSE FOR A WHILE THERE I THOUGHT YOU WERE.
HOW LONG WAS I OUT?
THE FIRST TIME? THIRTY-SIX HOURS. THE TIME BEFORE THIS? ANOTHER TWENTY-FOUR.
REALLY?
WOULD I LIE ABOUT SITTING HERE HOPING YOU WEREN'T GOING TO DIE ON ME? I'VE BEEN GOING CRAZY!

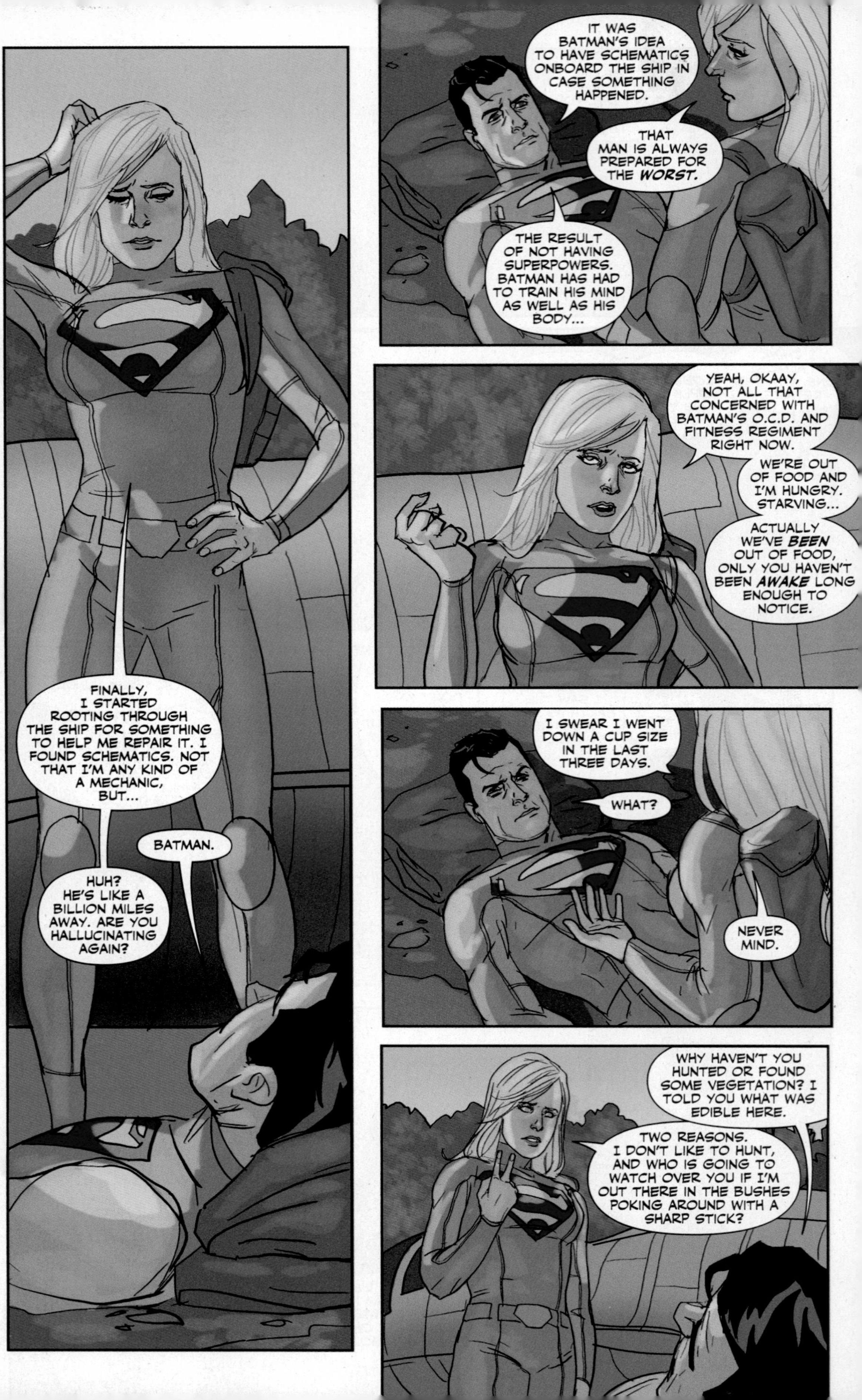

FINALLY, I STARTED ROOTING THROUGH THE SHIP FOR SOMETHING TO HELP ME REPAIR IT. I FOUND SCHEMATICS. NOT THAT I'M ANY KIND OF A MECHANIC, BUT...
BATMAN.
HUH? HE'S LIKE A BILLION MILES AWAY. ARE YOU HALLUCINATING AGAIN?
IT WAS BATMAN'S IDEA TO HAVE SCHEMATICS ONBOARD THE SHIP IN CASE SOMETHING HAPPENED.
THAT MAN IS ALWAYS PREPARED FOR THE *WORST.*
THE RESULT OF NOT HAVING SUPERPOWERS. BATMAN HAS HAD TO TRAIN HIS MIND AS WELL AS HIS BODY...
YEAH, OKAAY, NOT ALL THAT CONCERNED WITH BATMAN'S O.C.D. AND FITNESS REGIMENT RIGHT NOW.
WE'RE OUT OF FOOD AND I'M HUNGRY. STARVING...
ACTUALLY WE'VE *BEEN* OUT OF FOOD, ONLY YOU HAVEN'T BEEN *AWAKE* LONG ENOUGH TO NOTICE.
I SWEAR I WENT DOWN A CUP SIZE IN THE LAST THREE DAYS.
WHAT?
NEVER MIND.
WHY HAVEN'T YOU HUNTED OR FOUND SOME VEGETATION? I TOLD YOU WHAT WAS EDIBLE HERE.
TWO REASONS. I DON'T LIKE TO HUNT, AND WHO IS GOING TO WATCH OVER YOU IF I'M OUT THERE IN THE BUSHES POKING AROUND WITH A SHARP STICK?

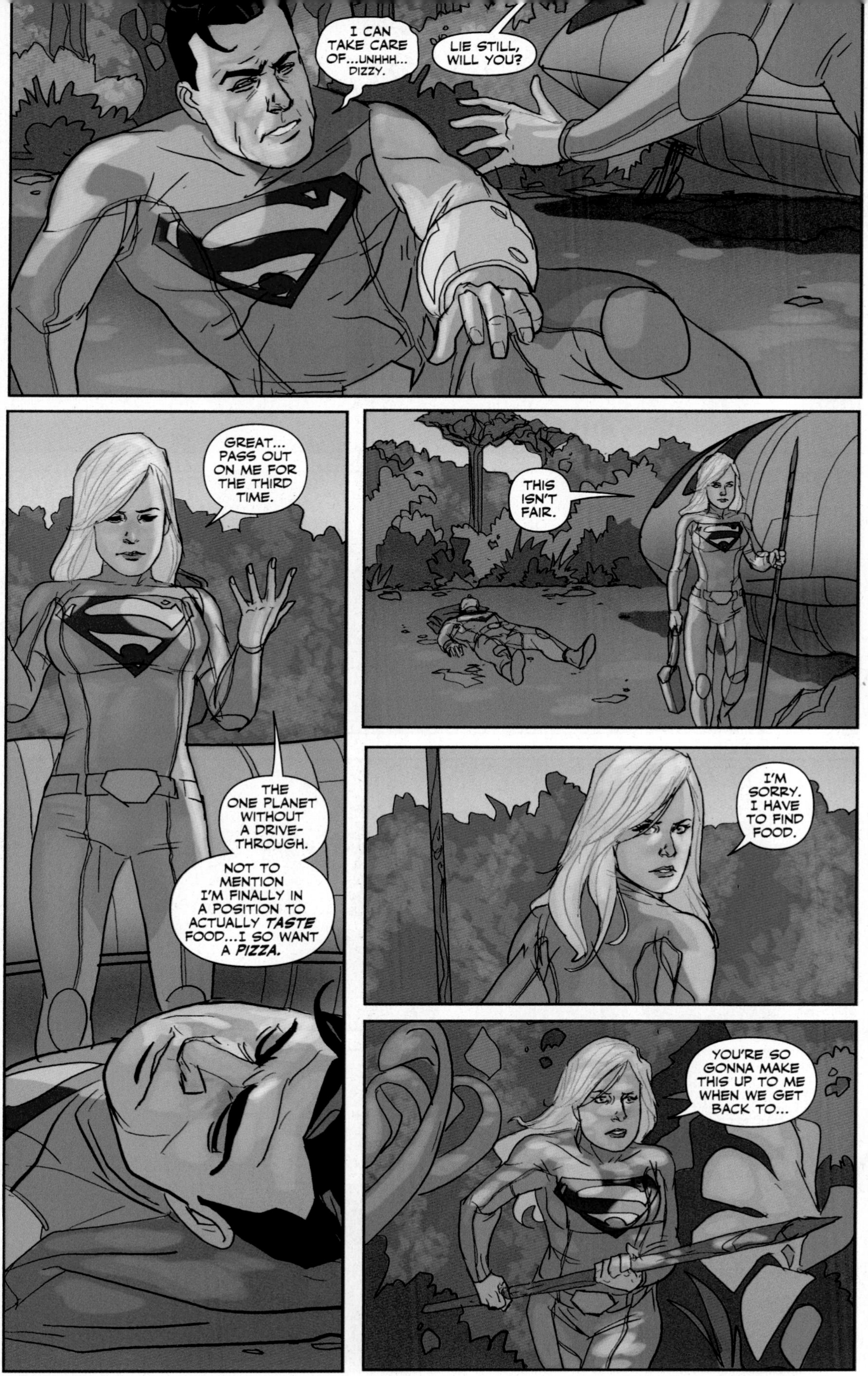

I CAN TAKE CARE OF...UNHHH... DIZZY.
LIE STILL, WILL YOU?
GREAT... PASS OUT ON ME FOR THE THIRD TIME.
THE ONE PLANET WITHOUT A DRIVE-THROUGH.
NOT TO MENTION I'M FINALLY IN A POSITION TO ACTUALLY *TASTE* FOOD...I SO WANT A *PIZZA.*
THIS ISN'T FAIR.
I'M SORRY. I HAVE TO FIND FOOD.
YOU'RE SO GONNA MAKE THIS UP TO ME WHEN WE GET BACK TO...

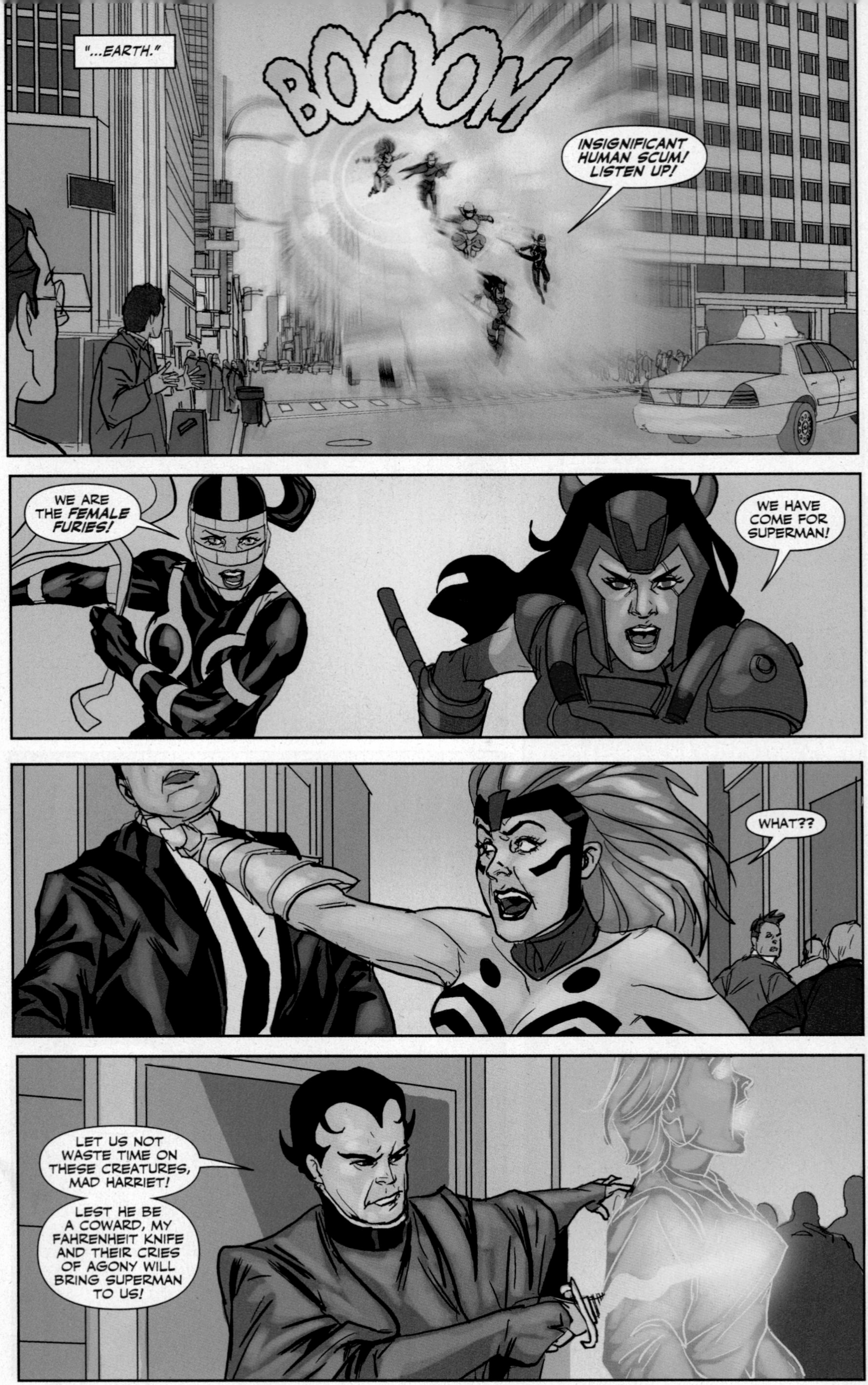
"...EARTH."
BOOOM
INSIGNIFICANT HUMAN SCUM! LISTEN UP!
WE ARE THE FEMALE FURIES!
WE HAVE COME FOR SUPERMAN!
WHAT??
LET US NOT WASTE TIME ON THESE CREATURES, MAD HARRIET!
LEST HE BE A COWARD, MY FAHRENHEIT KNIFE AND THEIR CRIES OF AGONY WILL BRING SUPERMAN TO US!

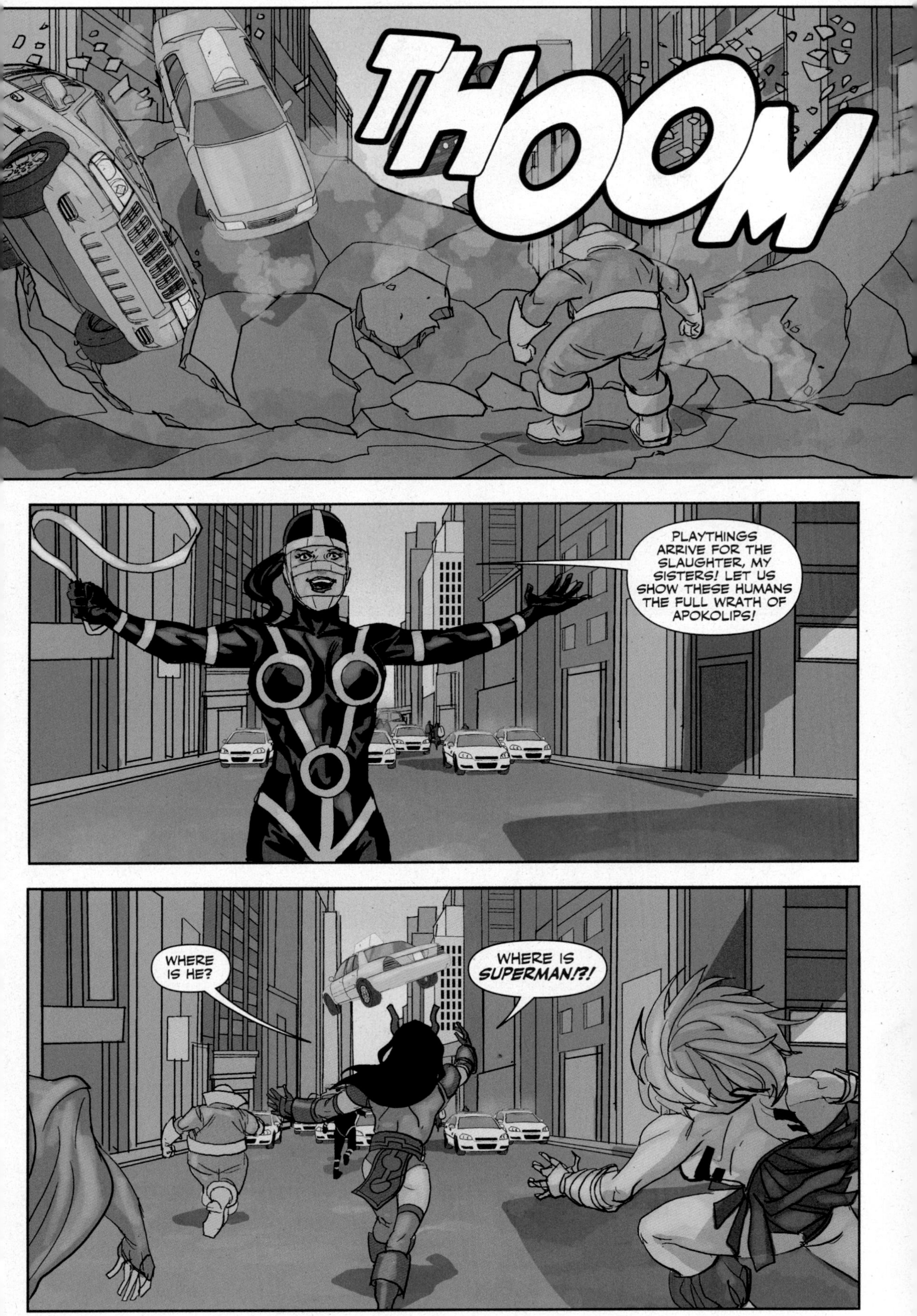
THOOM
PLAYTHINGS ARRIVE FOR THE SLAUGHTER, MY SISTERS! LET US SHOW THESE HUMANS THE FULL WRATH OF APOKOLIPS!
WHERE IS HE?
WHERE IS *SUPERMAN!?!*

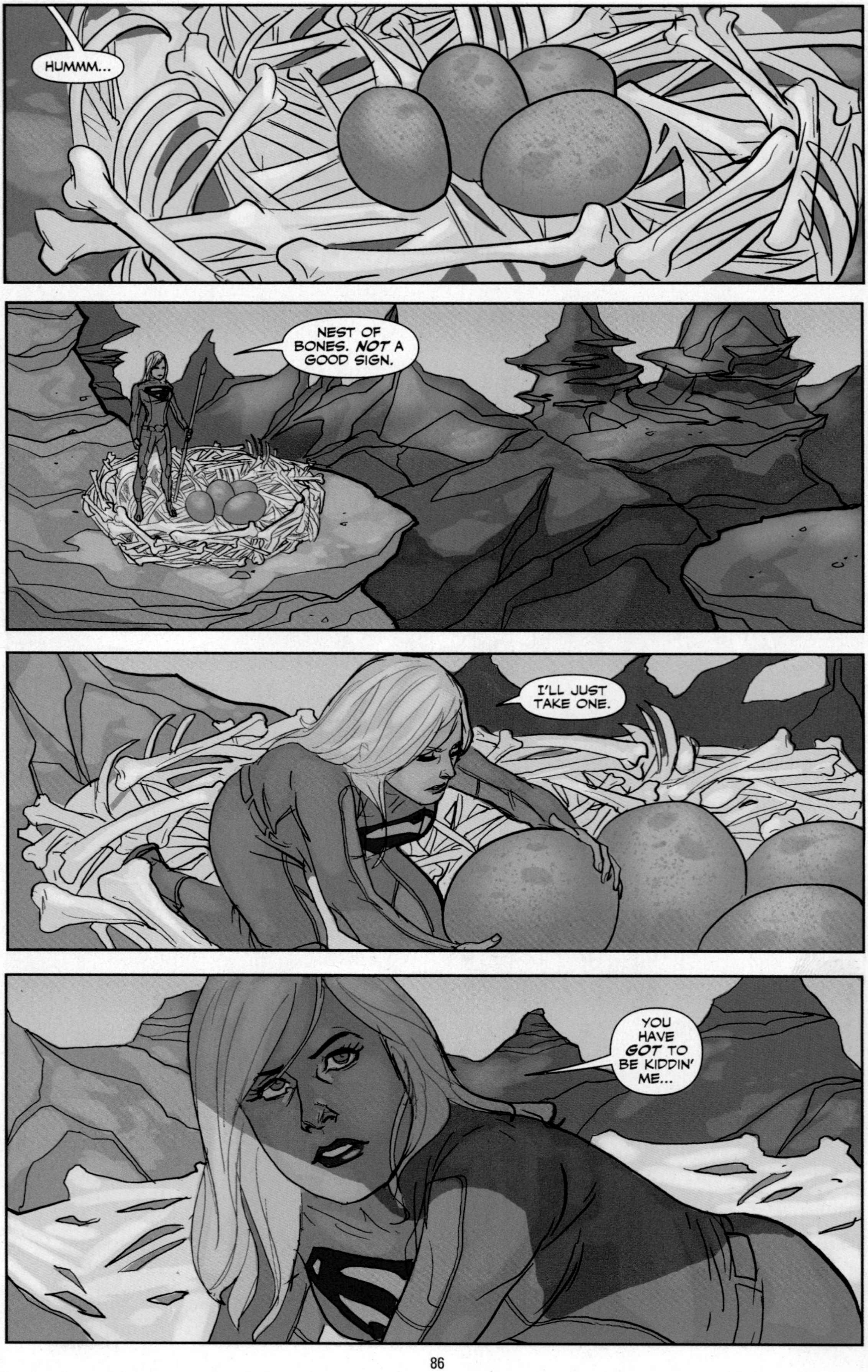
HUMMM...
NEST OF BONES. *NOT* A GOOD SIGN.
I'LL JUST TAKE ONE.
YOU HAVE *GOT* TO BE KIDDIN' ME...

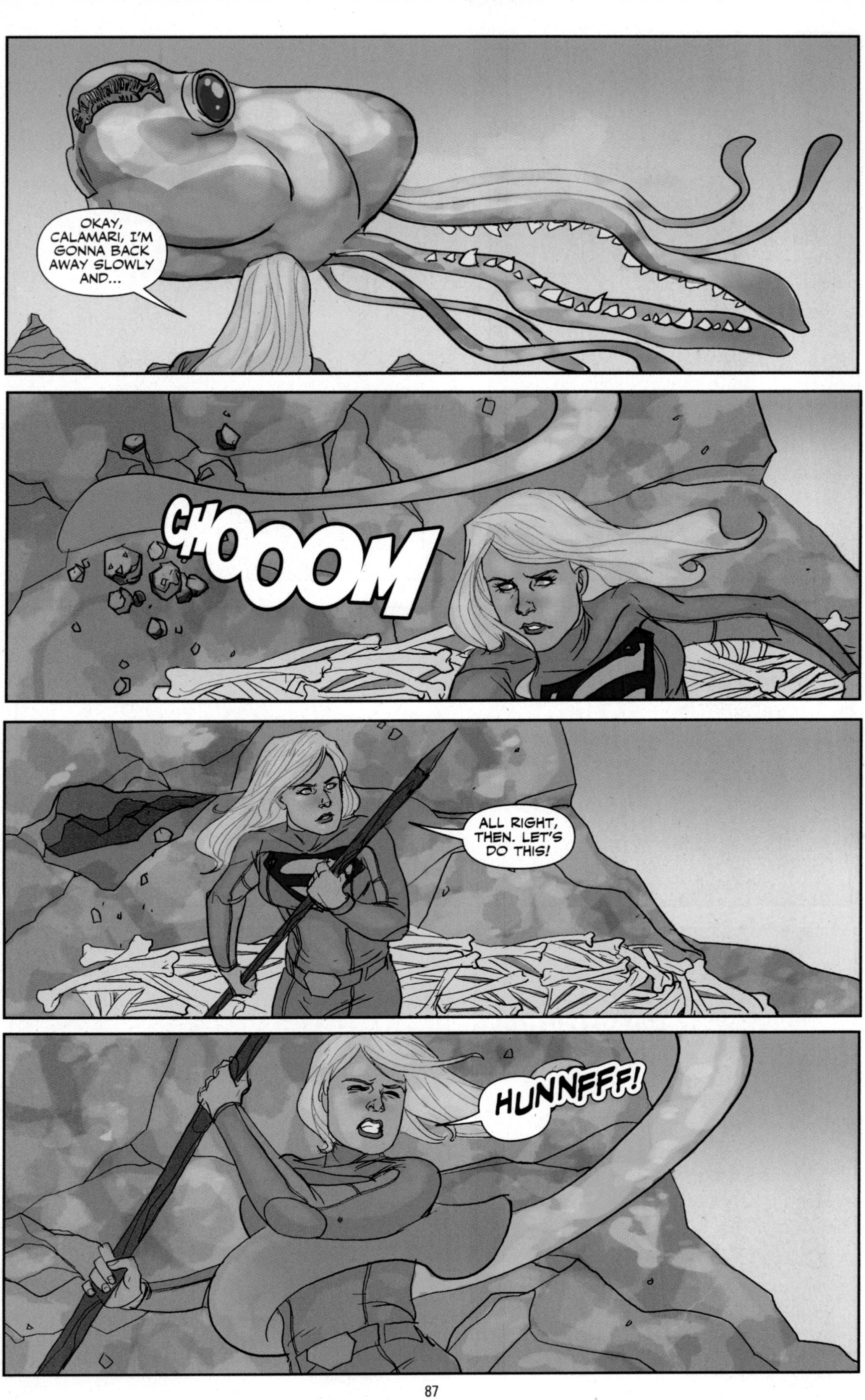
OKAY, CALAMARI, I'M GONNA BACK AWAY SLOWLY AND...
CHOOOM
ALL RIGHT, THEN. LET'S DO THIS!
HUNNFFF!

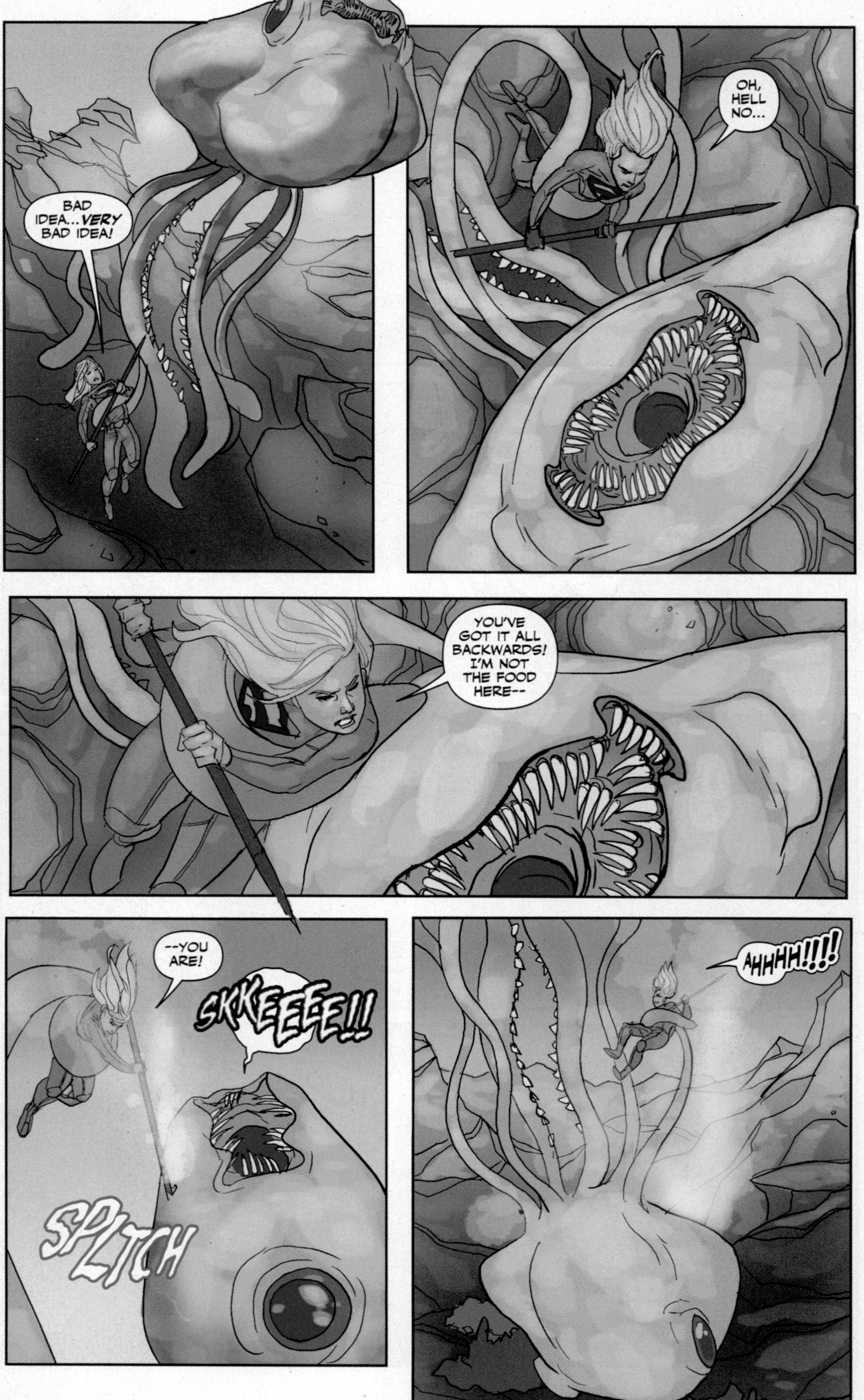
BAD IDEA...VERY BAD IDEA!
OH, HELL NO...
YOU'VE GOT IT ALL BACKWARDS! I'M NOT THE FOOD HERE--
--YOU ARE!
SKKEEEEE!!
SPLTCH
AHHHH!!!!

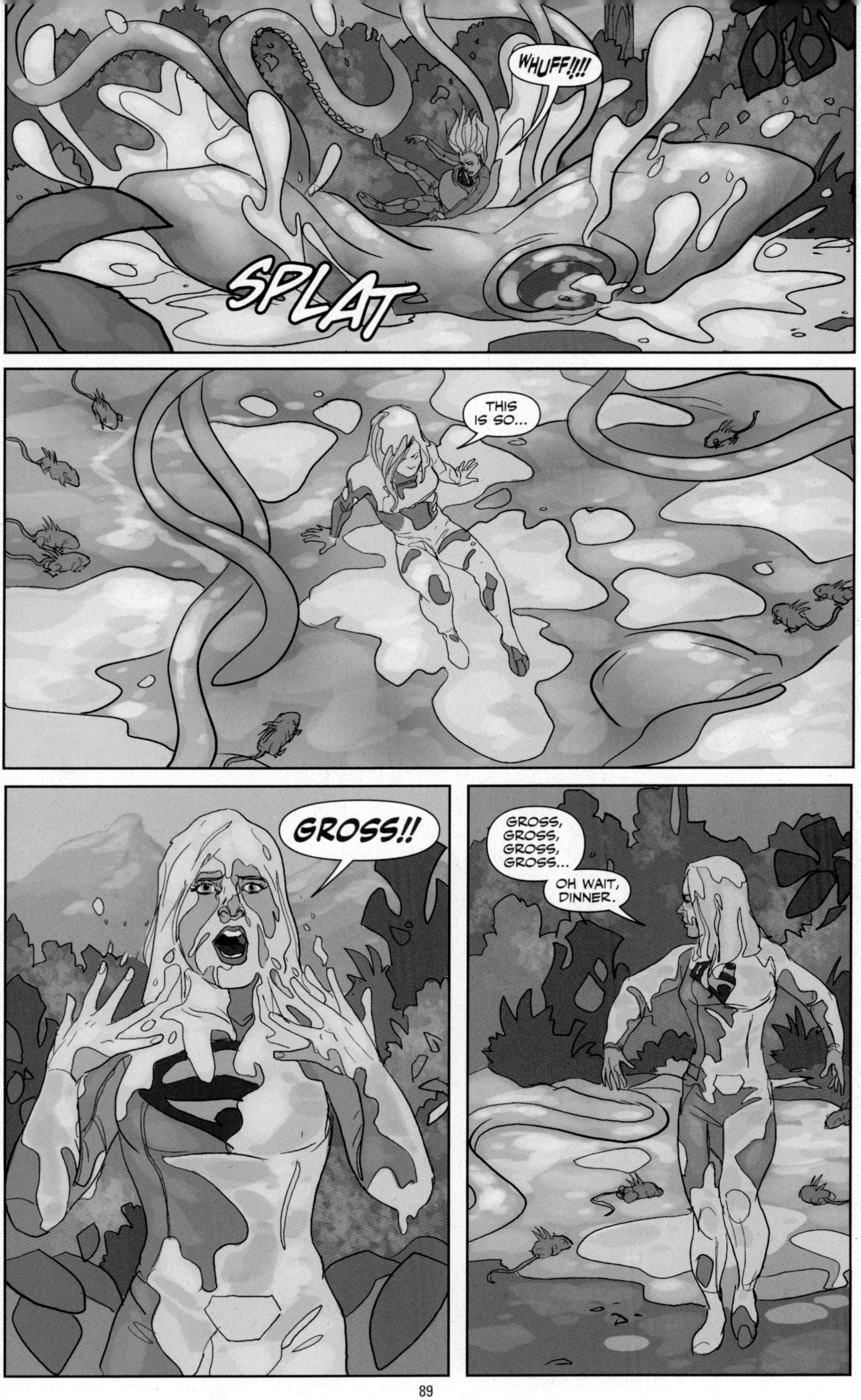
WHUFF!!!!
SPLAT
THIS IS SO...
GROSS!!
GROSS, GROSS, GROSS, GROSS...
OH WAIT, DINNER.

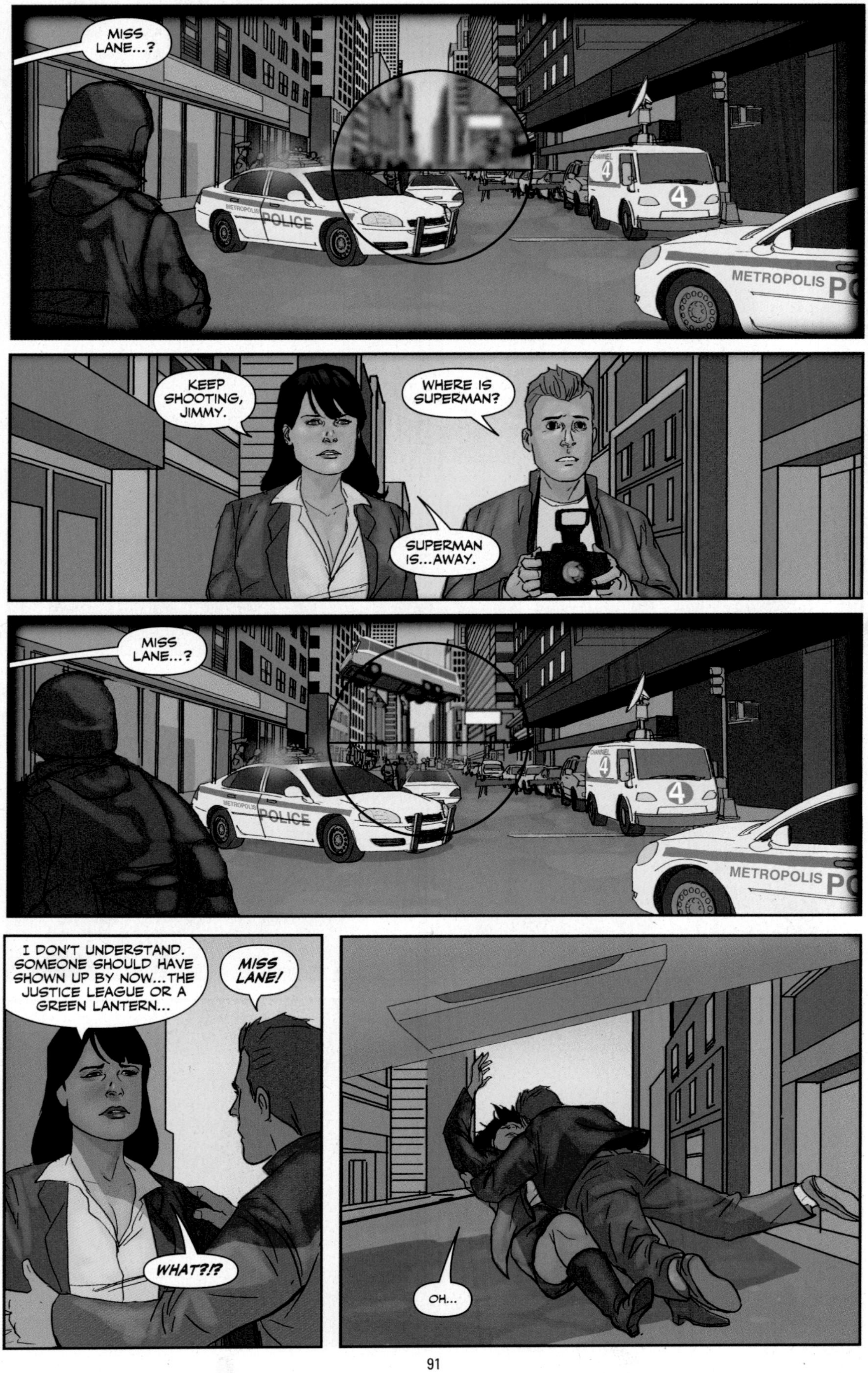
MISS LANE...?
METROPOLIS POLICE
CHANNEL 4
METROPOLIS PO
KEEP SHOOTING, JIMMY.
WHERE IS SUPERMAN?
SUPERMAN IS...AWAY.
MISS LANE...?
METROPOLIS POLICE
CHANNEL 4
METROPOLIS PO
I DON'T UNDERSTAND. SOMEONE SHOULD HAVE SHOWN UP BY NOW...THE JUSTICE LEAGUE OR A GREEN LANTERN...
MISS LANE!
WHAT?!?
OH...

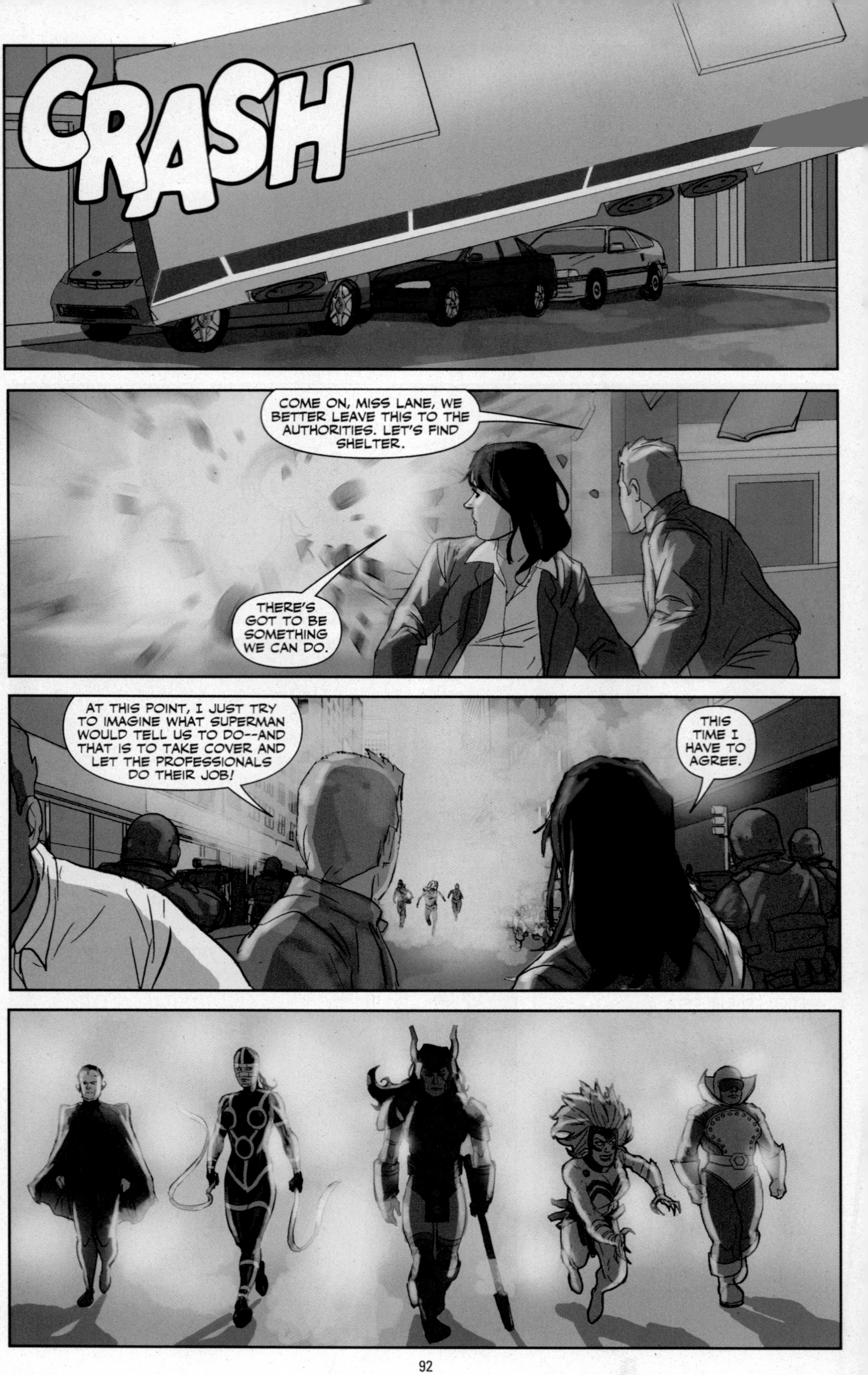
CRASH
COME ON, MISS LANE, WE BETTER LEAVE THIS TO THE AUTHORITIES. LET'S FIND SHELTER.
THERE'S GOT TO BE SOMETHING WE CAN DO.
AT THIS POINT, I JUST TRY TO IMAGINE WHAT SUPERMAN WOULD TELL US TO DO--AND THAT IS TO TAKE COVER AND LET THE PROFESSIONALS DO THEIR JOB!
THIS TIME I HAVE TO AGREE.

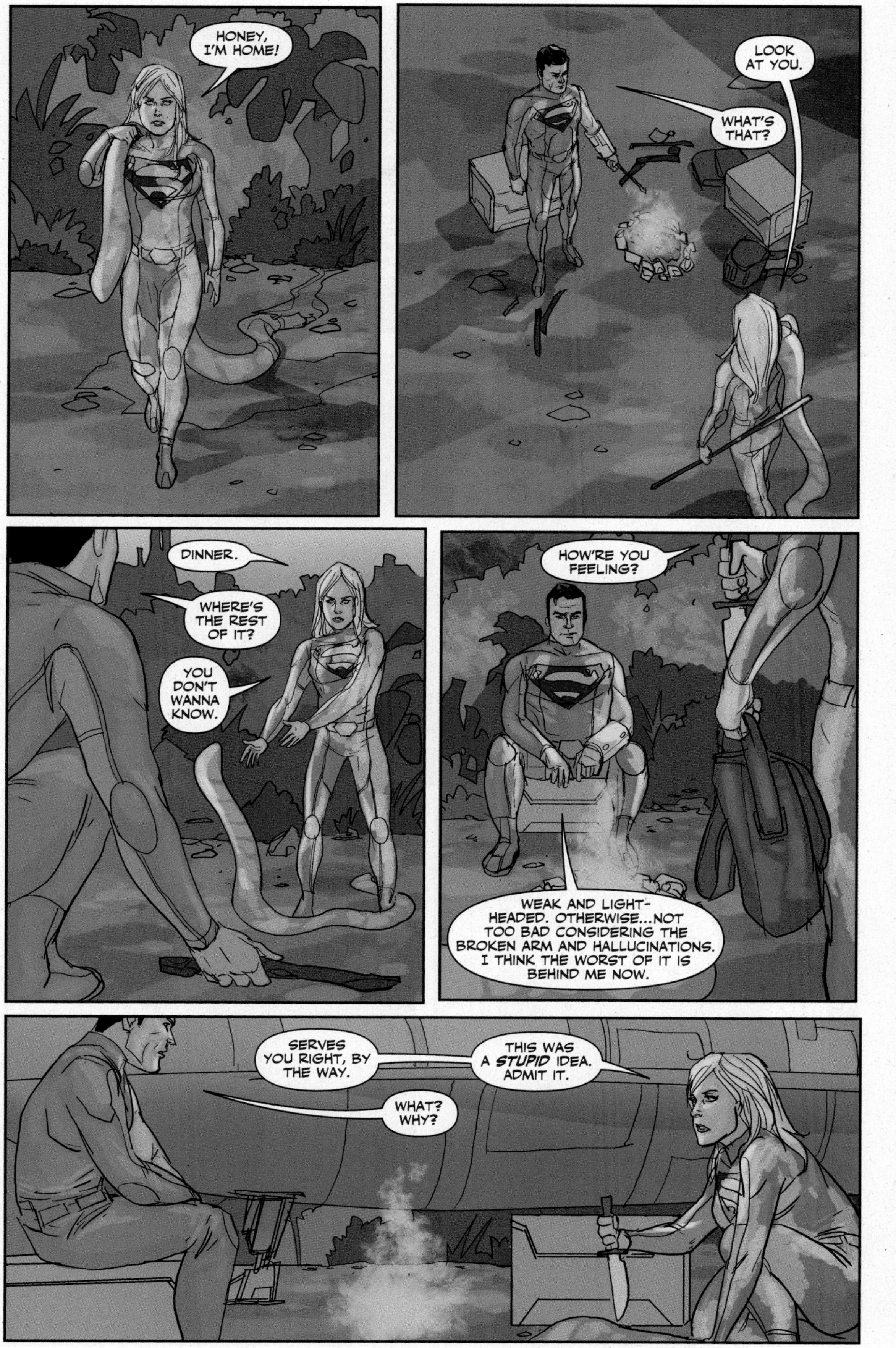
HONEY, I'M HOME!
LOOK AT YOU.
WHAT'S THAT?
DINNER.
WHERE'S THE REST OF IT?
YOU DON'T WANNA KNOW.
HOW'RE YOU FEELING?
WEAK AND LIGHT-HEADED. OTHERWISE...NOT TOO BAD CONSIDERING THE BROKEN ARM AND HALLUCINATIONS. I THINK THE WORST OF IT IS BEHIND ME NOW.
SERVES YOU RIGHT, BY THE WAY.
THIS WAS A *STUPID* IDEA. ADMIT IT.
WHAT? WHY?

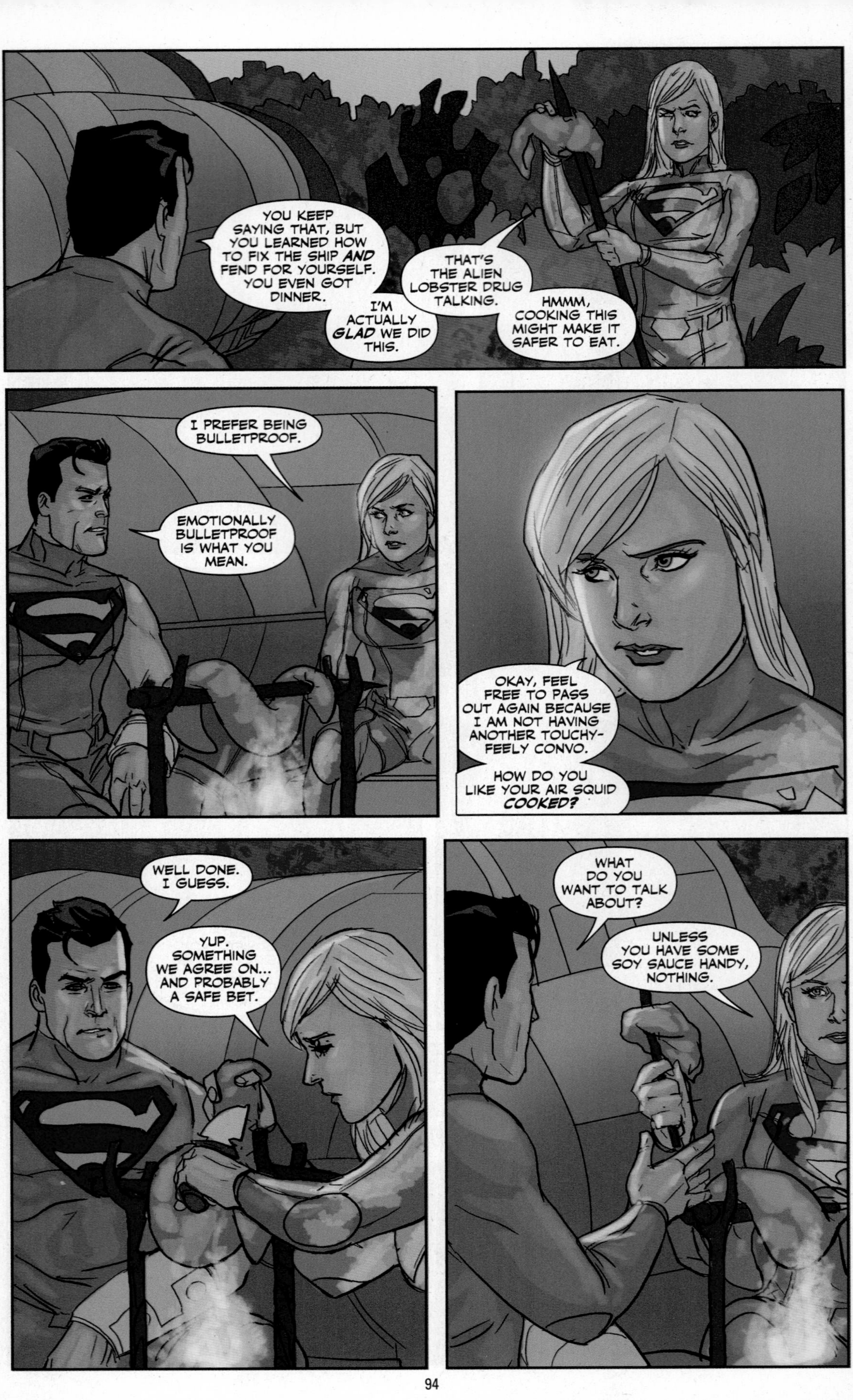
YOU KEEP SAYING THAT, BUT YOU LEARNED HOW TO FIX THE SHIP AND FEND FOR YOURSELF. YOU EVEN GOT DINNER.
I'M ACTUALLY GLAD WE DID THIS.
THAT'S THE ALIEN LOBSTER DRUG TALKING.
HMMM, COOKING THIS MIGHT MAKE IT SAFER TO EAT.
I PREFER BEING BULLETPROOF.
EMOTIONALLY BULLETPROOF IS WHAT YOU MEAN.
OKAY, FEEL FREE TO PASS OUT AGAIN BECAUSE I AM NOT HAVING ANOTHER TOUCHY-FEELY CONVO.
HOW DO YOU LIKE YOUR AIR SQUID COOKED?
WELL DONE. I GUESS.
YUP. SOMETHING WE AGREE ON... AND PROBABLY A SAFE BET.
WHAT DO YOU WANT TO TALK ABOUT?
UNLESS YOU HAVE SOME SOY SAUCE HANDY, NOTHING.

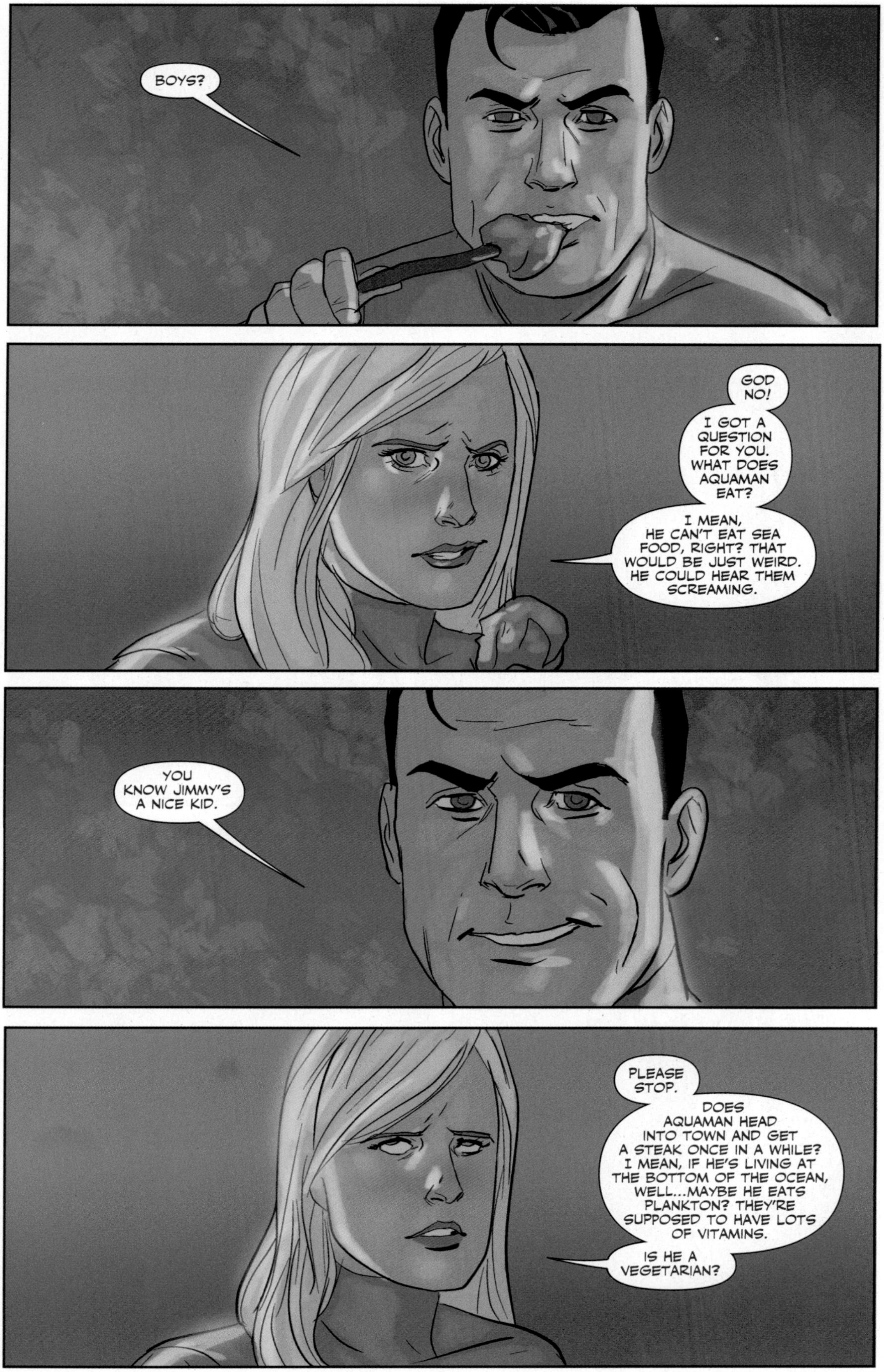
BOYS?
GOD NO!
I GOT A QUESTION FOR YOU. WHAT DOES AQUAMAN EAT?
I MEAN, HE CAN'T EAT SEA FOOD, RIGHT? THAT WOULD BE JUST WEIRD. HE COULD HEAR THEM SCREAMING.
YOU KNOW JIMMY'S A NICE KID.
PLEASE STOP.
DOES AQUAMAN HEAD INTO TOWN AND GET A STEAK ONCE IN A WHILE? I MEAN, IF HE'S LIVING AT THE BOTTOM OF THE OCEAN, WELL...MAYBE HE EATS PLANKTON? THEY'RE SUPPOSED TO HAVE LOTS OF VITAMINS.
IS HE A VEGETARIAN?

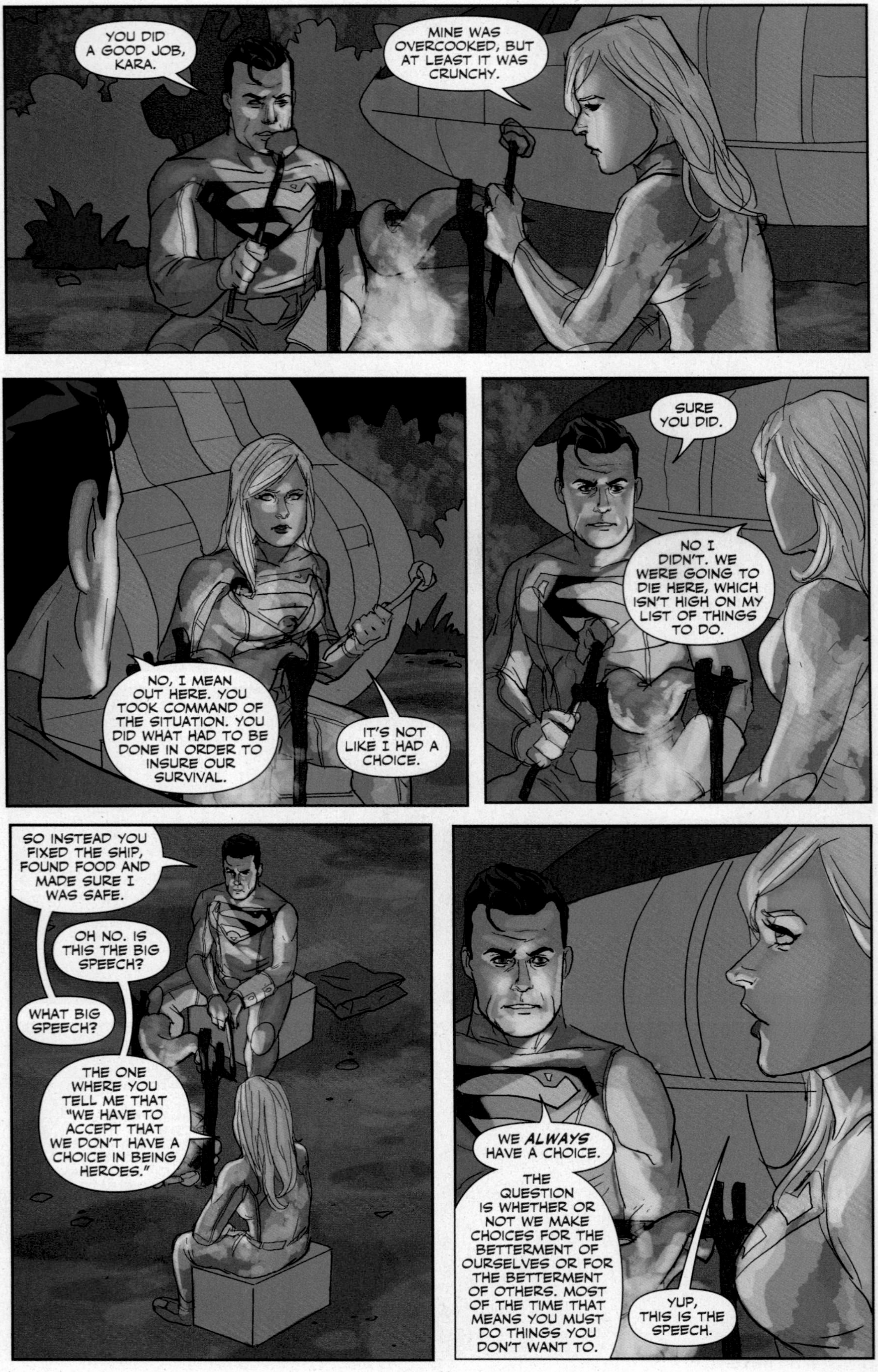
YOU DID A GOOD JOB, KARA.
MINE WAS OVERCOOKED, BUT AT LEAST IT WAS CRUNCHY.
NO, I MEAN OUT HERE. YOU TOOK COMMAND OF THE SITUATION. YOU DID WHAT HAD TO BE DONE IN ORDER TO INSURE OUR SURVIVAL.
IT'S NOT LIKE I HAD A CHOICE.
SURE YOU DID.
NO I DIDN'T. WE WERE GOING TO DIE HERE, WHICH ISN'T HIGH ON MY LIST OF THINGS TO DO.
SO INSTEAD YOU FIXED THE SHIP, FOUND FOOD AND MADE SURE I WAS SAFE.
OH NO. IS THIS THE BIG SPEECH?
WHAT BIG SPEECH?
THE ONE WHERE YOU TELL ME THAT "WE HAVE TO ACCEPT THAT WE DON'T HAVE A CHOICE IN BEING HEROES."
WE *ALWAYS* HAVE A CHOICE.
THE QUESTION IS WHETHER OR NOT WE MAKE CHOICES FOR THE BETTERMENT OF OURSELVES OR FOR THE BETTERMENT OF OTHERS. MOST OF THE TIME THAT MEANS YOU MUST DO THINGS YOU DON'T WANT TO.
YUP, THIS IS THE SPEECH.

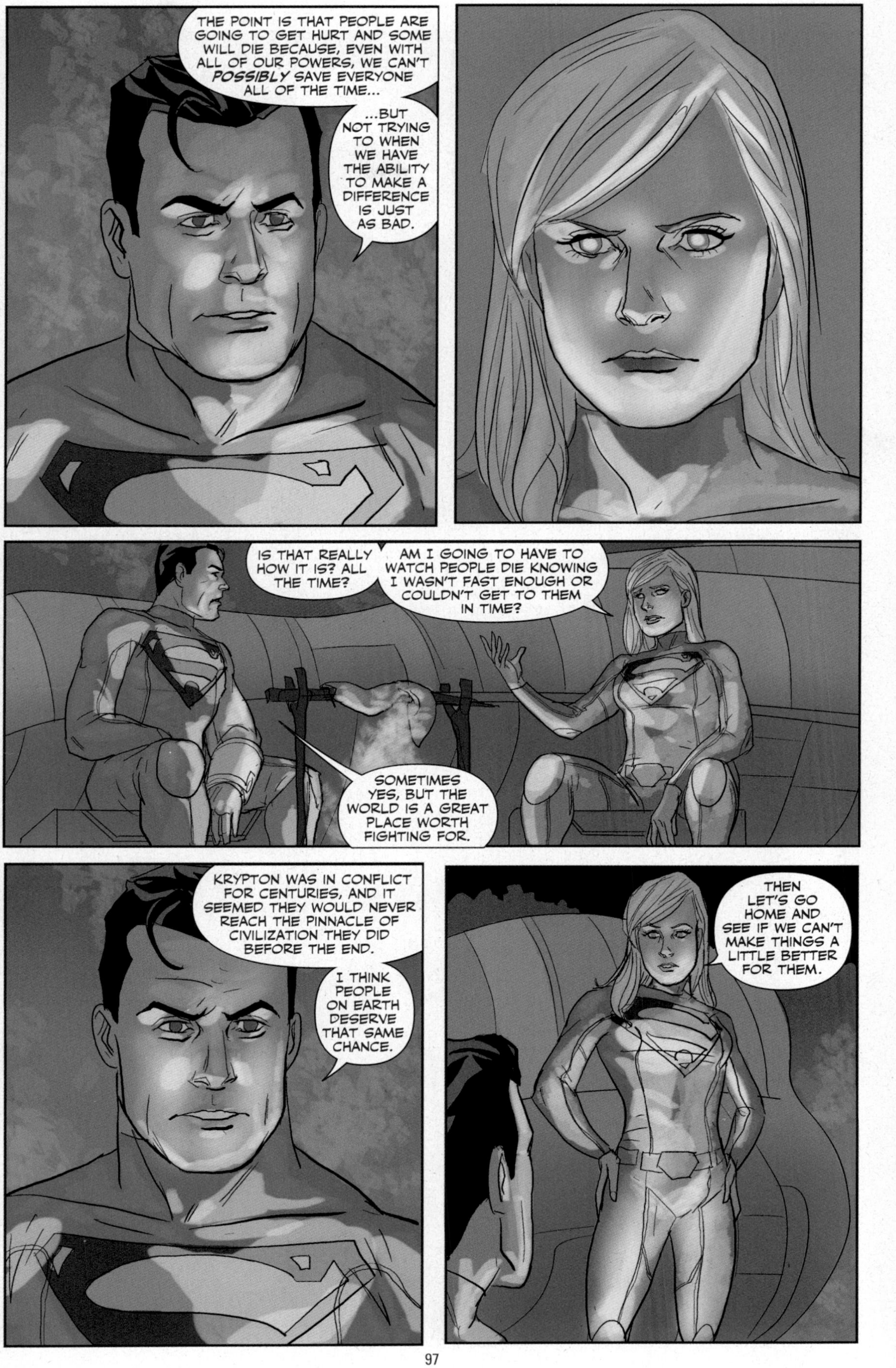
THE POINT IS THAT PEOPLE ARE GOING TO GET HURT AND SOME WILL DIE BECAUSE, EVEN WITH ALL OF OUR POWERS, WE CAN'T *POSSIBLY* SAVE EVERYONE ALL OF THE TIME...
...BUT NOT TRYING TO WHEN WE HAVE THE ABILITY TO MAKE A DIFFERENCE IS JUST AS BAD.
IS THAT REALLY HOW IT IS? ALL THE TIME?
AM I GOING TO HAVE TO WATCH PEOPLE DIE KNOWING I WASN'T FAST ENOUGH OR COULDN'T GET TO THEM IN TIME?
SOMETIMES YES, BUT THE WORLD IS A GREAT PLACE WORTH FIGHTING FOR.
KRYPTON WAS IN CONFLICT FOR CENTURIES, AND IT SEEMED THEY WOULD NEVER REACH THE PINNACLE OF CIVILIZATION THEY DID BEFORE THE END.
I THINK PEOPLE ON EARTH DESERVE THAT SAME CHANCE.
THEN LET'S GO HOME AND SEE IF WE CAN'T MAKE THINGS A LITTLE BETTER FOR THEM.

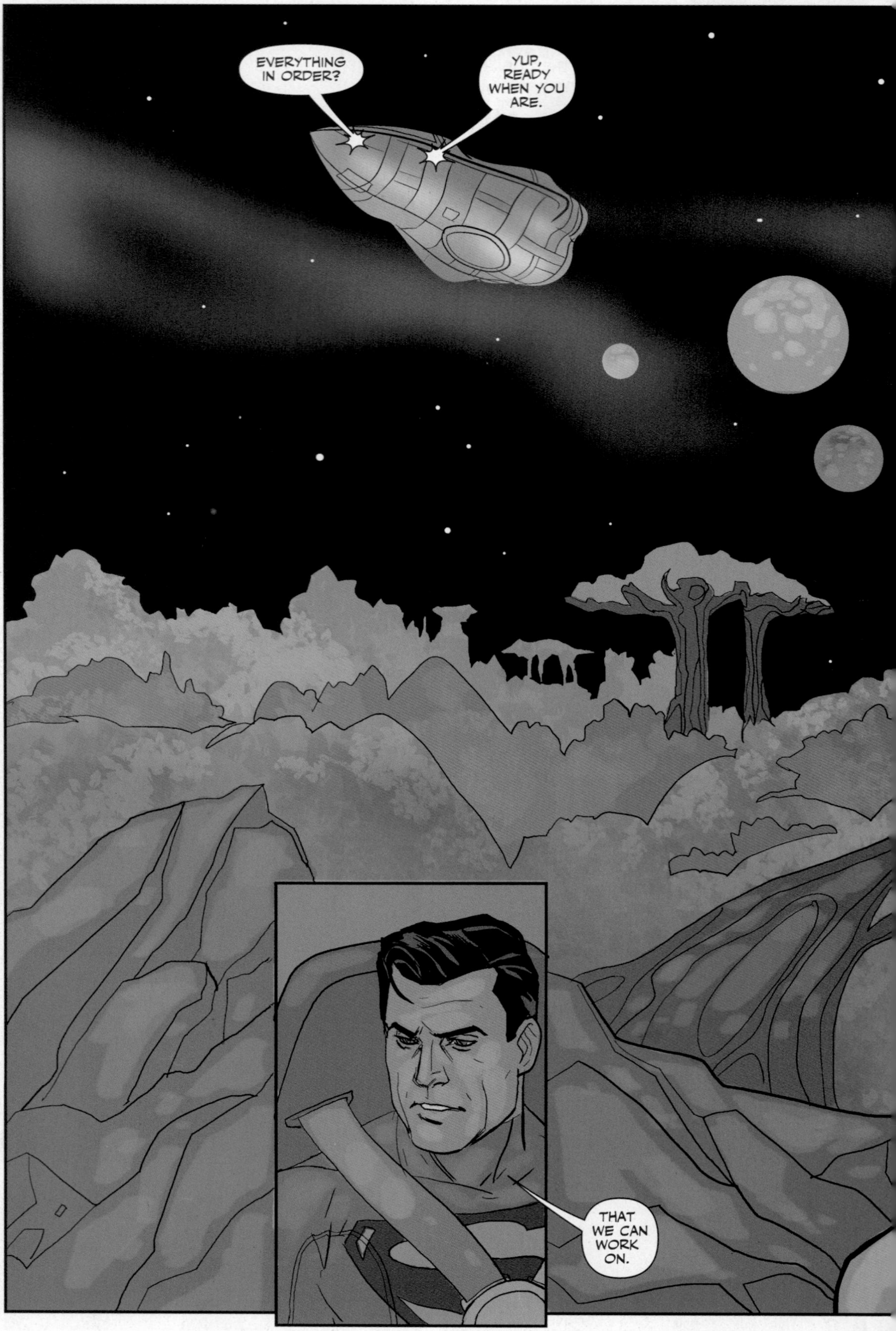
EVERYTHING IN ORDER?
YUP, READY WHEN YOU ARE.
THAT WE CAN WORK ON.

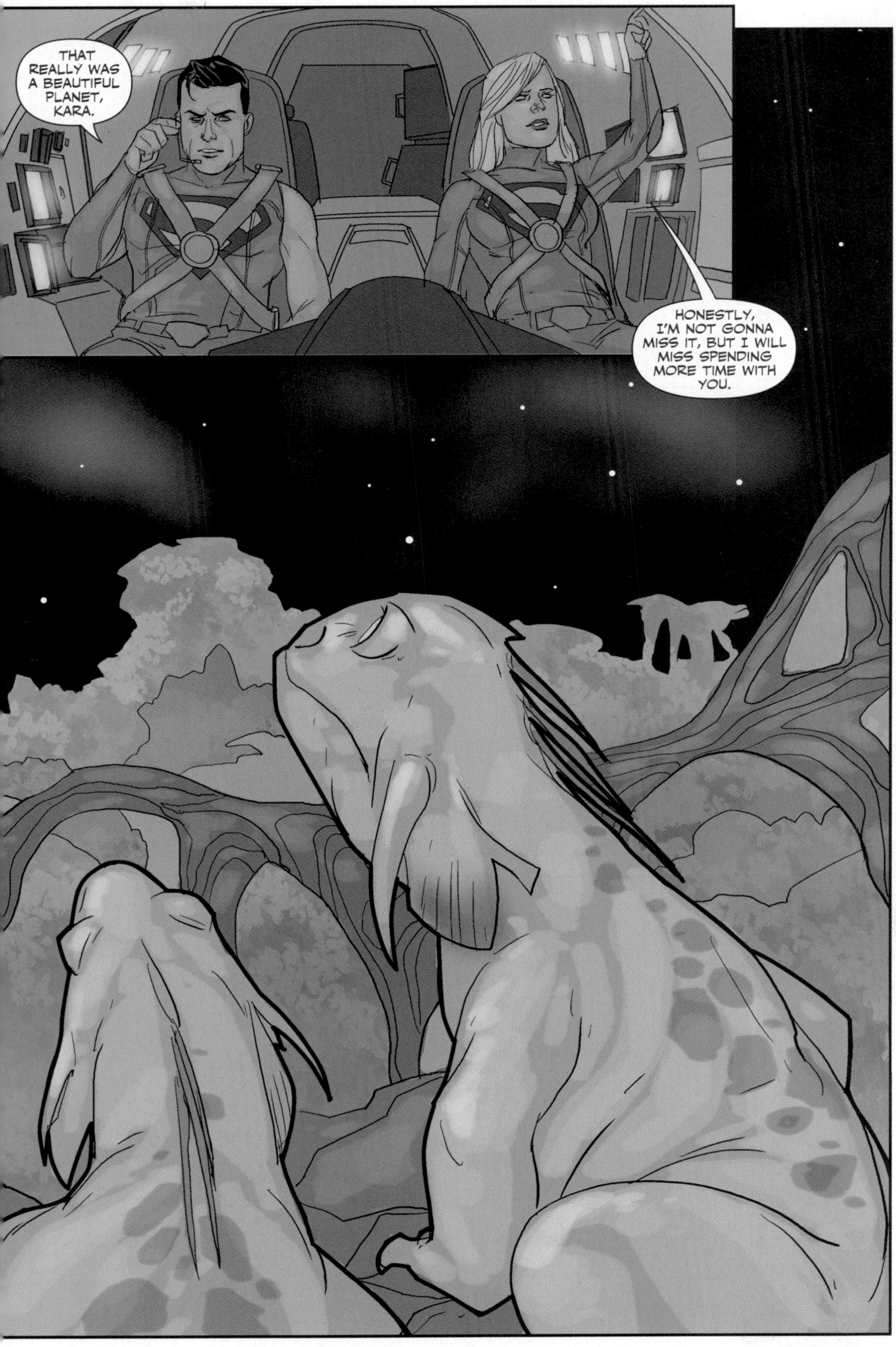

THAT REALLY WAS A BEAUTIFUL PLANET, KARA.
HONESTLY, I'M NOT GONNA MISS IT, BUT I WILL MISS SPENDING MORE TIME WITH YOU.

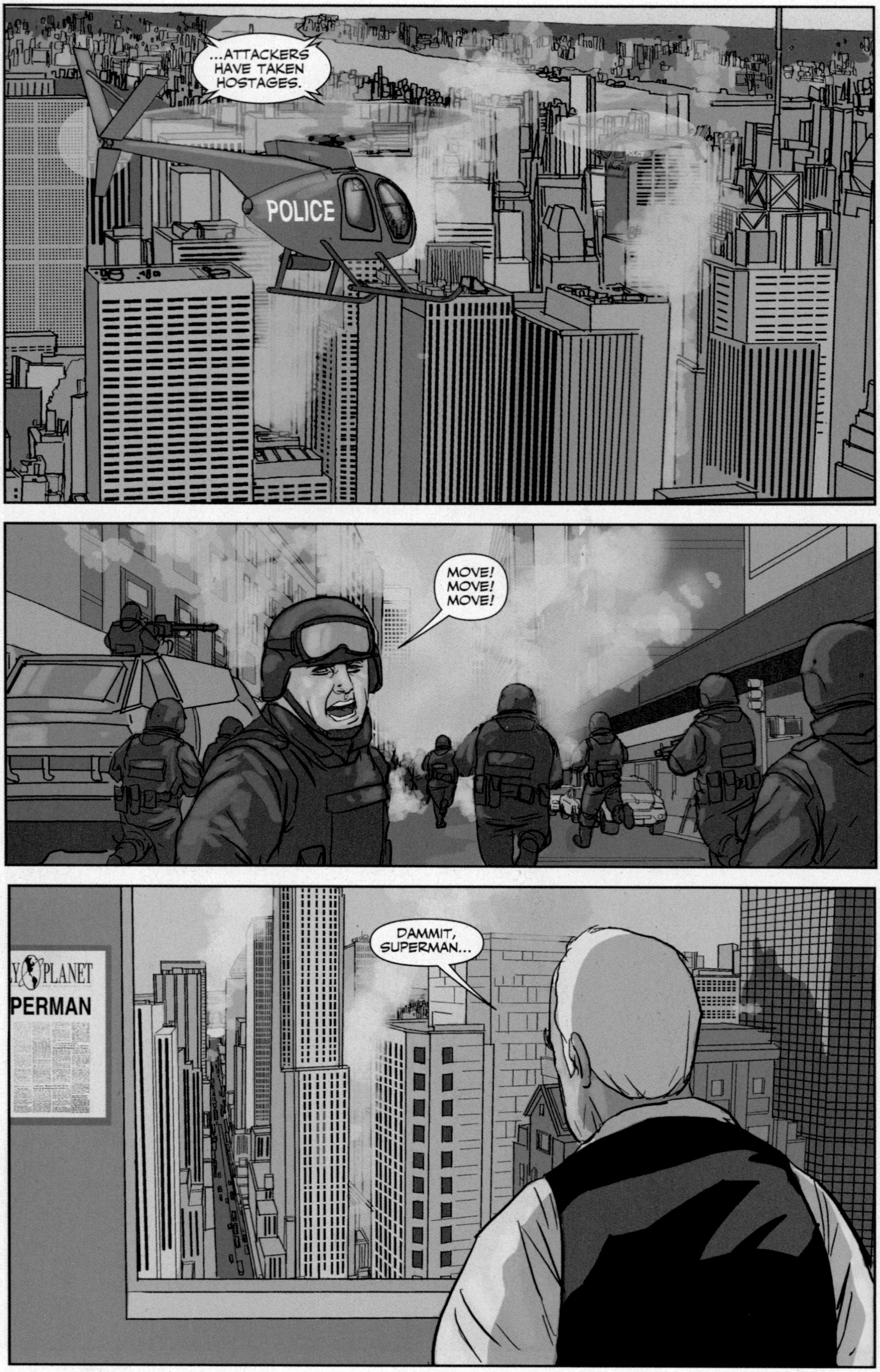
...ATTACKERS HAVE TAKEN HOSTAGES.
POLICE
MOVE! MOVE! MOVE!
PLANET
PERMAN
DAMMIT, SUPERMAN...

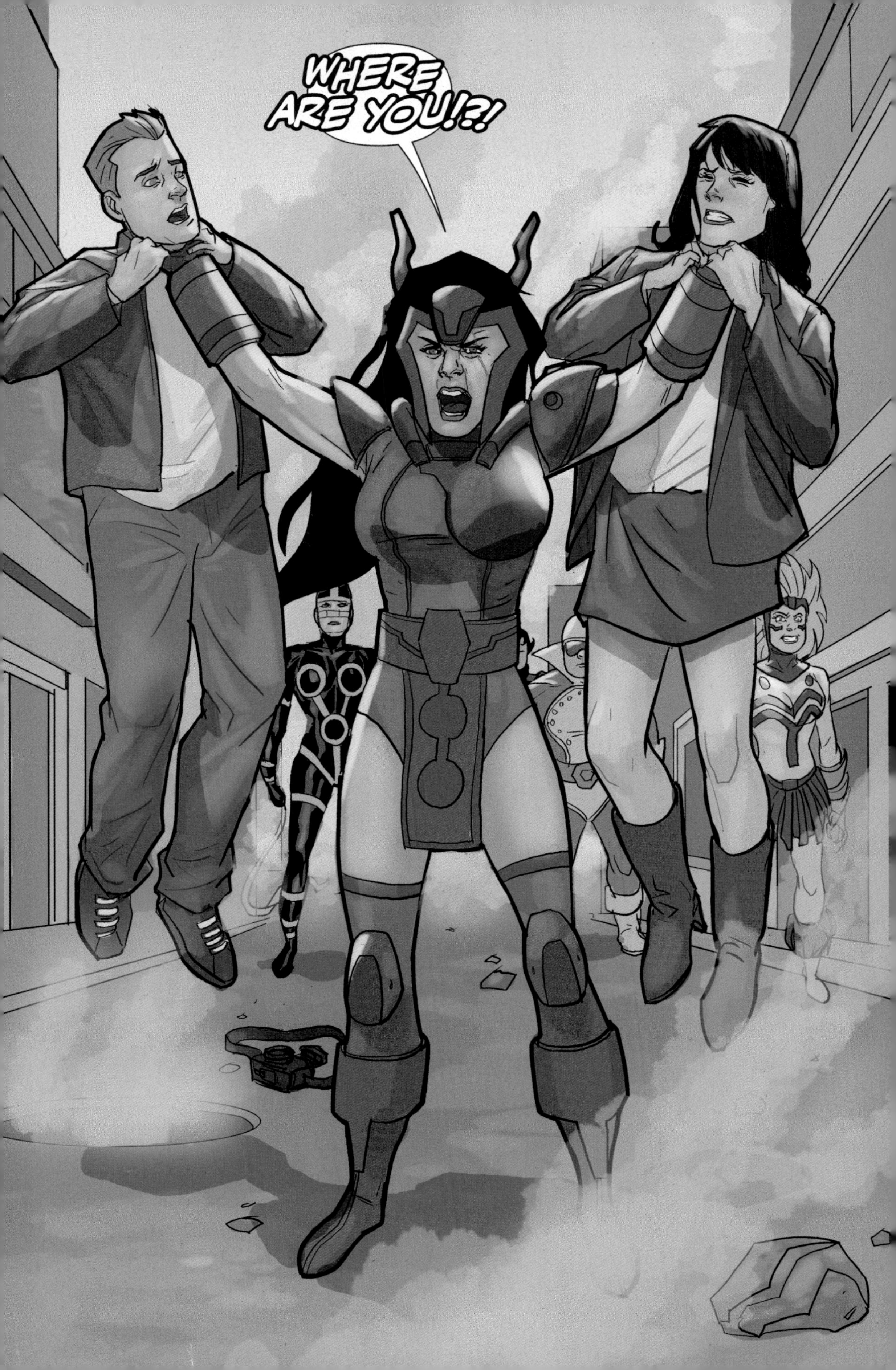
WHERE ARE YOU!?!

SUPERMAN / SUPERGIRL: MAELSTROM #5

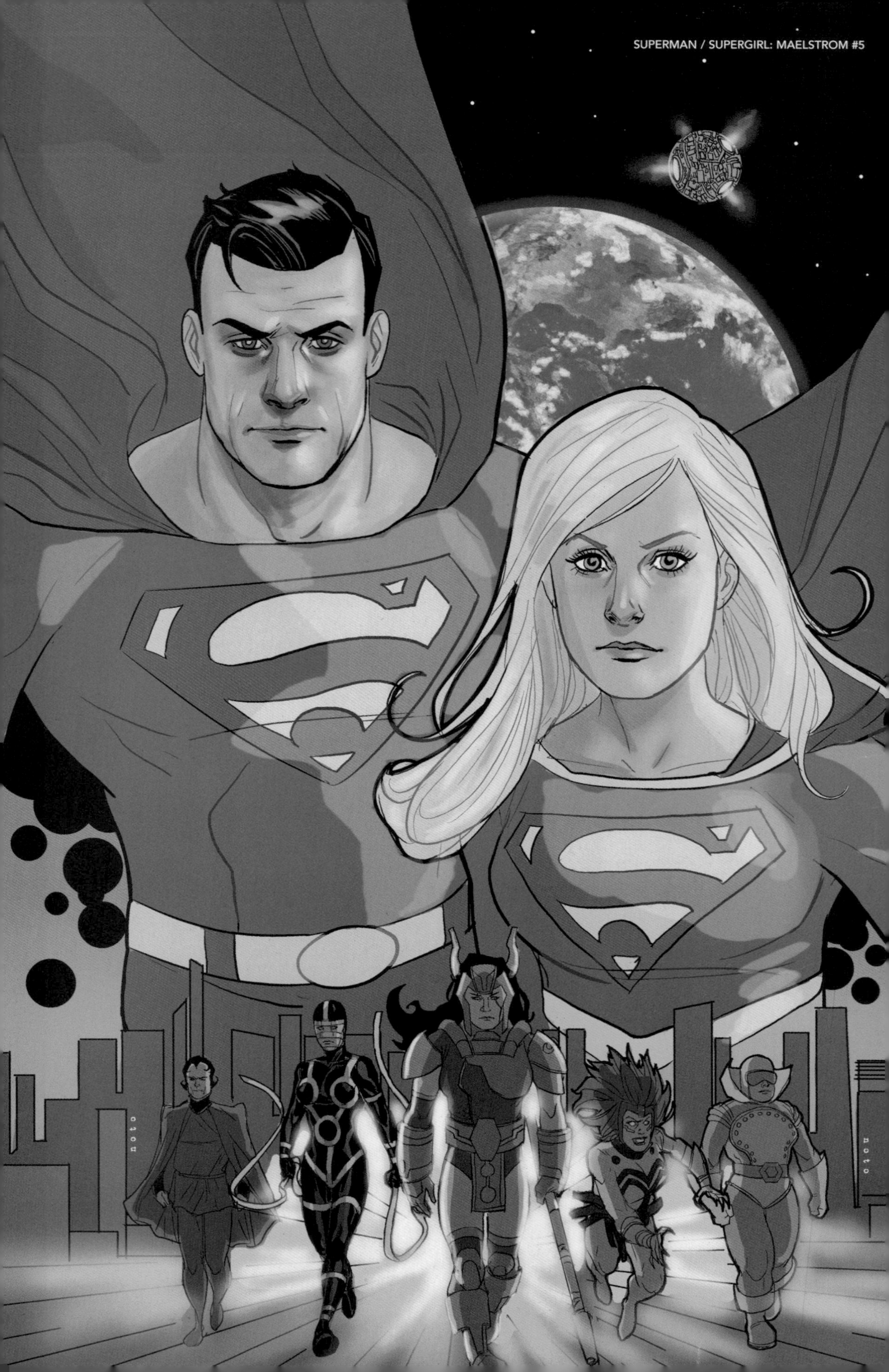

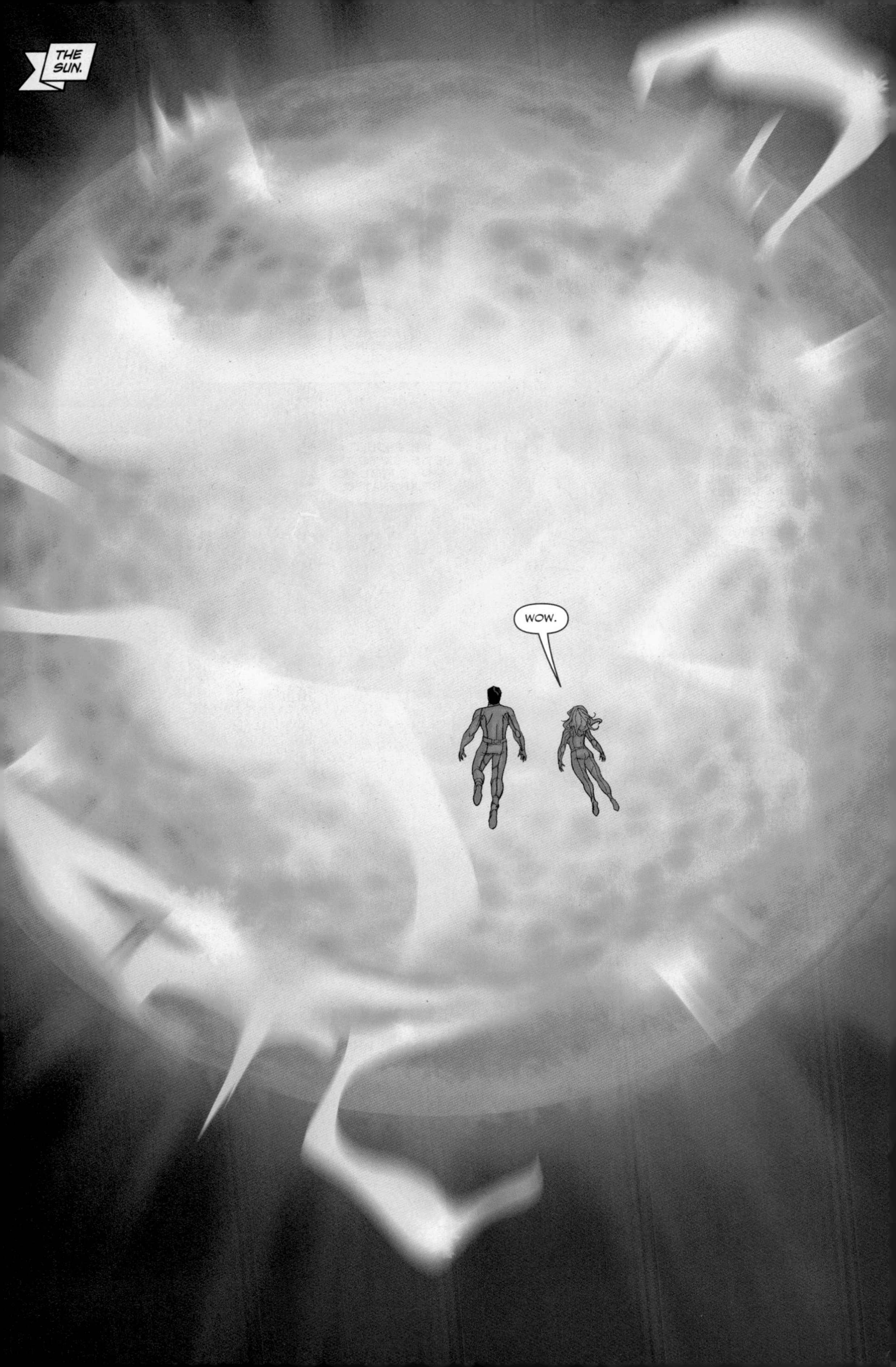
THE SUN.
WOW.

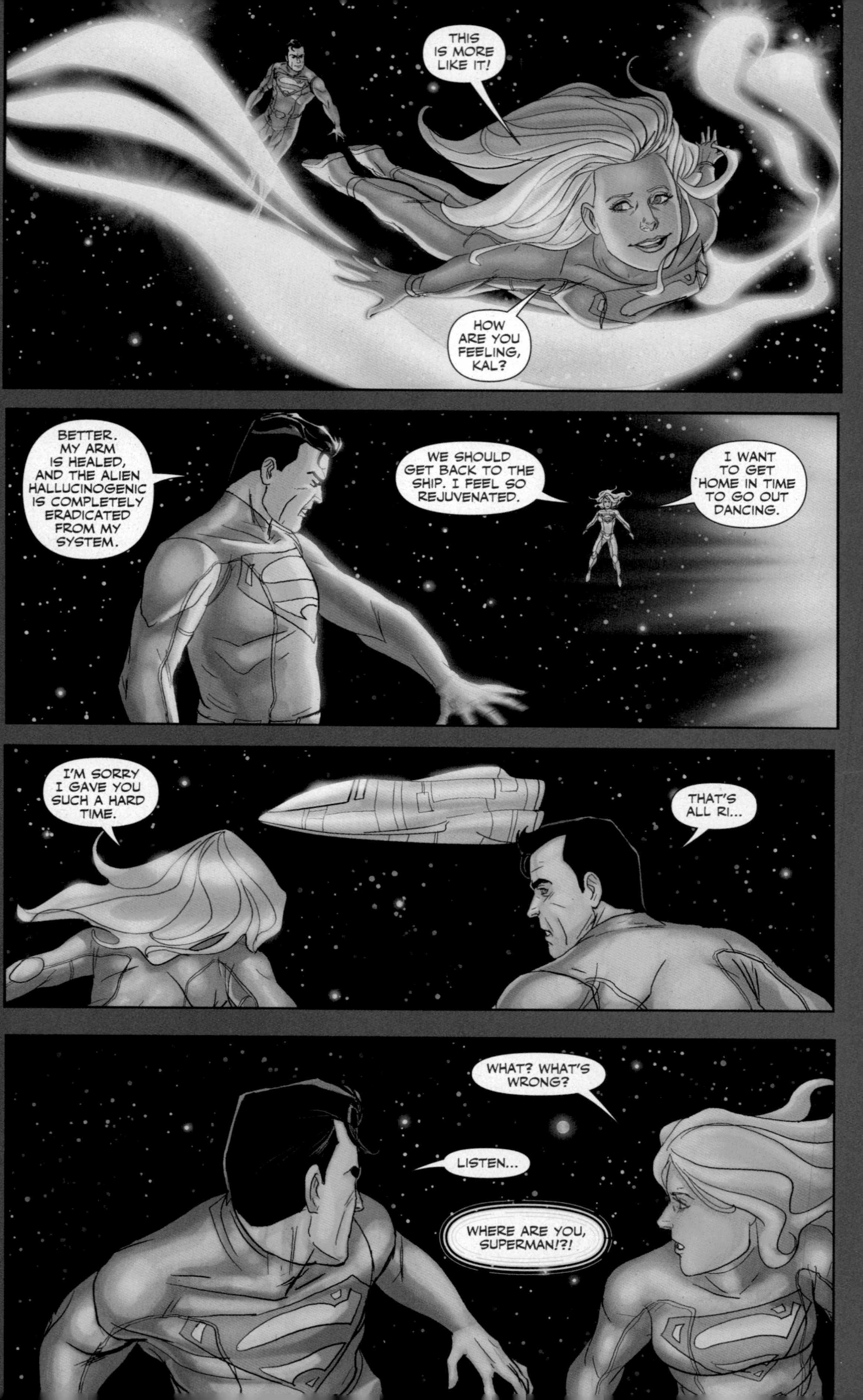
THIS IS MORE LIKE IT!
HOW ARE YOU FEELING, KAL?
BETTER. MY ARM IS HEALED, AND THE ALIEN HALLUCINOGENIC IS COMPLETELY ERADICATED FROM MY SYSTEM.
WE SHOULD GET BACK TO THE SHIP. I FEEL SO REJUVENATED.
I WANT TO GET HOME IN TIME TO GO OUT DANCING.
I'M SORRY I GAVE YOU SUCH A HARD TIME.
THAT'S ALL RI...
WHAT? WHAT'S WRONG?
LISTEN...
WHERE ARE YOU, SUPERMAN!?!

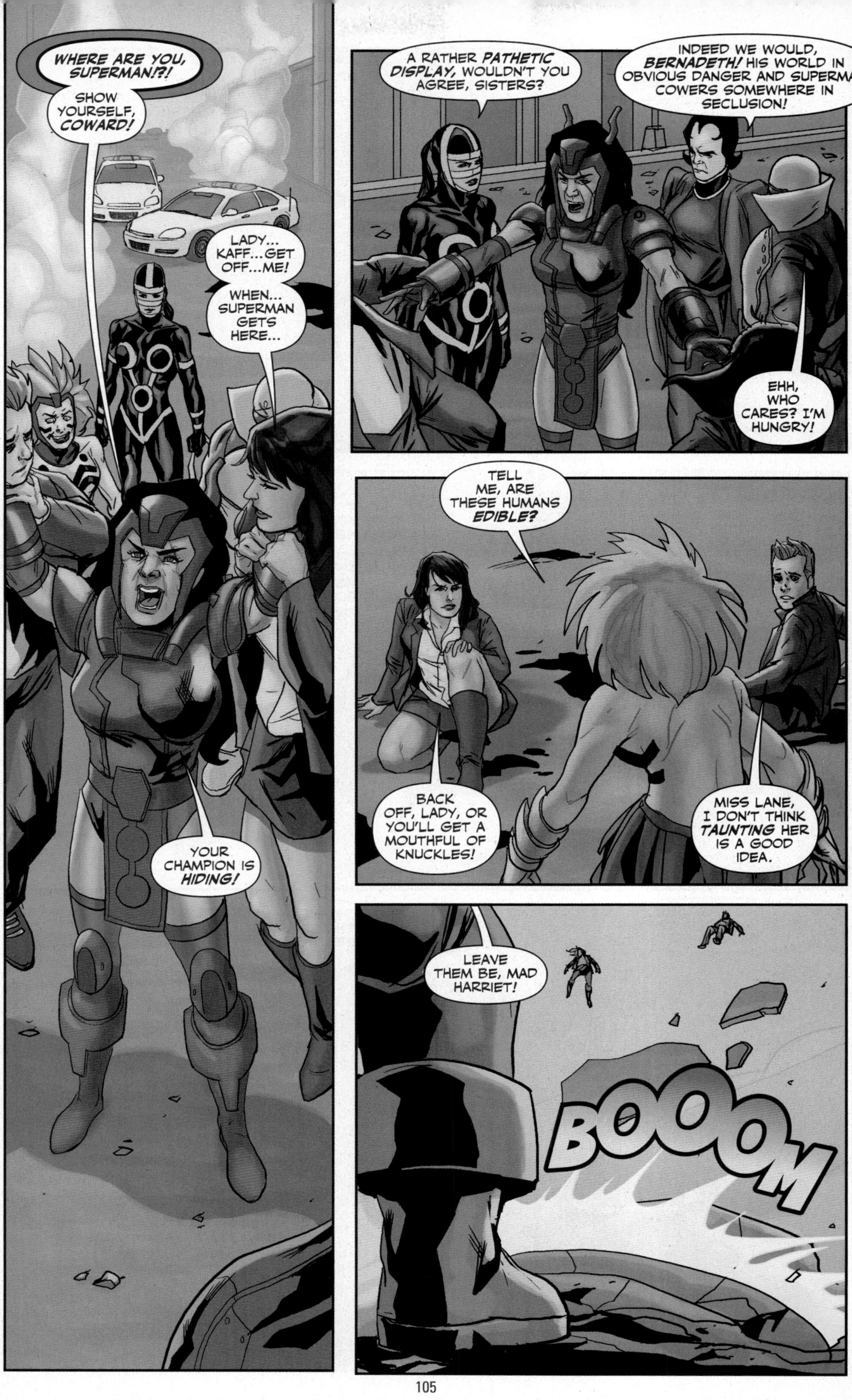
WHERE ARE YOU, SUPERMAN!?!
SHOW YOURSELF, COWARD!
LADY... KAFF...GET OFF...ME!
WHEN... SUPERMAN GETS HERE...
YOUR CHAMPION IS HIDING!
A RATHER PATHETIC DISPLAY, WOULDN'T YOU AGREE, SISTERS?
INDEED WE WOULD, BERNADETH! HIS WORLD IN OBVIOUS DANGER AND SUPERMAN COWERS SOMEWHERE IN SECLUSION!
EHH, WHO CARES? I'M HUNGRY!
TELL ME, ARE THESE HUMANS EDIBLE?
BACK OFF, LADY, OR YOU'LL GET A MOUTHFUL OF KNUCKLES!
MISS LANE, I DON'T THINK TAUNTING HER IS A GOOD IDEA.
LEAVE THEM BE, MAD HARRIET!
BOOOOM

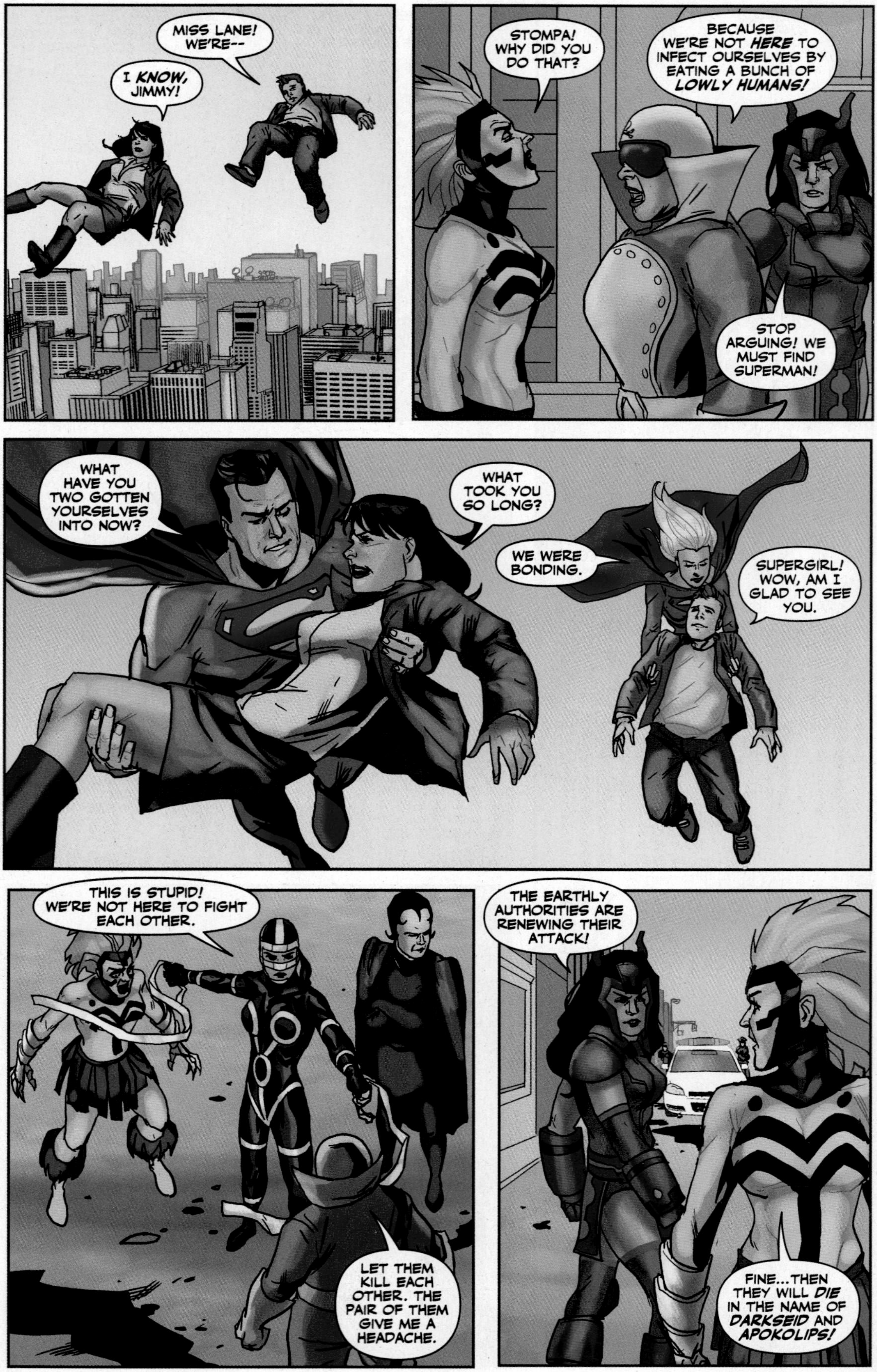
MISS LANE! WE'RE--
I KNOW, JIMMY!
STOMPA! WHY DID YOU DO THAT?
BECAUSE WE'RE NOT HERE TO INFECT OURSELVES BY EATING A BUNCH OF LOWLY HUMANS!
STOP ARGUING! WE MUST FIND SUPERMAN!
WHAT HAVE YOU TWO GOTTEN YOURSELVES INTO NOW?
WHAT TOOK YOU SO LONG?
WE WERE BONDING.
SUPERGIRL! WOW, AM I GLAD TO SEE YOU.
THIS IS STUPID! WE'RE NOT HERE TO FIGHT EACH OTHER.
LET THEM KILL EACH OTHER. THE PAIR OF THEM GIVE ME A HEADACHE.
THE EARTHLY AUTHORITIES ARE RENEWING THEIR ATTACK!
FINE...THEN THEY WILL DIE IN THE NAME OF DARKSEID AND APOKOLIPS!

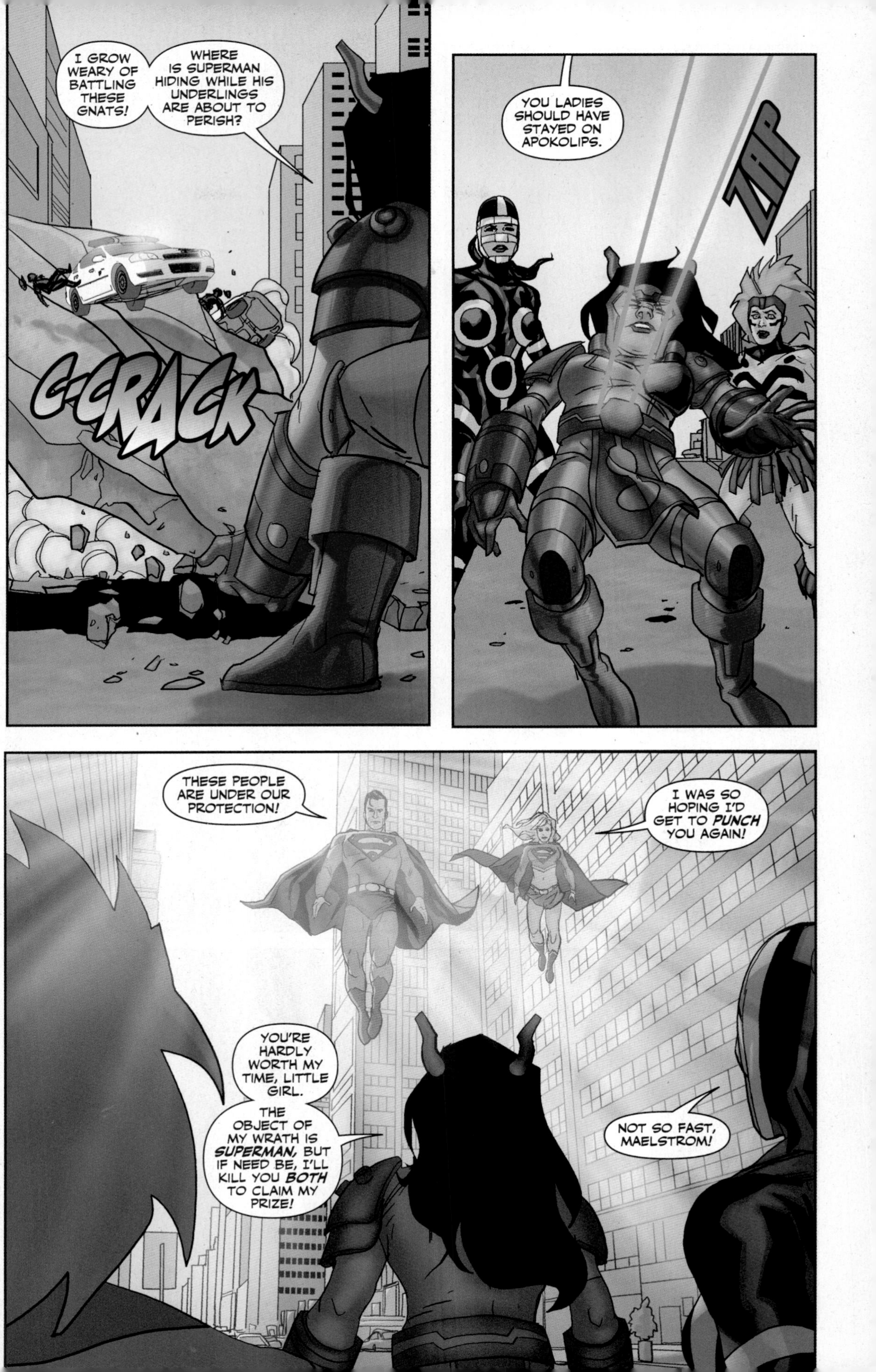
I GROW WEARY OF BATTLING THESE GNATS!
WHERE IS SUPERMAN HIDING WHILE HIS UNDERLINGS ARE ABOUT TO PERISH?
C-CRACK
YOU LADIES SHOULD HAVE STAYED ON APOKOLIPS.
ZAP
THESE PEOPLE ARE UNDER OUR PROTECTION!
I WAS SO HOPING I'D GET TO PUNCH YOU AGAIN!
YOU'RE HARDLY WORTH MY TIME, LITTLE GIRL.
THE OBJECT OF MY WRATH IS SUPERMAN, BUT IF NEED BE, I'LL KILL YOU BOTH TO CLAIM MY PRIZE!
NOT SO FAST, MAELSTROM!

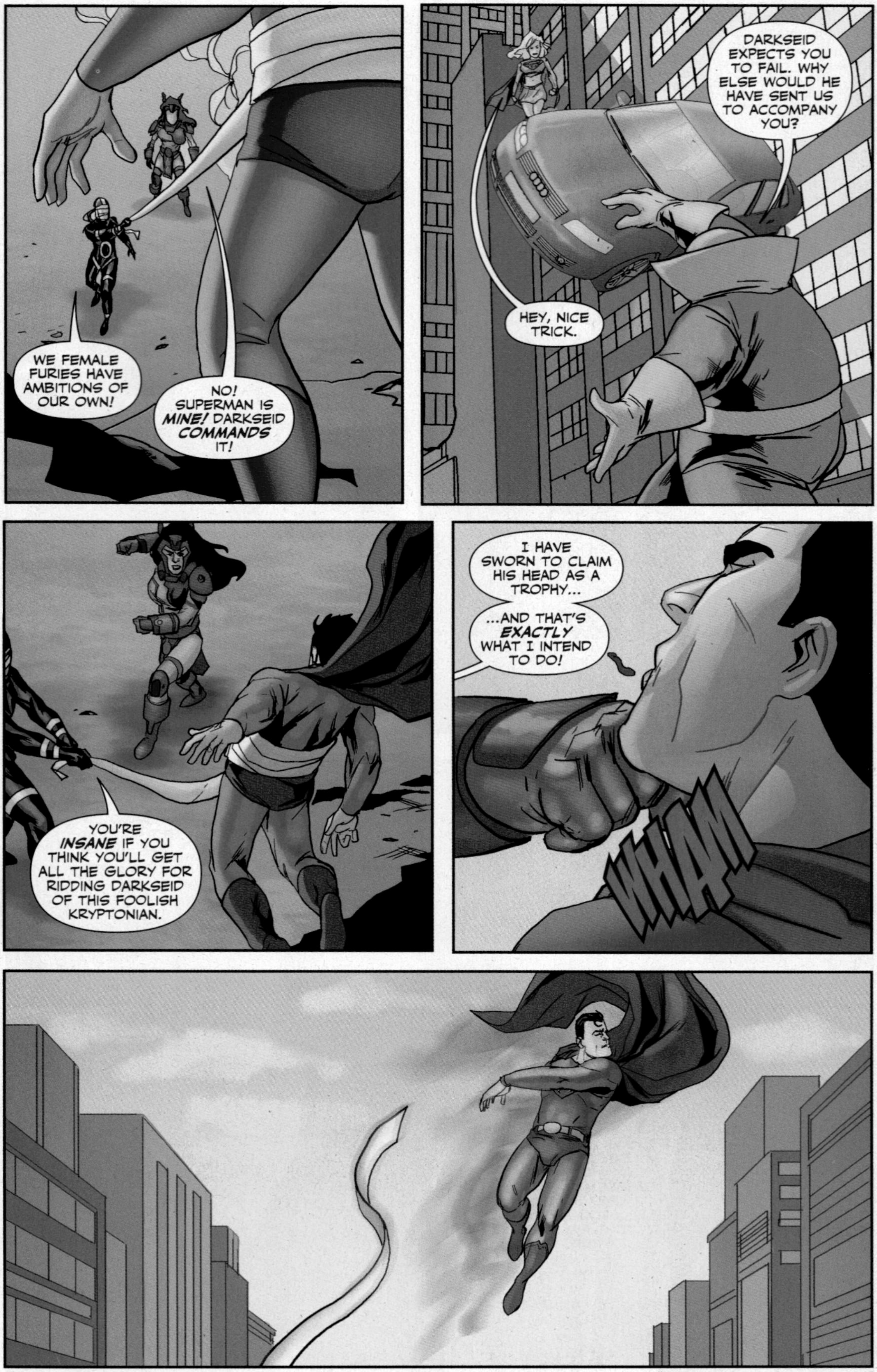

WE FEMALE FURIES HAVE AMBITIONS OF OUR OWN!
NO! SUPERMAN IS MINE! DARKSEID COMMANDS IT!
DARKSEID EXPECTS YOU TO FAIL. WHY ELSE WOULD HE HAVE SENT US TO ACCOMPANY YOU?
HEY, NICE TRICK.
YOU'RE INSANE IF YOU THINK YOU'LL GET ALL THE GLORY FOR RIDDING DARKSEID OF THIS FOOLISH KRYPTONIAN.
I HAVE SWORN TO CLAIM HIS HEAD AS A TROPHY...
...AND THAT'S EXACTLY WHAT I INTEND TO DO!
WHAM

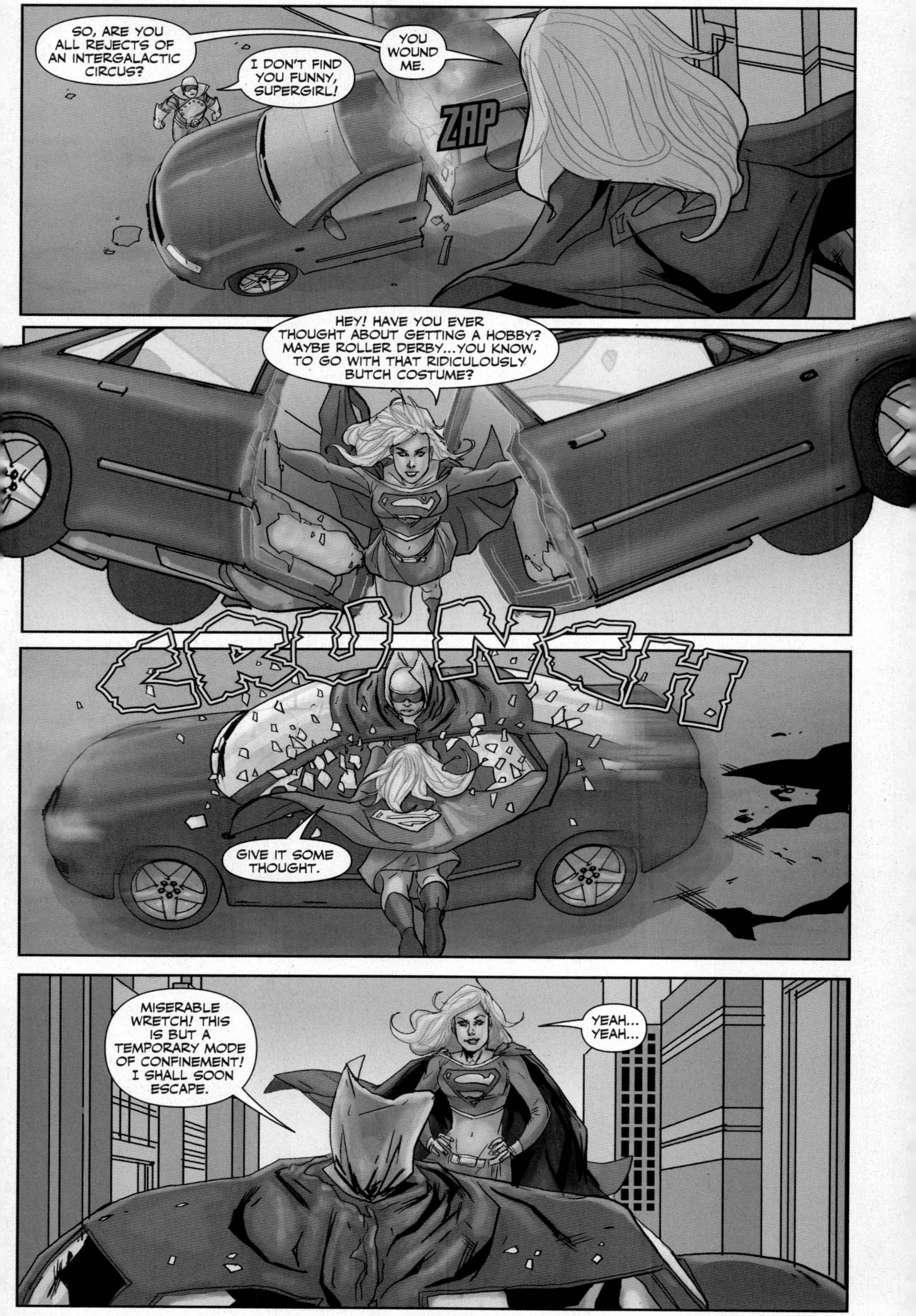
SO, ARE YOU ALL REJECTS OF AN INTERGALACTIC CIRCUS?
I DON'T FIND YOU FUNNY, SUPERGIRL!
YOU WOUND ME.
ZAP
HEY! HAVE YOU EVER THOUGHT ABOUT GETTING A HOBBY? MAYBE ROLLER DERBY...YOU KNOW, TO GO WITH THAT RIDICULOUSLY BUTCH COSTUME?
CRUNCH
GIVE IT SOME THOUGHT.
MISERABLE WRETCH! THIS IS BUT A TEMPORARY MODE OF CONFINEMENT! I SHALL SOON ESCAPE.
YEAH... YEAH...

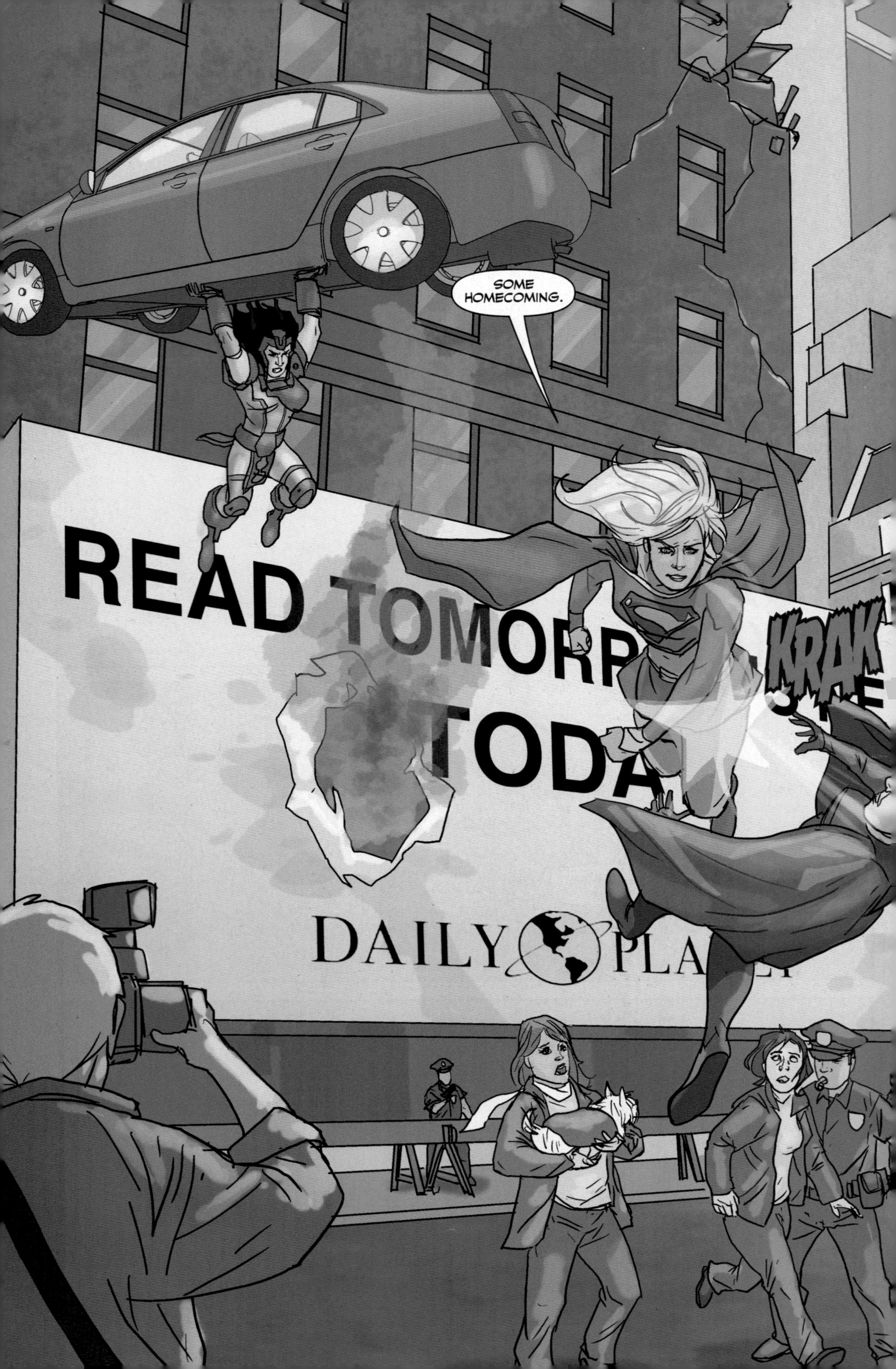
SOME HOMECOMING.
READ TOMORR
KRAK
TODA
DAILY PLA

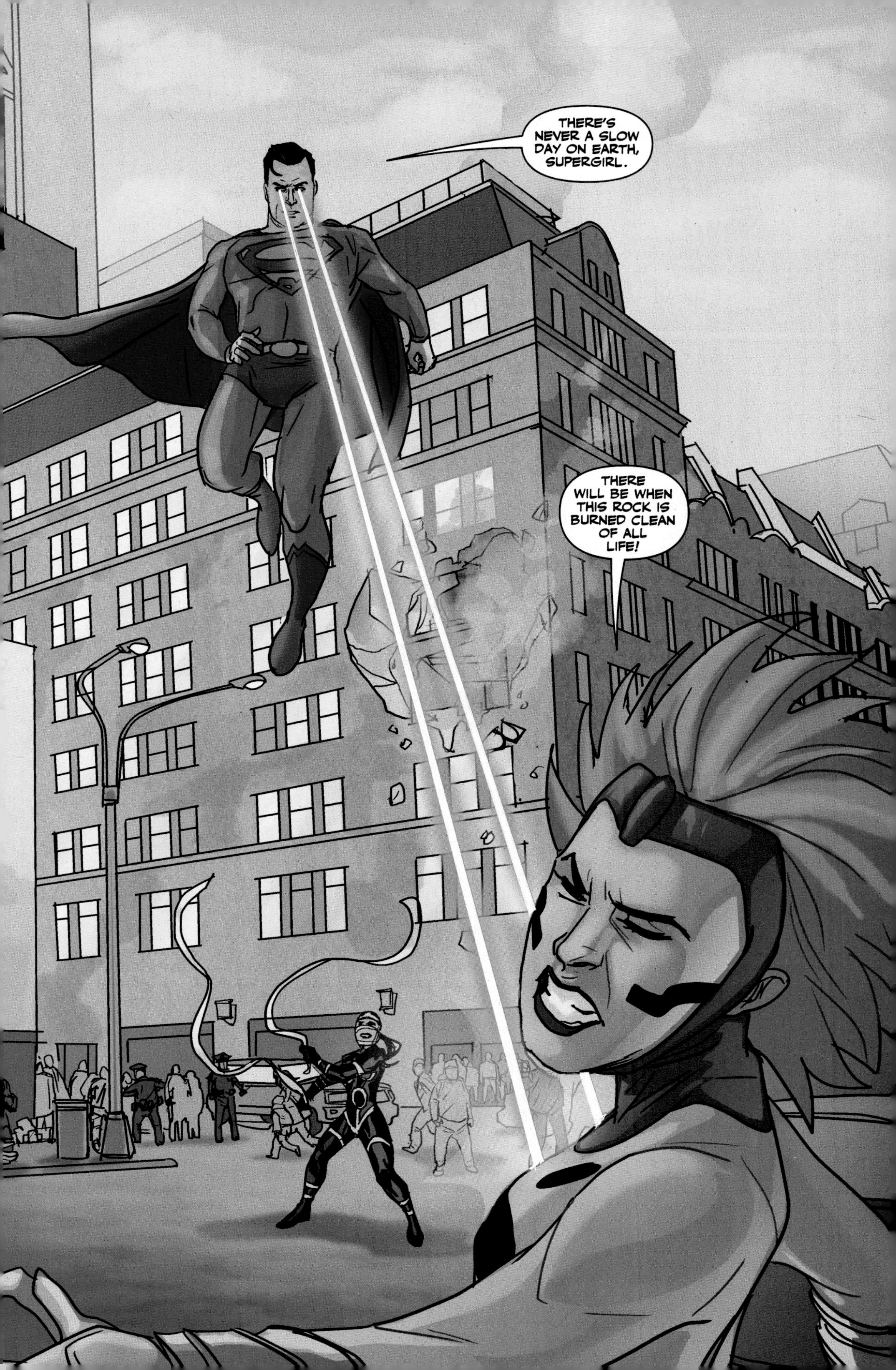
THERE'S NEVER A SLOW DAY ON EARTH, SUPERGIRL.
THERE WILL BE WHEN THIS ROCK IS BURNED CLEAN OF ALL LIFE!

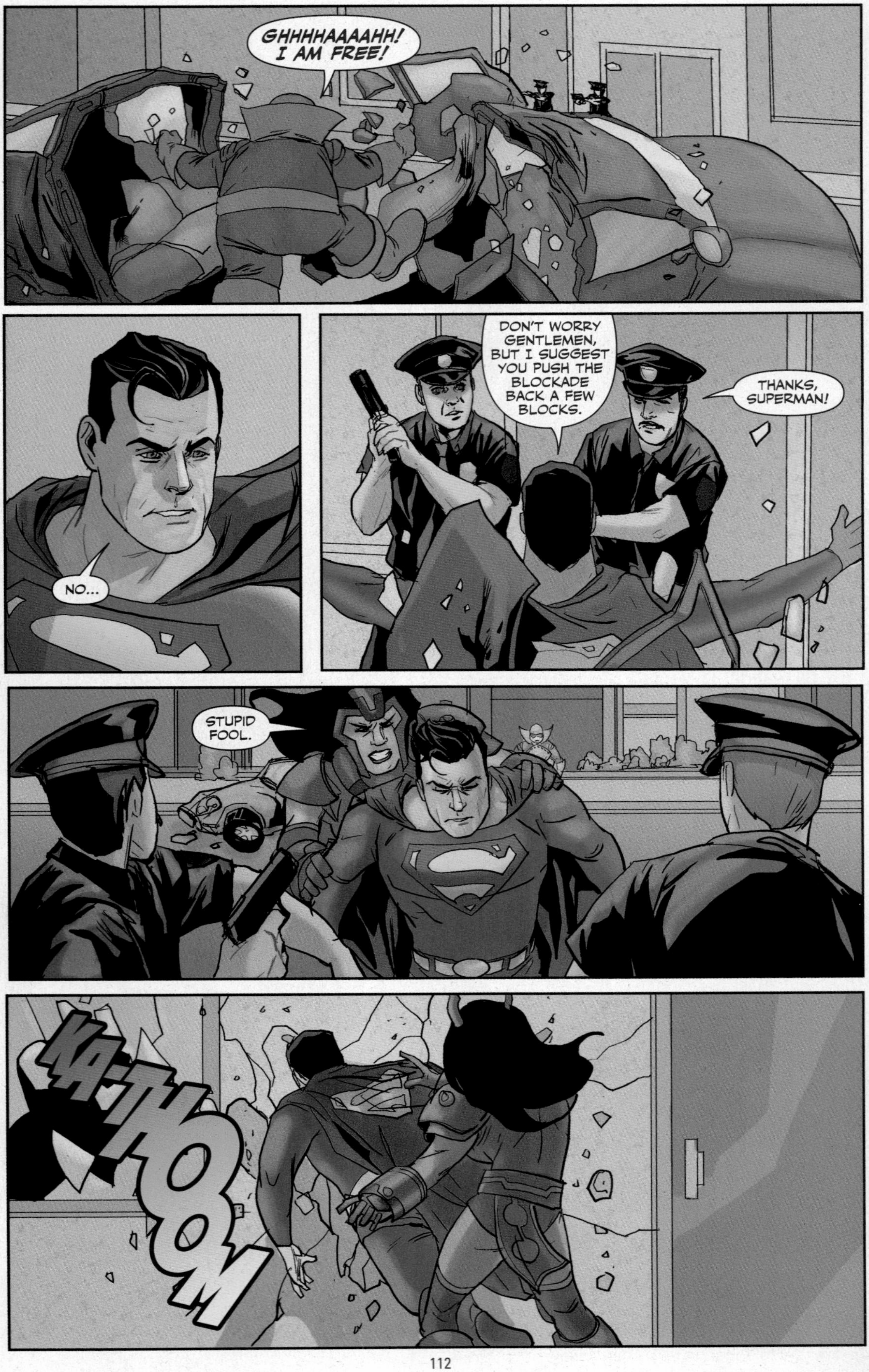
GHHHHAAAAHH! I AM FREE!
NO...
DON'T WORRY GENTLEMEN, BUT I SUGGEST YOU PUSH THE BLOCKADE BACK A FEW BLOCKS.
THANKS, SUPERMAN!
STUPID FOOL.
KA-THOOM

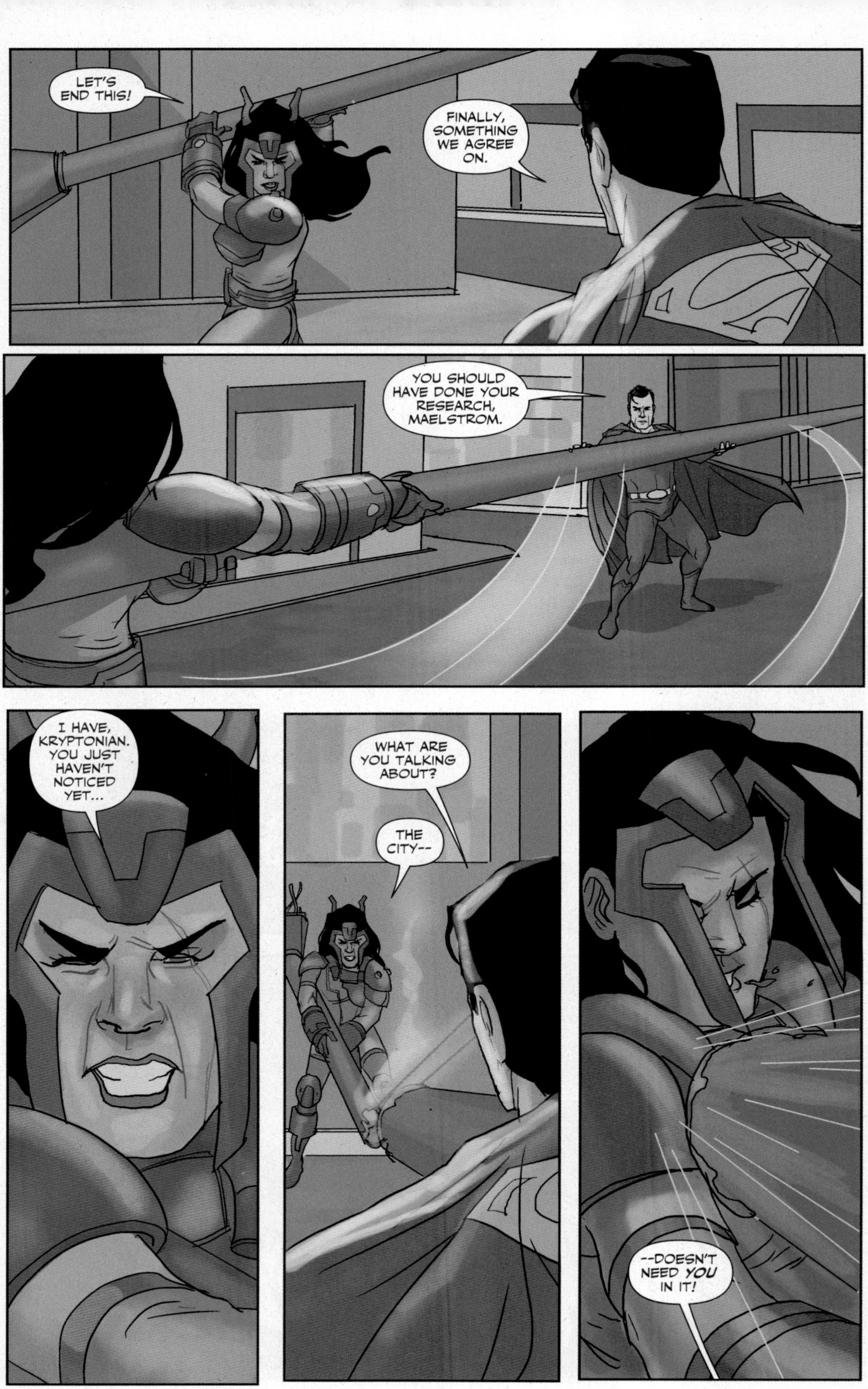
LET'S END THIS!
FINALLY, SOMETHING WE AGREE ON.
YOU SHOULD HAVE DONE YOUR RESEARCH, MAELSTROM.
I HAVE, KRYPTONIAN. YOU JUST HAVEN'T NOTICED YET...
WHAT ARE YOU TALKING ABOUT?
THE CITY--
--DOESN'T NEED *YOU* IN IT!

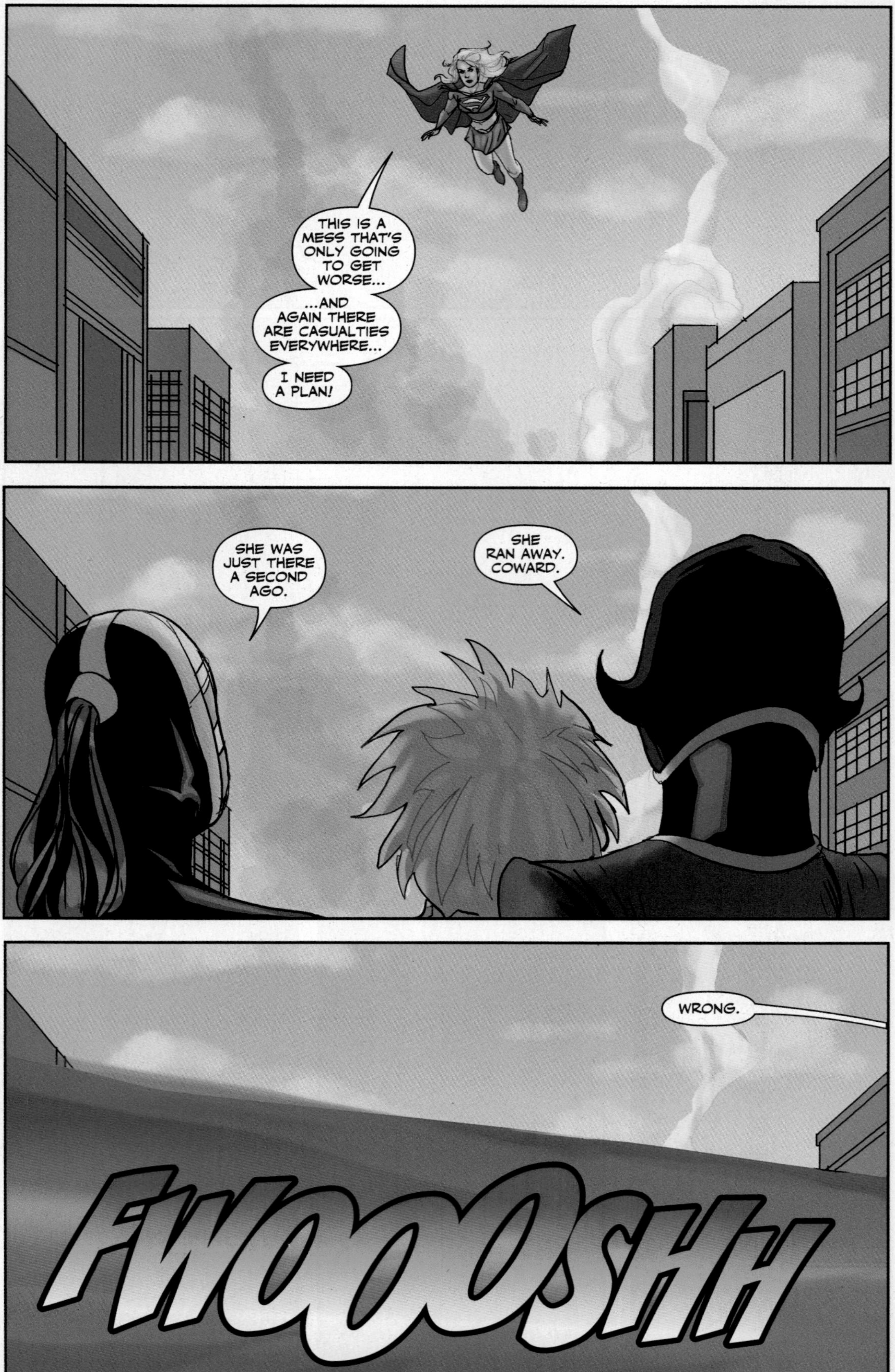
THIS IS A MESS THAT'S ONLY GOING TO GET WORSE...
...AND AGAIN THERE ARE CASUALTIES EVERYWHERE...
I NEED A PLAN!
SHE WAS JUST THERE A SECOND AGO.
SHE RAN AWAY. COWARD.
WRONG.
FWOOOSHH

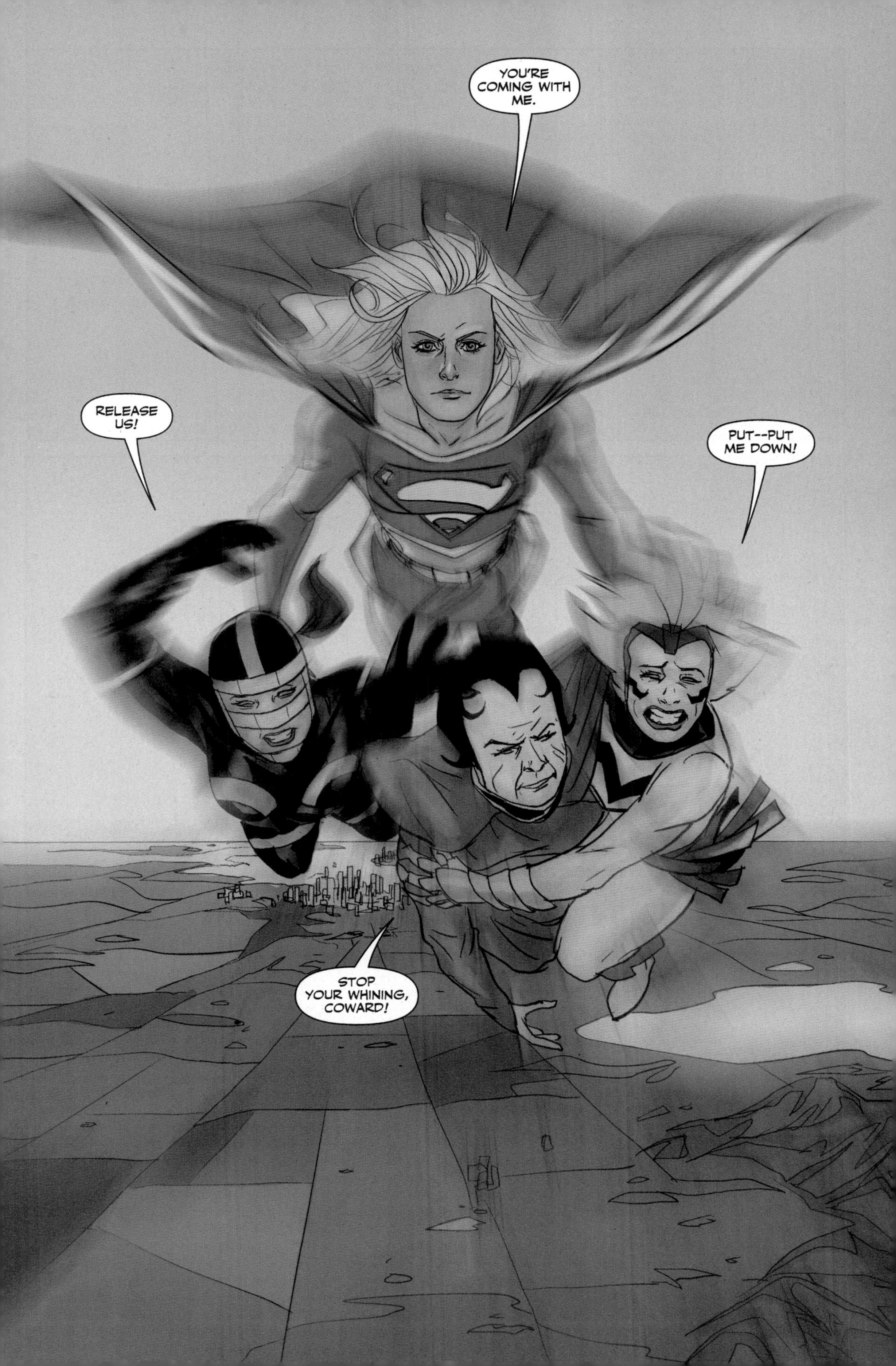
YOU'RE COMING WITH ME.
RELEASE US!
PUT--PUT ME DOWN!
STOP YOUR WHINING, COWARD!

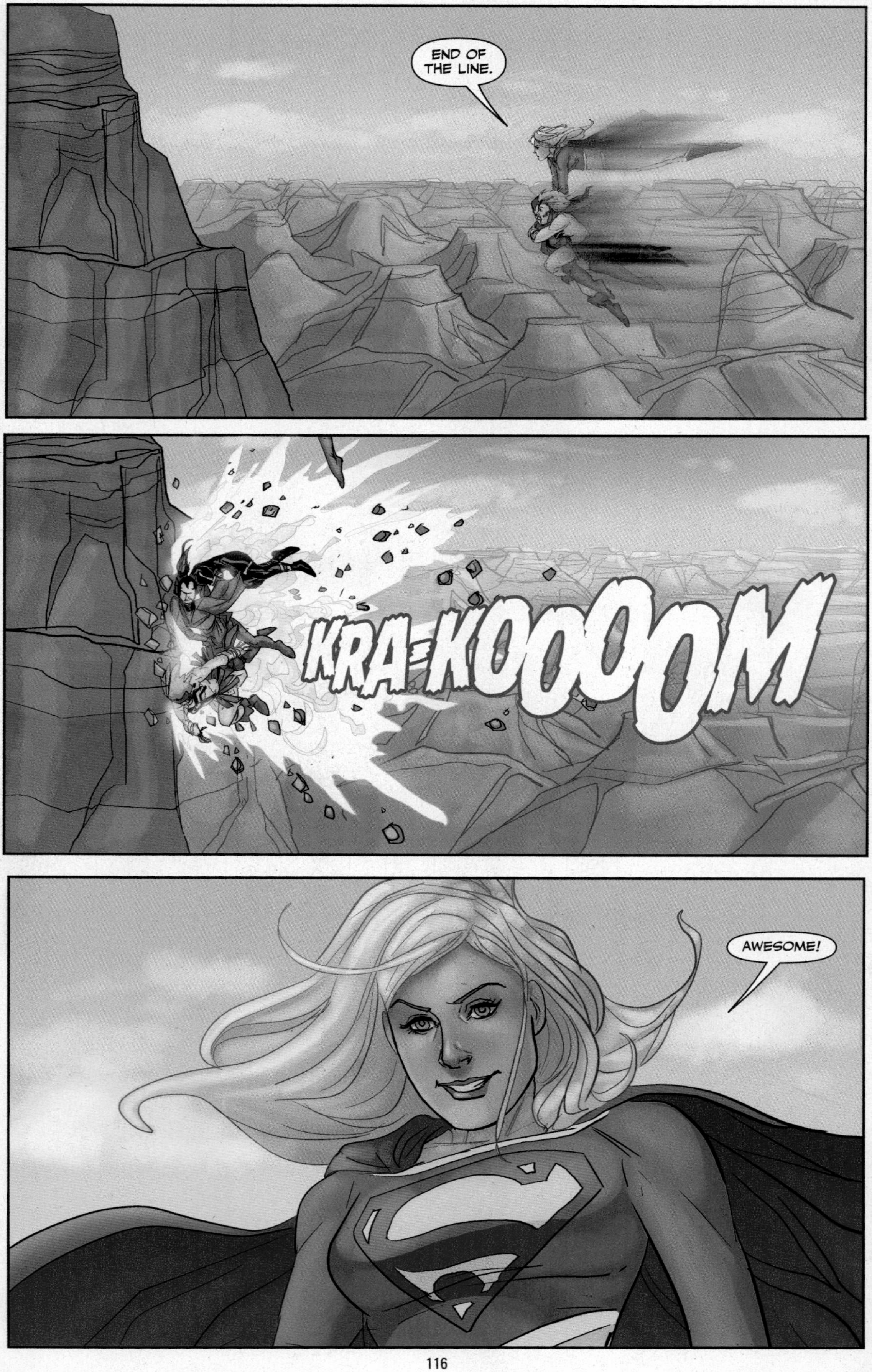
END OF THE LINE.
KRA-KOOOOOM
AWESOME!

LOOK AROUND. WE'RE DESTROYING THIS CITY!
THERE'S YOUR WEAKNESS, SUPERMAN. YOU CARE TOO MUCH ABOUT THESE MAGGOTS.
NOW HOLD STILL. I DON'T NEED ALL OF YOU...
FWAM
...JUST YOUR HEAD.
NOT A CHANCE...
UNHAND ME!
UNHAND YOU?
HONESTLY... WHO TALKS LIKE THAT?

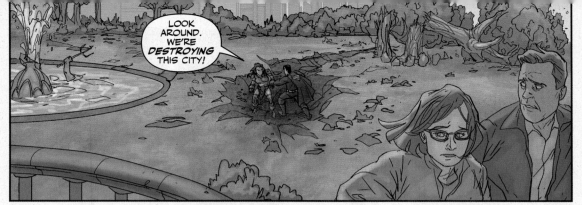

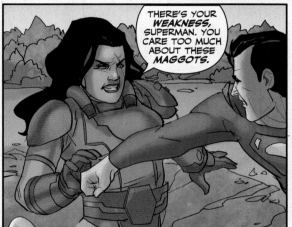

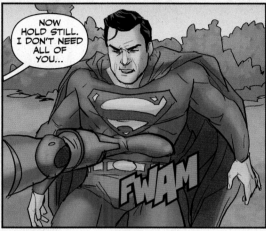

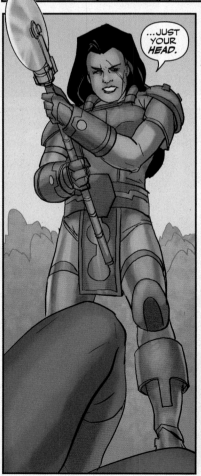

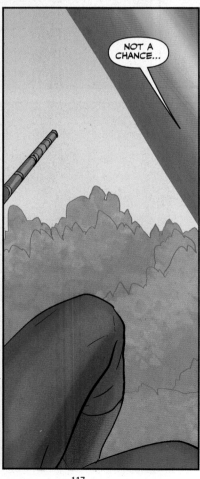

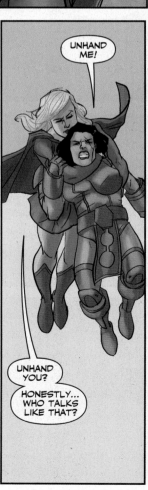

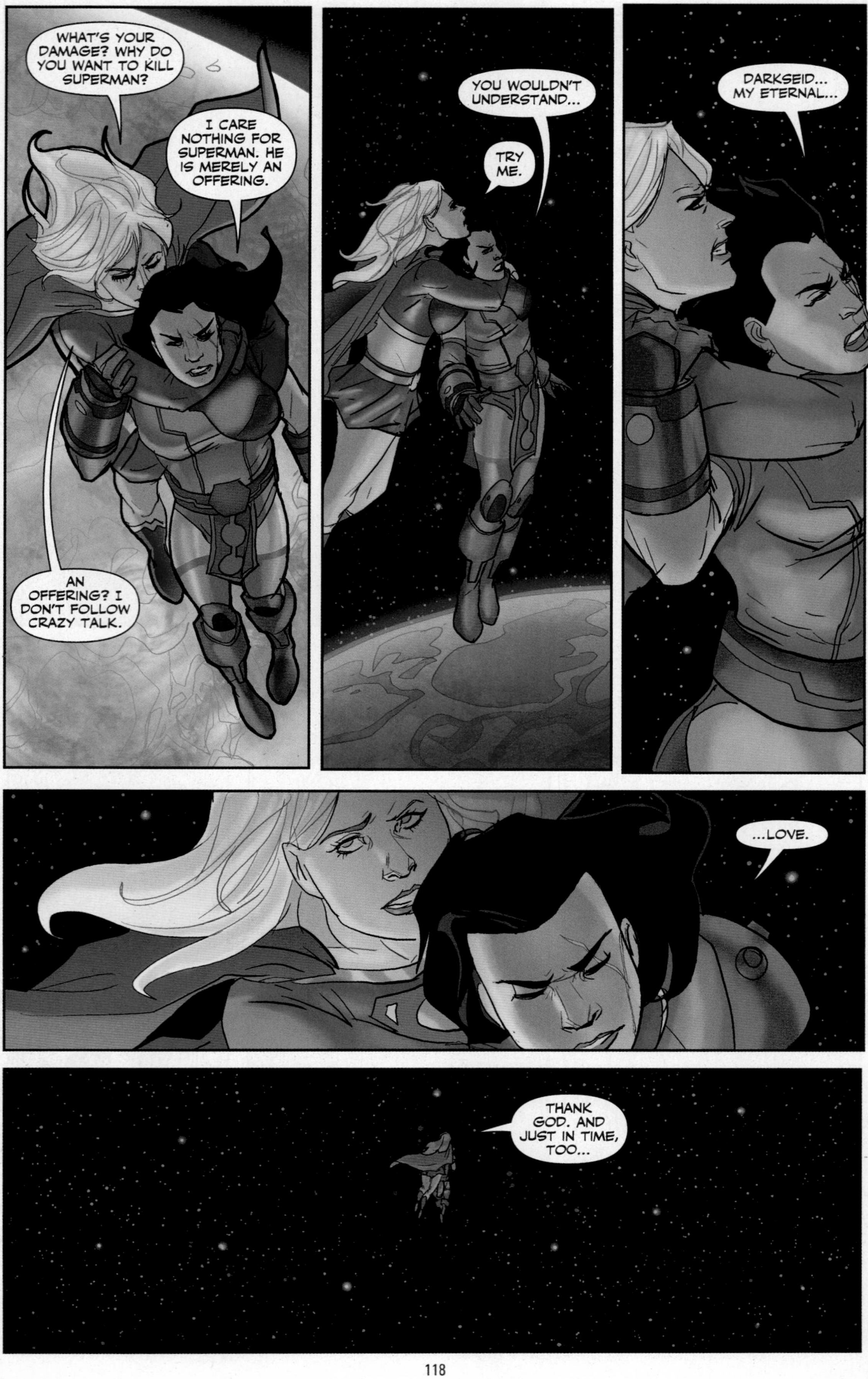
WHAT'S YOUR DAMAGE? WHY DO YOU WANT TO KILL SUPERMAN?
I CARE NOTHING FOR SUPERMAN. HE IS MERELY AN OFFERING.
AN OFFERING? I DON'T FOLLOW CRAZY TALK.
YOU WOULDN'T UNDERSTAND...
TRY ME.
DARKSEID... MY ETERNAL...
...LOVE.
THANK GOD. AND JUST IN TIME, TOO...

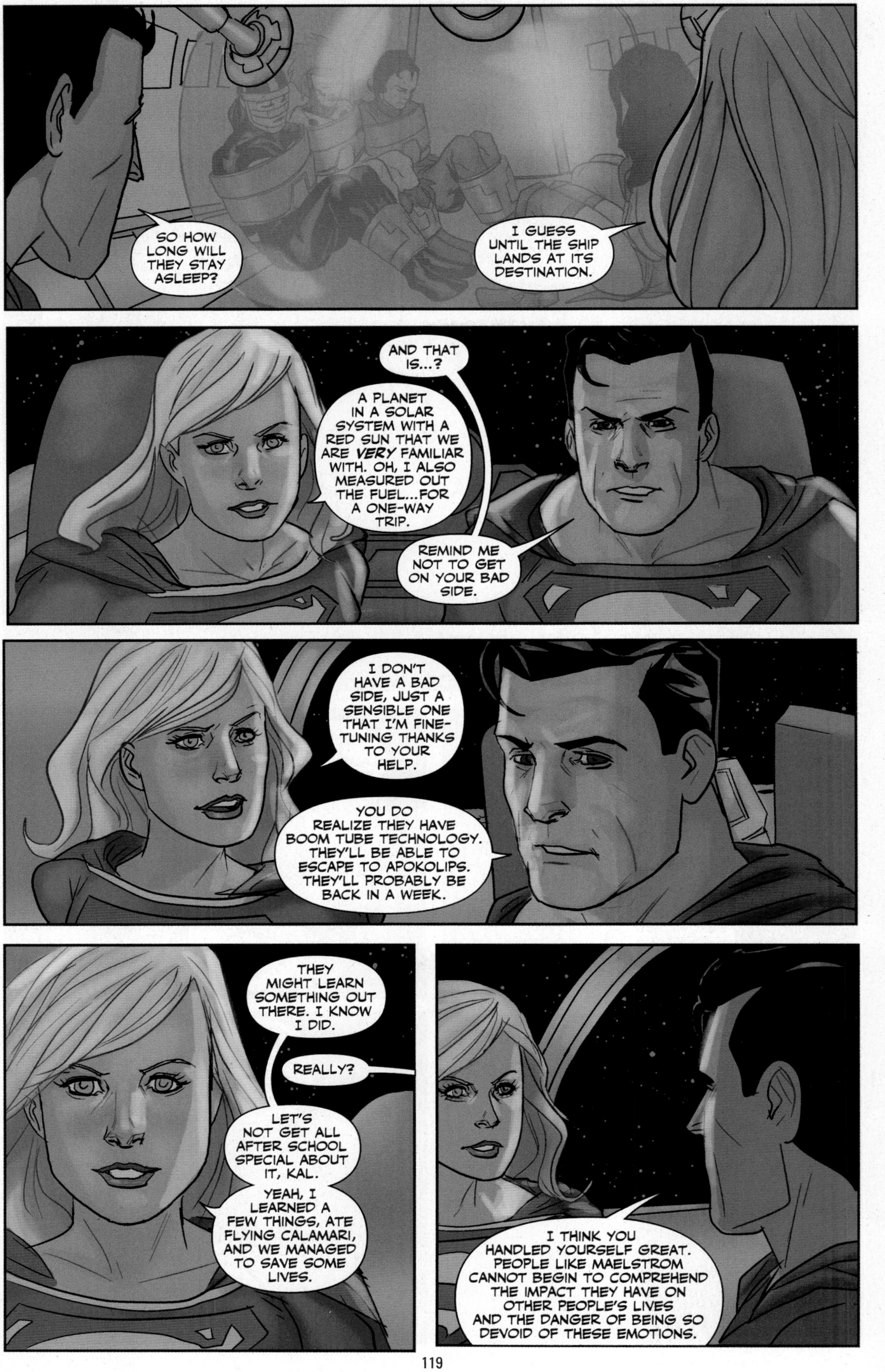
SO HOW LONG WILL THEY STAY ASLEEP?
I GUESS UNTIL THE SHIP LANDS AT ITS DESTINATION.
AND THAT IS...?
A PLANET IN A SOLAR SYSTEM WITH A RED SUN THAT WE ARE *VERY* FAMILIAR WITH. OH, I ALSO MEASURED OUT THE FUEL...FOR A ONE-WAY TRIP.
REMIND ME NOT TO GET ON YOUR BAD SIDE.
I DON'T HAVE A BAD SIDE, JUST A SENSIBLE ONE THAT I'M FINE-TUNING THANKS TO YOUR HELP.
YOU DO REALIZE THEY HAVE BOOM TUBE TECHNOLOGY. THEY'LL BE ABLE TO ESCAPE TO APOKOLIPS. THEY'LL PROBABLY BE BACK IN A WEEK.
THEY MIGHT LEARN SOMETHING OUT THERE. I KNOW I DID.
REALLY?
LET'S NOT GET ALL AFTER SCHOOL SPECIAL ABOUT IT, KAL.
YEAH, I LEARNED A FEW THINGS, ATE FLYING CALAMARI, AND WE MANAGED TO SAVE SOME LIVES.
I THINK YOU HANDLED YOURSELF GREAT. PEOPLE LIKE MAELSTROM CANNOT BEGIN TO COMPREHEND THE IMPACT THEY HAVE ON OTHER PEOPLE'S LIVES AND THE DANGER OF BEING SO DEVOID OF THESE EMOTIONS.

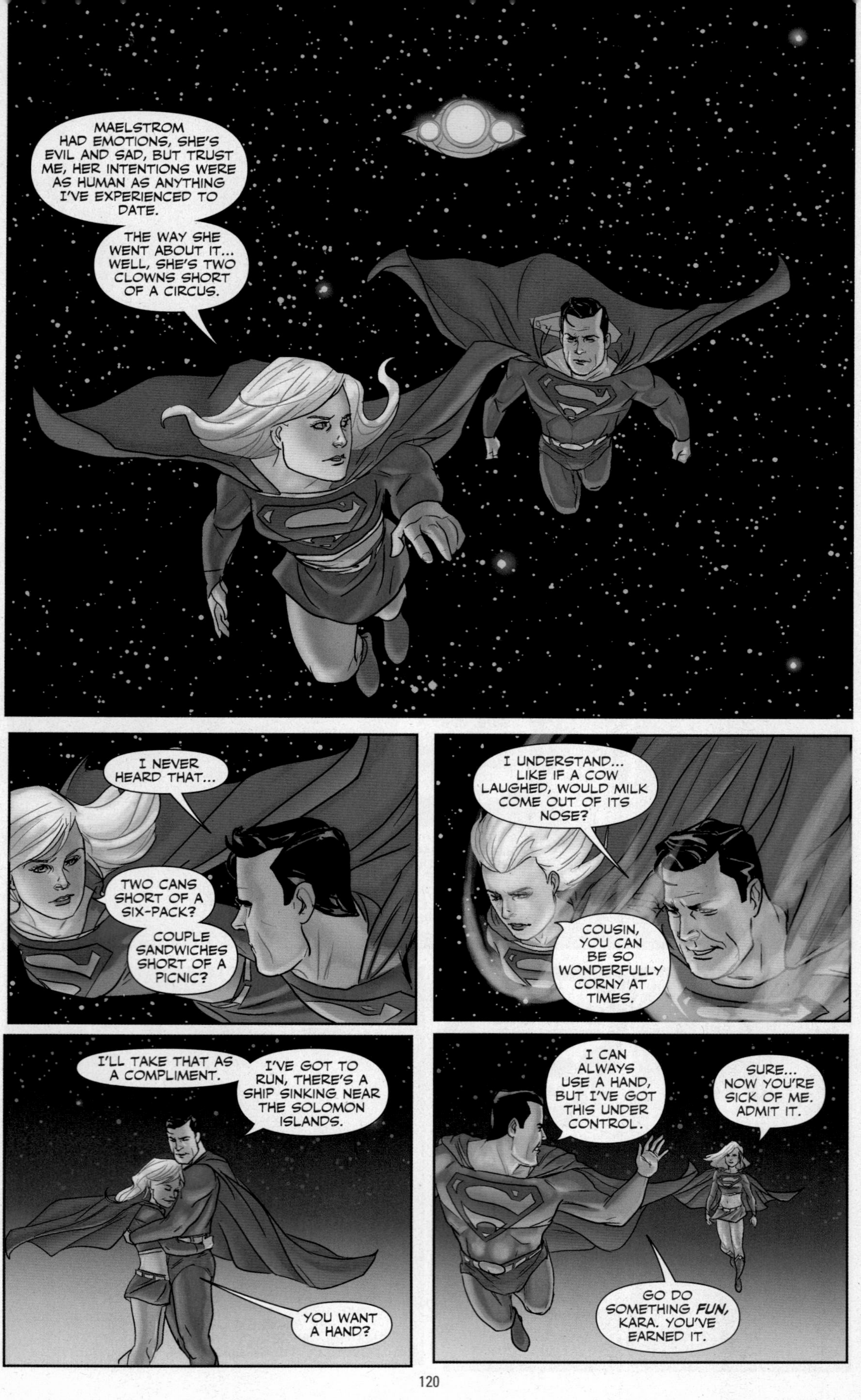

MAELSTROM HAD EMOTIONS, SHE'S EVIL AND SAD, BUT TRUST ME, HER INTENTIONS WERE AS HUMAN AS ANYTHING I'VE EXPERIENCED TO DATE.
THE WAY SHE WENT ABOUT IT... WELL, SHE'S TWO CLOWNS SHORT OF A CIRCUS.
I NEVER HEARD THAT...
TWO CANS SHORT OF A SIX-PACK?
COUPLE SANDWICHES SHORT OF A PICNIC?
I UNDERSTAND... LIKE IF A COW LAUGHED, WOULD MILK COME OUT OF ITS NOSE?
COUSIN, YOU CAN BE SO WONDERFULLY CORNY AT TIMES.
I'LL TAKE THAT AS A COMPLIMENT.
I'VE GOT TO RUN, THERE'S A SHIP SINKING NEAR THE SOLOMON ISLANDS.
YOU WANT A HAND?
I CAN ALWAYS USE A HAND, BUT I'VE GOT THIS UNDER CONTROL.
SURE... NOW YOU'RE SICK OF ME. ADMIT IT.
GO DO SOMETHING *FUN*, KARA. YOU'VE EARNED IT.

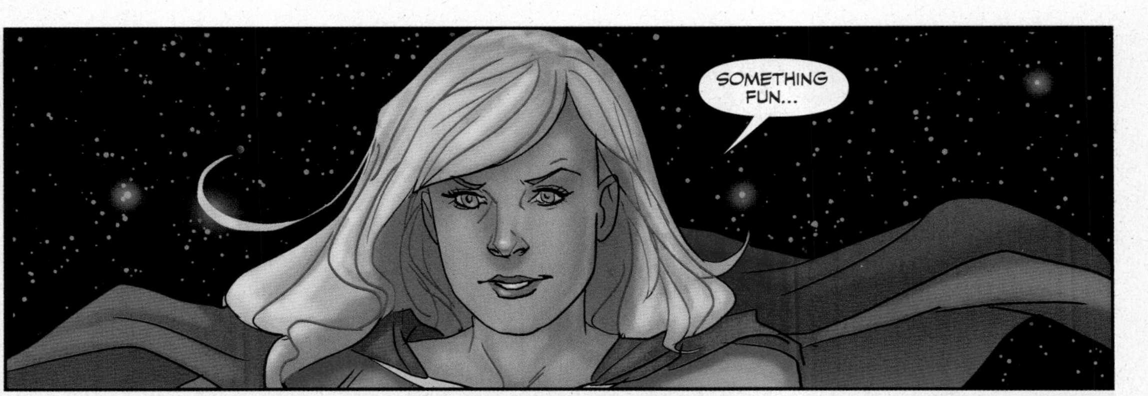
SOMETHING FUN...

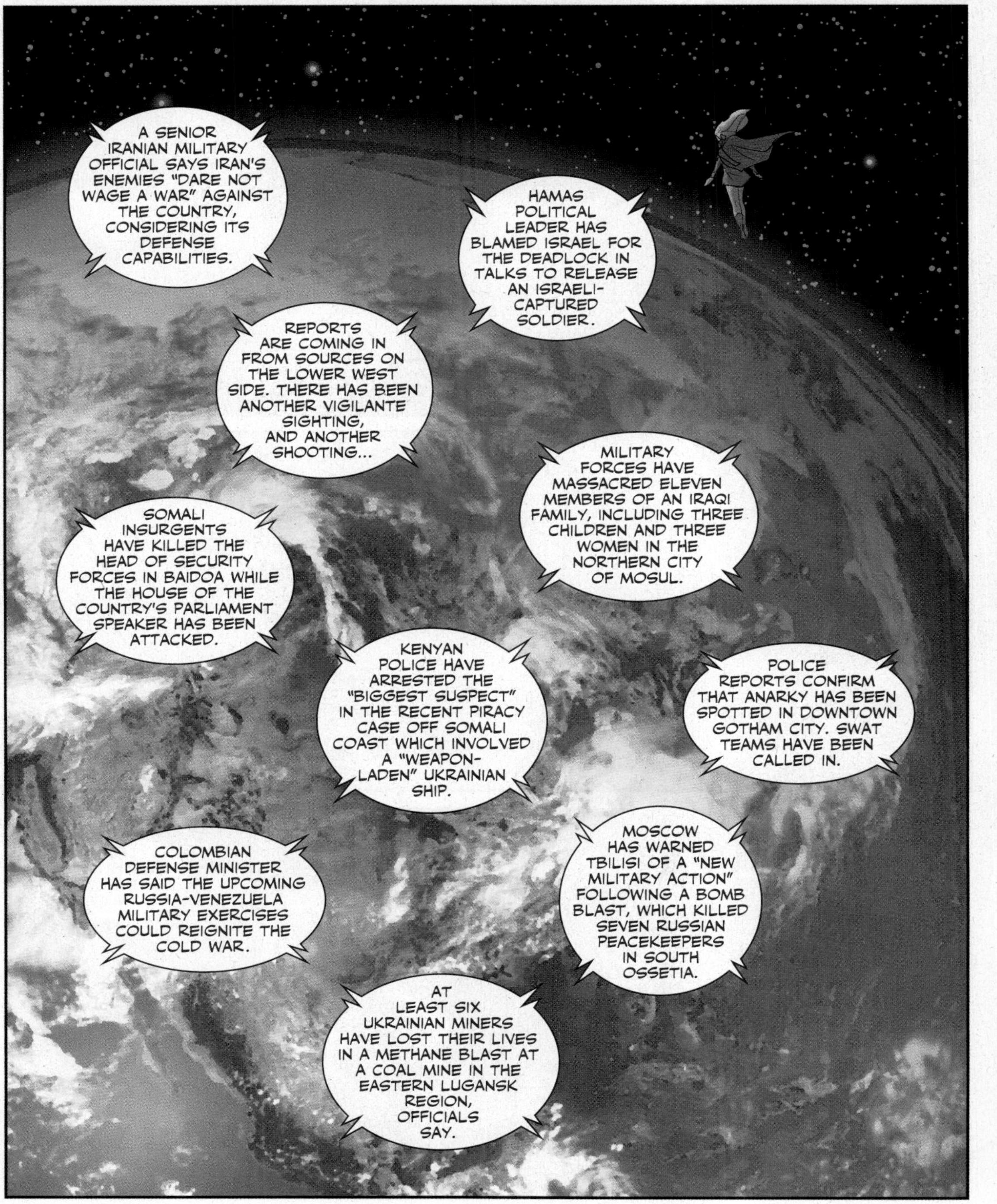
A SENIOR IRANIAN MILITARY OFFICIAL SAYS IRAN'S ENEMIES "DARE NOT WAGE A WAR" AGAINST THE COUNTRY, CONSIDERING ITS DEFENSE CAPABILITIES.
HAMAS POLITICAL LEADER HAS BLAMED ISRAEL FOR THE DEADLOCK IN TALKS TO RELEASE AN ISRAELI-CAPTURED SOLDIER.
REPORTS ARE COMING IN FROM SOURCES ON THE LOWER WEST SIDE. THERE HAS BEEN ANOTHER VIGILANTE SIGHTING, AND ANOTHER SHOOTING...
MILITARY FORCES HAVE MASSACRED ELEVEN MEMBERS OF AN IRAQI FAMILY, INCLUDING THREE CHILDREN AND THREE WOMEN IN THE NORTHERN CITY OF MOSUL.
SOMALI INSURGENTS HAVE KILLED THE HEAD OF SECURITY FORCES IN BAIDOA WHILE THE HOUSE OF THE COUNTRY'S PARLIAMENT SPEAKER HAS BEEN ATTACKED.
KENYAN POLICE HAVE ARRESTED THE "BIGGEST SUSPECT" IN THE RECENT PIRACY CASE OFF SOMALI COAST WHICH INVOLVED A "WEAPON-LADEN" UKRAINIAN SHIP.
POLICE REPORTS CONFIRM THAT ANARKY HAS BEEN SPOTTED IN DOWNTOWN GOTHAM CITY. SWAT TEAMS HAVE BEEN CALLED IN.
COLOMBIAN DEFENSE MINISTER HAS SAID THE UPCOMING RUSSIA-VENEZUELA MILITARY EXERCISES COULD REIGNITE THE COLD WAR.
MOSCOW HAS WARNED TBILISI OF A "NEW MILITARY ACTION" FOLLOWING A BOMB BLAST, WHICH KILLED SEVEN RUSSIAN PEACEKEEPERS IN SOUTH OSSETIA.
AT LEAST SIX UKRAINIAN MINERS HAVE LOST THEIR LIVES IN A METHANE BLAST AT A COAL MINE IN THE EASTERN LUGANSK REGION, OFFICIALS SAY.

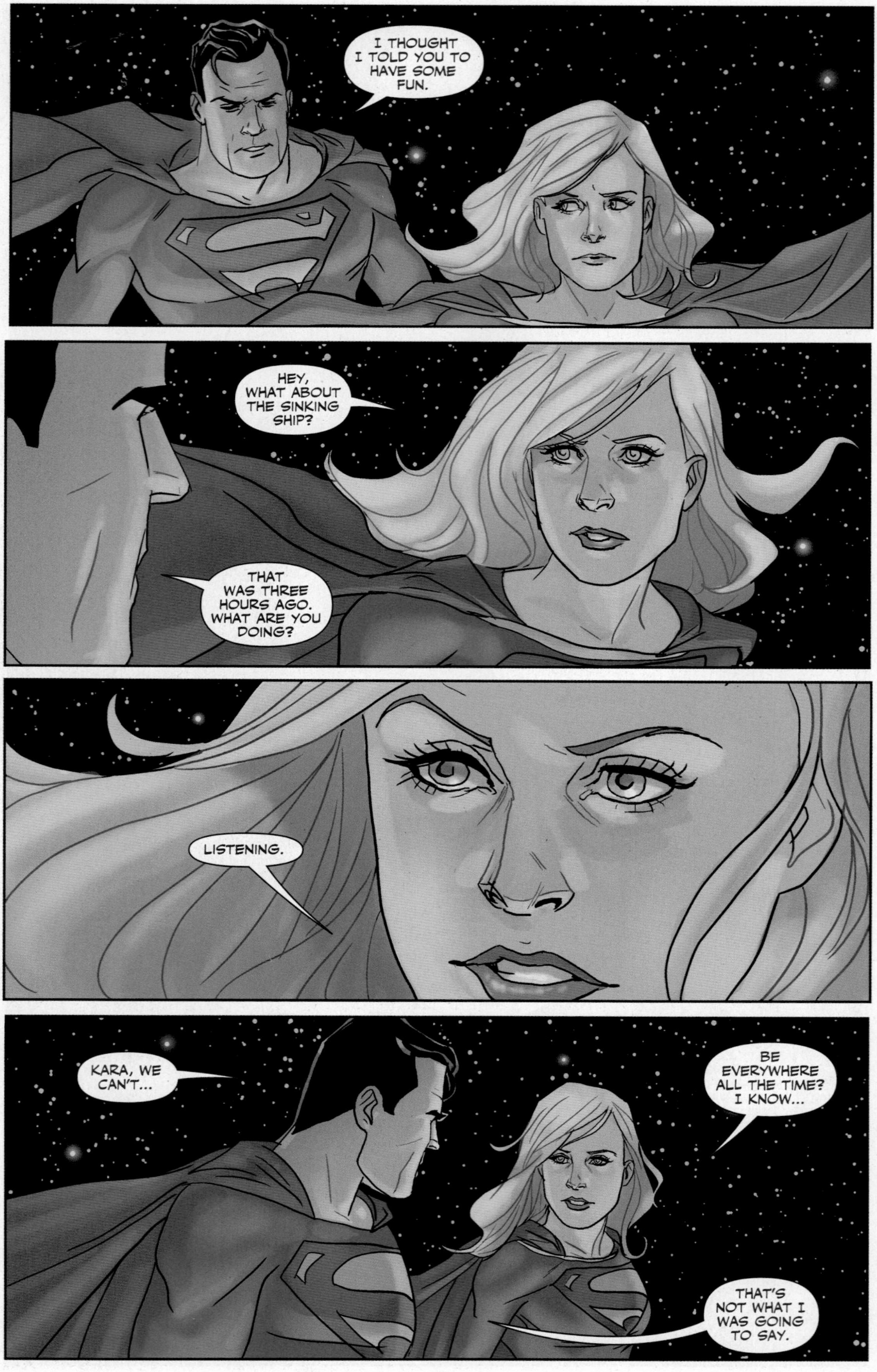
I THOUGHT I TOLD YOU TO HAVE SOME FUN.
HEY, WHAT ABOUT THE SINKING SHIP?
THAT WAS THREE HOURS AGO. WHAT ARE YOU DOING?
LISTENING.
KARA, WE CAN'T...
BE EVERYWHERE ALL THE TIME? I KNOW...
THAT'S NOT WHAT I WAS GOING TO SAY.

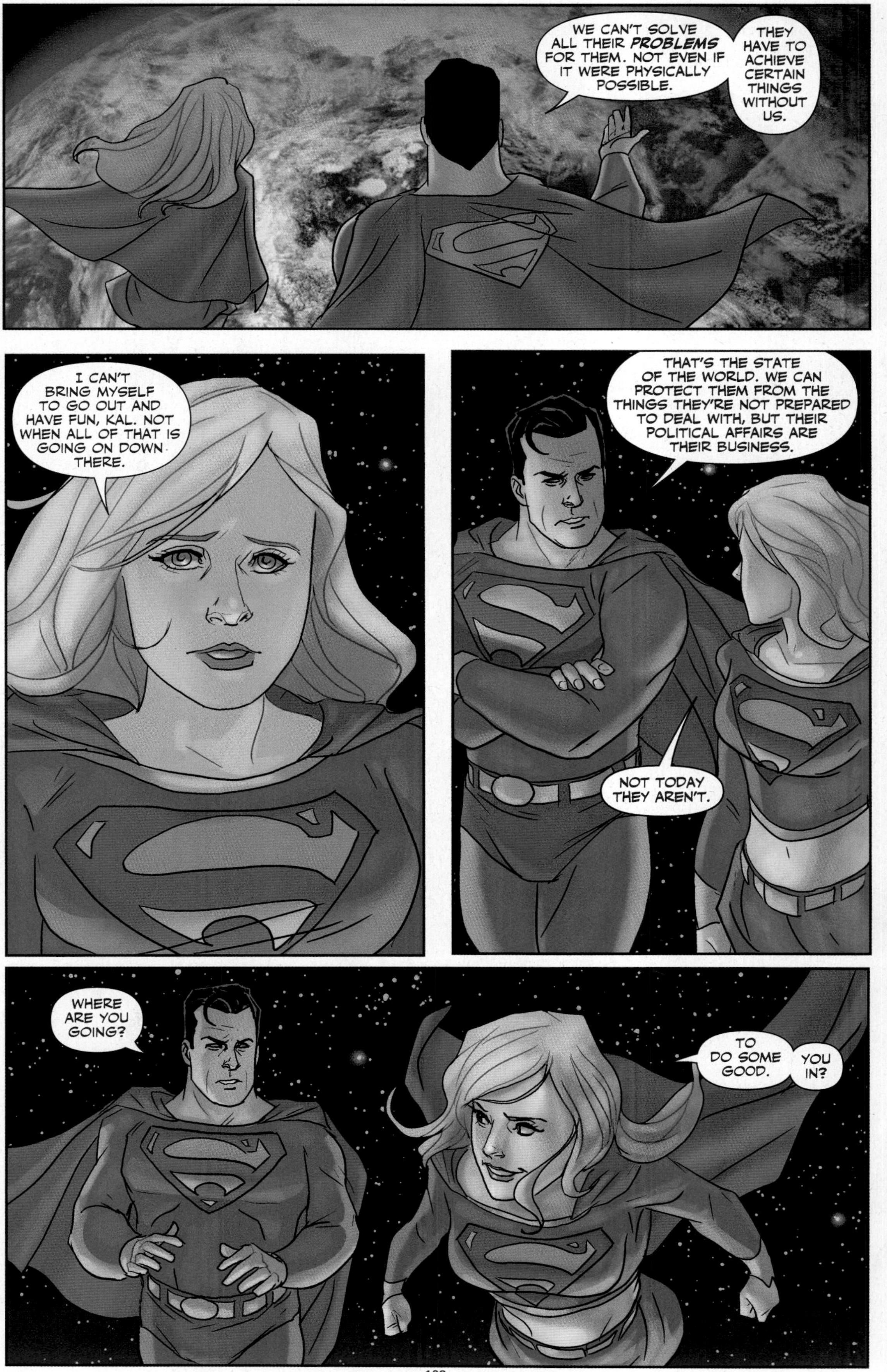
WE CAN'T SOLVE ALL THEIR *PROBLEMS* FOR THEM. NOT EVEN IF IT WERE PHYSICALLY POSSIBLE.
THEY HAVE TO ACHIEVE CERTAIN THINGS WITHOUT US.
I CAN'T BRING MYSELF TO GO OUT AND HAVE FUN, KAL. NOT WHEN ALL OF THAT IS GOING ON DOWN THERE.
THAT'S THE STATE OF THE WORLD. WE CAN PROTECT THEM FROM THE THINGS THEY'RE NOT PREPARED TO DEAL WITH, BUT THEIR POLITICAL AFFAIRS ARE THEIR BUSINESS.
NOT TODAY THEY AREN'T.
WHERE ARE YOU GOING?
TO DO SOME GOOD.
YOU IN?

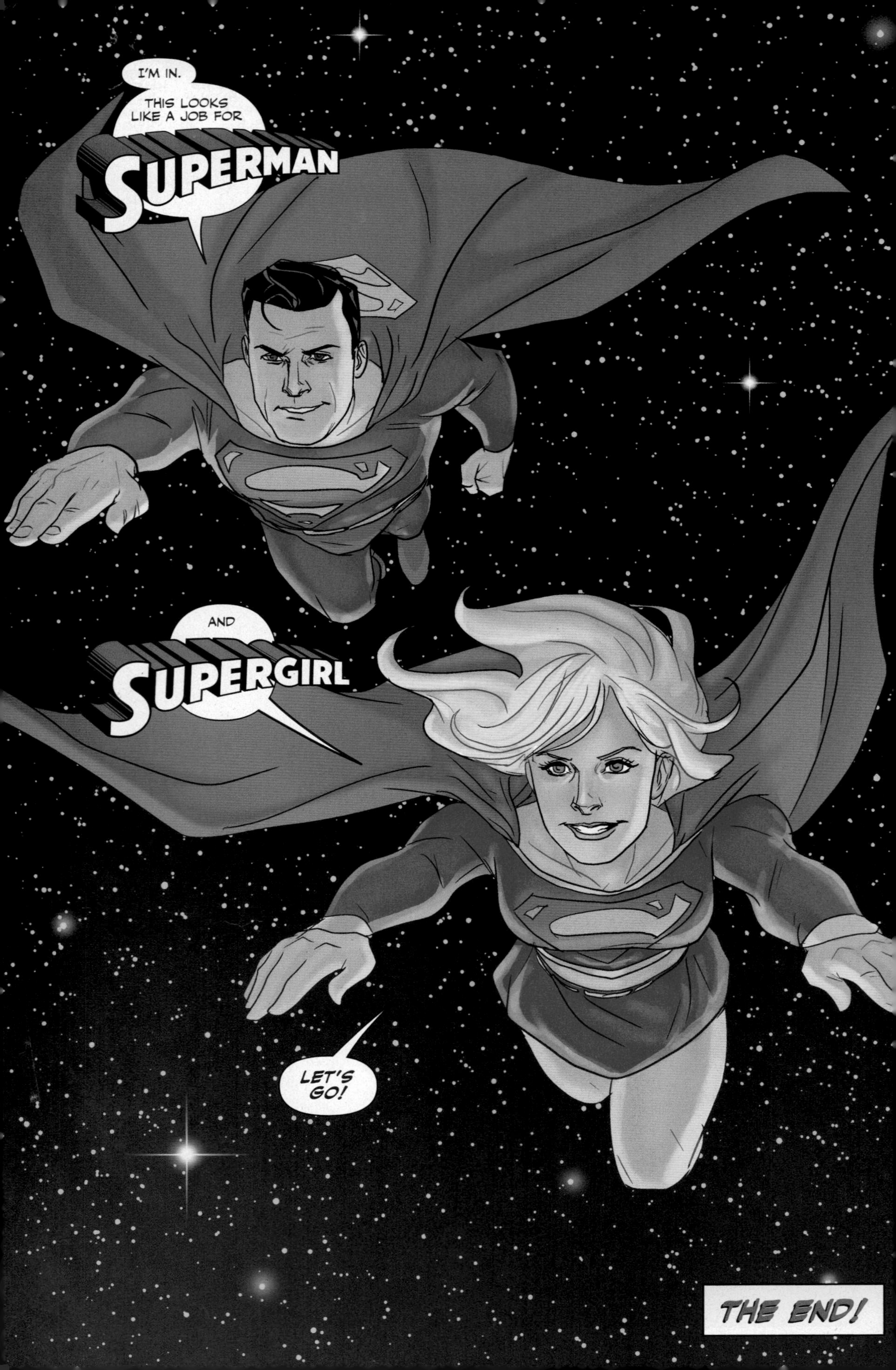
I'M IN.
THIS LOOKS LIKE A JOB FOR
SUPERMAN
AND
SUPERGIRL
LET'S GO!
THE END!

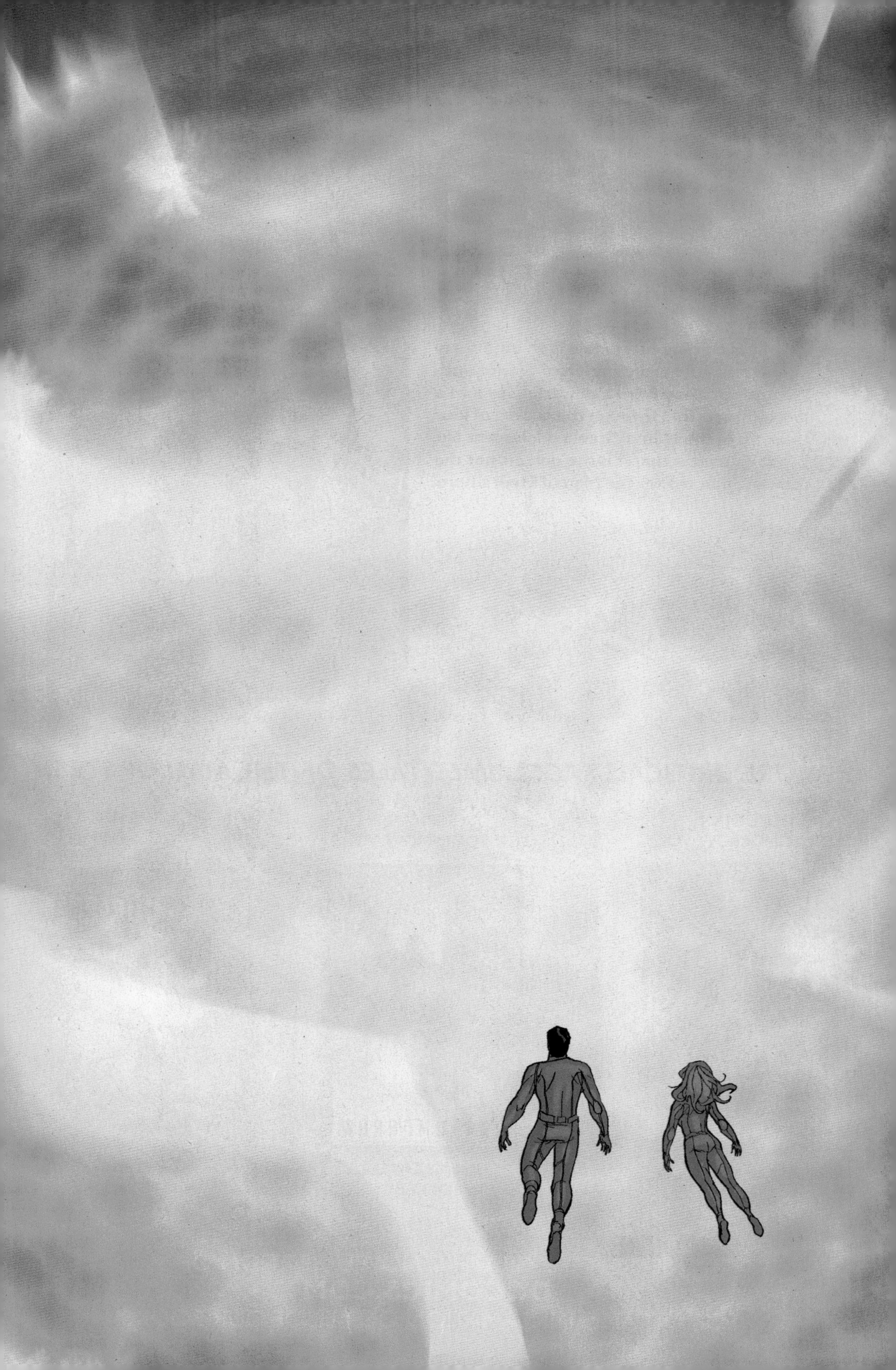

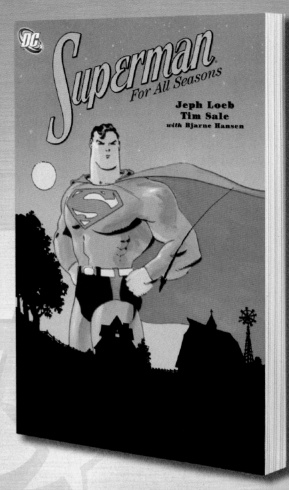

MORE CLASSIC TALES OF THE MAN OF STEEL

SUPERMAN:
THE MAN OF STEEL
VOLS. 1 - 6

SUPERMAN:
BIRTHRIGHT

SUPERMAN:
CAMELOT FALLS
VOLS. 1 - 2

JOHN BYRNE

MARK WAID
LEINIL YU

KURT BUSIEK
CARLOS PACHECO

SUPERMAN:
OUR WORLDS AT WAR

SUPERMAN:
RED SON

SUPERMAN:
SECRET IDENTITY

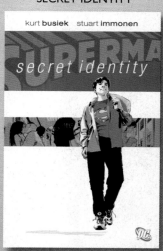

VARIOUS
WRITERS & ARTISTS

MARK MILLAR
DAVE JOHNSON
KILLIAN PLUNKETT

KURT BUSIEK
STUART IMMONEN

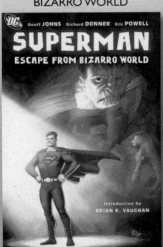